DEADWORLD

THE LAST
SIESTA

written by

Gary Reed
and
Gary Francis

illustrated by
Mark Bloodworth

lettered by
Jaymes Reed

IDW™

ISBN: 978-1-61377-044-3   14 13 12 11   1 2 3 4
www.IDWPUBLISHING.com

DESPERADO
www.desperadopublishing.com

Ted Adams, CEO & Publisher
Greg Goldstein, Chief Operating Officer
Robbie Robbins, EVP/Sr. Graphic Artist
Chris Ryall, Chief Creative Officer, Editor-In-Chief
Matthew Ruzicka, CPA, Chief Financial Officer
Alan Payne, VP of Sales

Joe Pruett, President & Publisher
Stephan Nilson, Creative Director
Gary Reed, Business Development
Malcolm Bourne, Special Projects Coordinator

DEADWORLD

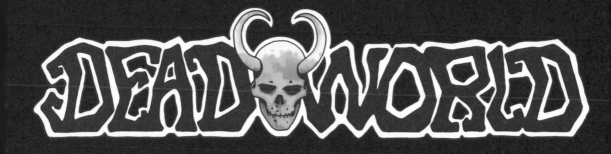

THE LAST SIESTA

INTRODUCTION

I've written a lot of Deadworld stories over the years. I don't know the exact count but it is well over 50 issues' worth. Thinking about that, there are not too many writers, especially in independent comics, who have had the opportunity to be immersed in one world for such a long time.

Deadworld: The Last Siesta was a very different project for me in many ways. First off, it was designed right from the beginning to be a self-contained graphic novel. It wasn't a mini-series or part of an ongoing series to be packaged later. It had to have a beginning, middle, and an end. It also had to be accessible to new readers, so there was no back story to bog it down. The only pre-existing character was King Zombie.

It was also a unique experience for me because I worked with another writer, Gary Francis. I've worked in collaboration with artists, of course, but never in a capacity of sharing the actual writing. But even though we share the writing credit and duties, the roles were still pretty well delineated. Francis wrote an outline of the entire story and even provided storyboard-type breakdowns. After that, the artist, Mark Bloodworth and I went through the outline, page by page, and retooled it. It wasn't that Gary's story needed changing but more fleshing out as he provided the outline. Then Mark drew the book and as he went through, he made some more changes, most of them being small subtle changes.

After Mark finished drawing the book, then I went through and scripted it. Some might refer to this as the "Marvel" way as often times they would have a writer provide a plot that the artist would draw from and then the writer would script the completed art. Having never worked on a Marvel book, I can't say for sure but I'll accept that designation.

It was hard. I'm used to doing full scripts broken down panel by panel.

Sometimes I'd go into great detail on a panel or add extraneous material that will never be drawn but done to convey a sense of mood or emotion to the artist. Here, there was no opportunity to do that. However, by the two of us going through it together (Mark and me), the emotional and spatial aspects were there when Mark drew the book.

I found it difficult because being the final creator on a joint effort like this pushed me into a different sense of pacing but it also was challenging. The narrative wasn't all mine as I'm used to but I also found it enjoyable in tackling it a different way. Probably the biggest change I made was to move some of the pages around from the original sequence and even Mark's.

It is satisfying knowing that the project will be read in its entirety and not having to take into consideration ending and starting points that you have to consider when breaking a story into the comic issues. And one thing that is a vital part of doing comics in general is the collaboration aspect.

If you haven't read Deadworld before, the hope is that you will enjoy the work and venture into more tales of the zombie-infested world. And if you're a fan of Deadworld already, hopefully it will be a welcome addition that measures up.

Gary Reed

Prelude

~one~

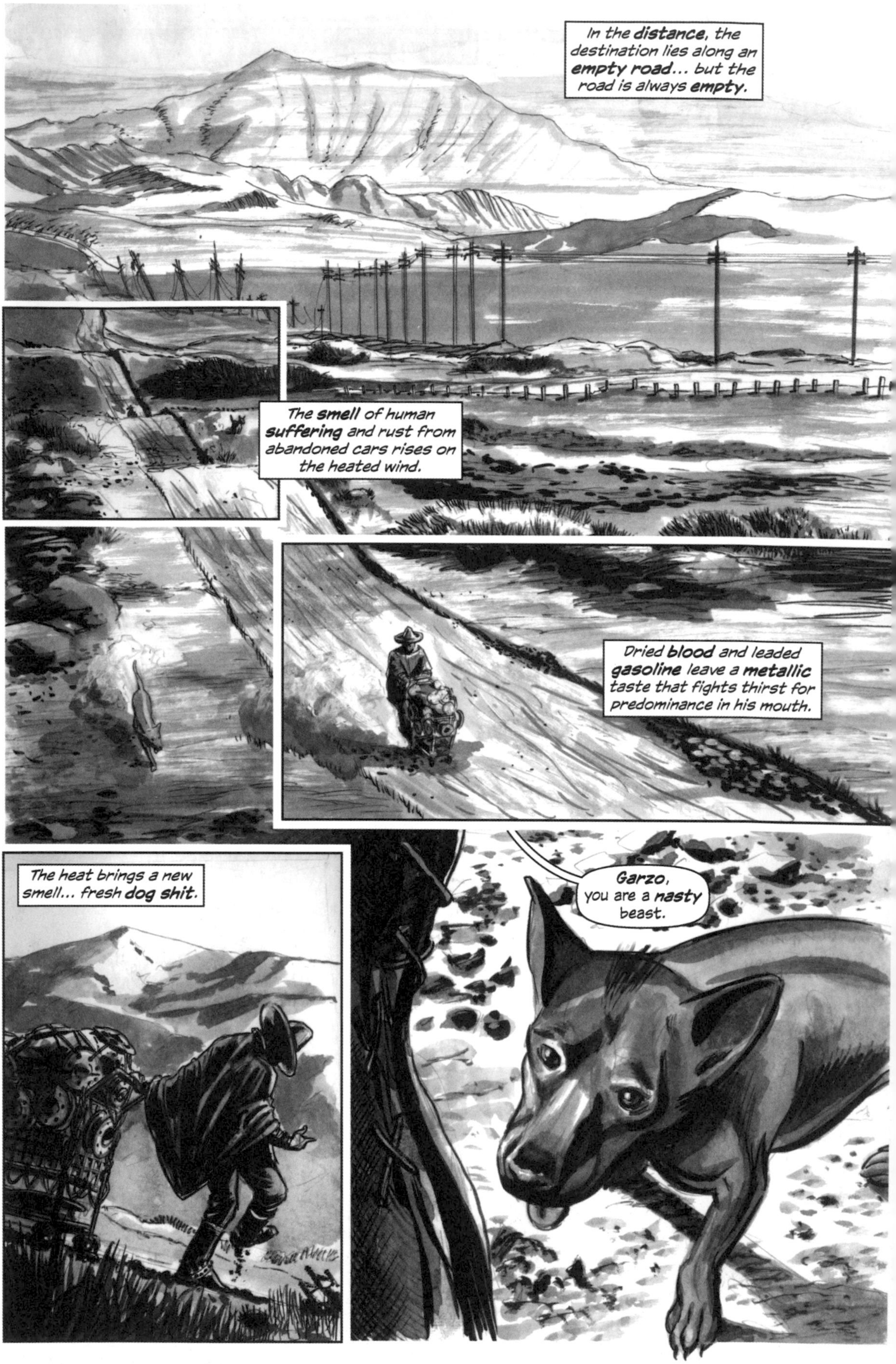

In the **distance**, the destination lies along an **empty road**... but the road is always **empty.**
The **smell** of human **suffering** and rust from abandoned cars rises on the heated wind.
Dried **blood** and leaded **gasoline** leave a **metallic** taste that fights thirst for predominance in his mouth.
The heat brings a new smell... fresh **dog shit**.
Garzo, you are a **nasty** beast.

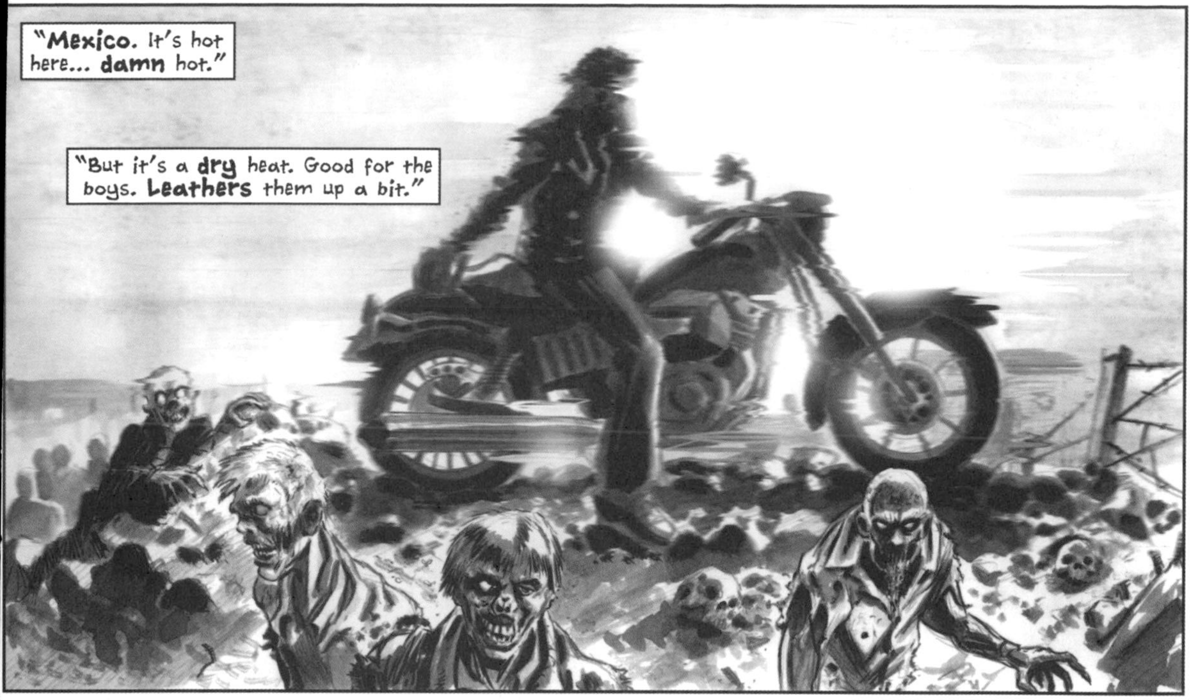
"Mexico. It's hot here... damn hot."
"But it's a dry heat. Good for the boys. Leathers them up a bit."

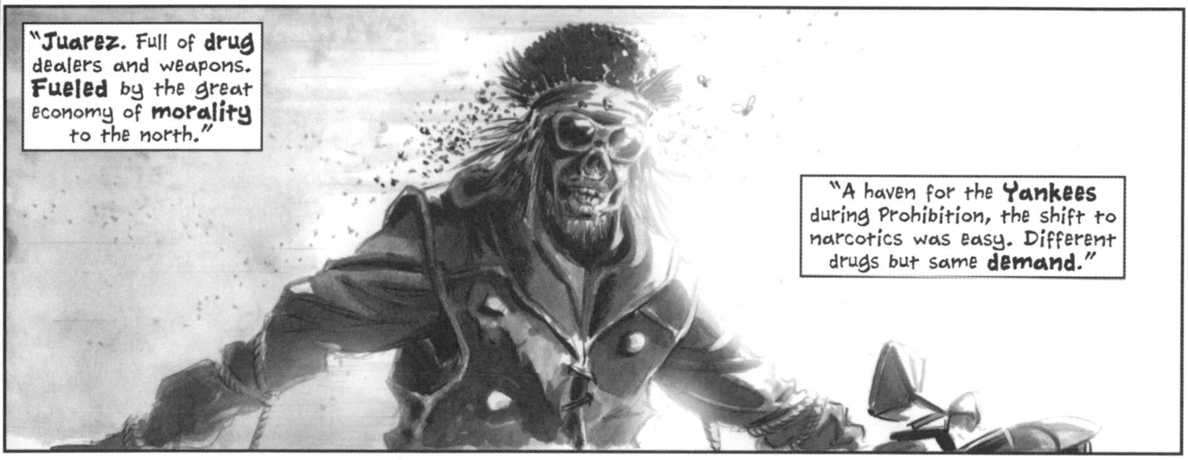
"Juarez. Full of drug dealers and weapons. Fueled by the great economy of morality to the north."
"A haven for the Yankees during Prohibition, the shift to narcotics was easy. Different drugs but same demand."

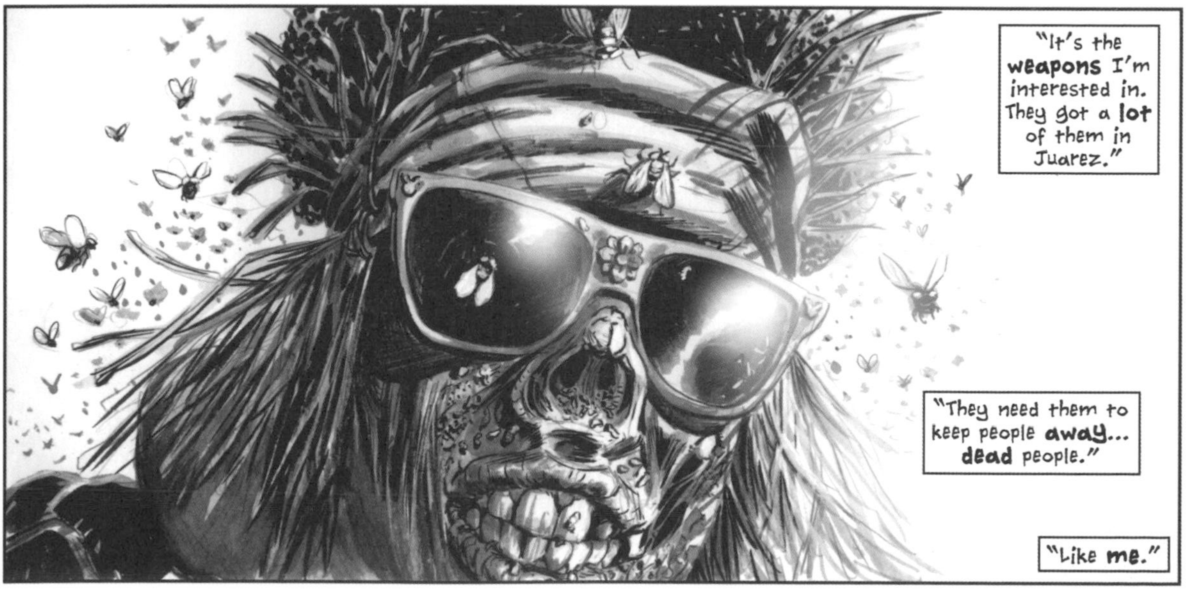
"It's the weapons I'm interested in. They got a lot of them in Juarez."
"They need them to keep people away... dead people."
"Like me."

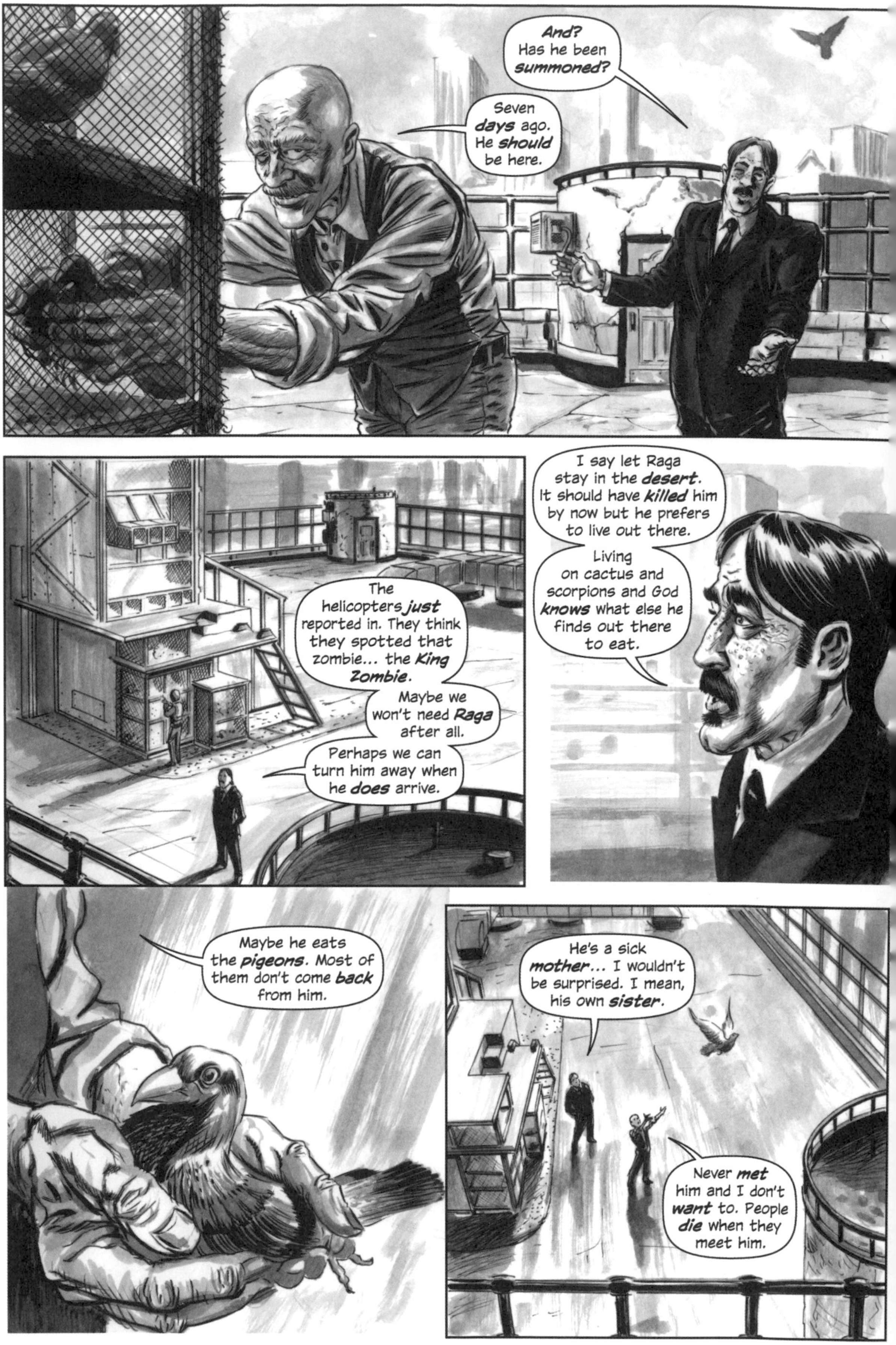
And? Has he been summoned?
Seven days ago. He should be here.
The helicopters just reported in. They think they spotted that zombie... the King Zombie.
Maybe we won't need Raga after all.
Perhaps we can turn him away when he does arrive.
I say let Raga stay in the desert. It should have killed him by now but he prefers to live out there.
Living on cactus and scorpions and God knows what else he finds out there to eat.
Maybe he eats the pigeons. Most of them don't come back from him.
He's a sick mother... I wouldn't be surprised. I mean, his own sister.
Never met him and I don't want to. People die when they meet him.

Prelude

~two~

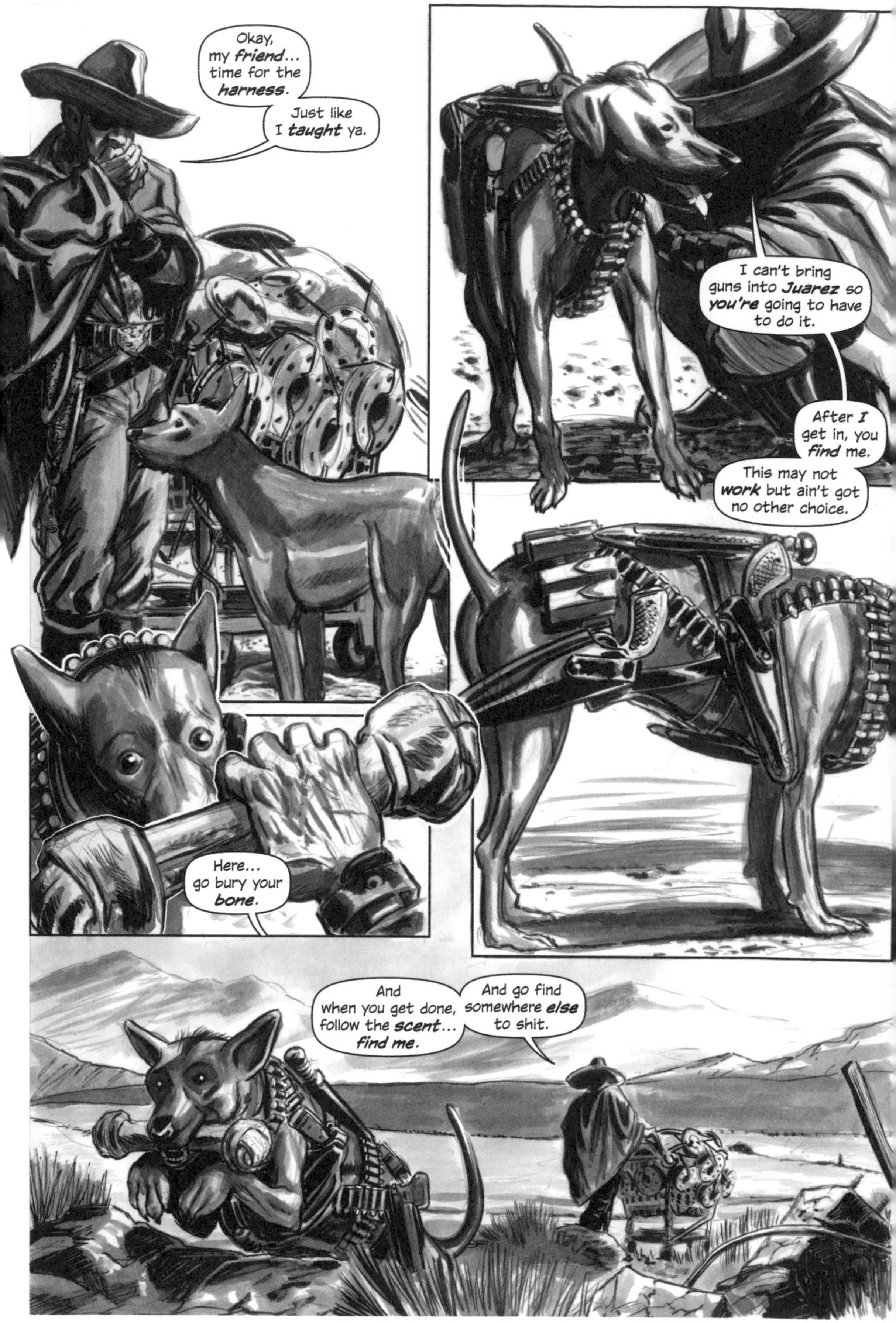
Okay, my friend... time for the harness.
Just like I taught ya.
I can't bring guns into Juarez so you're going to have to do it.
After I get in, you find me.
This may not work but ain't got no other choice.
Here... go bury your bone.
And when you get done, follow the scent... find me.
And go find somewhere else to shit.

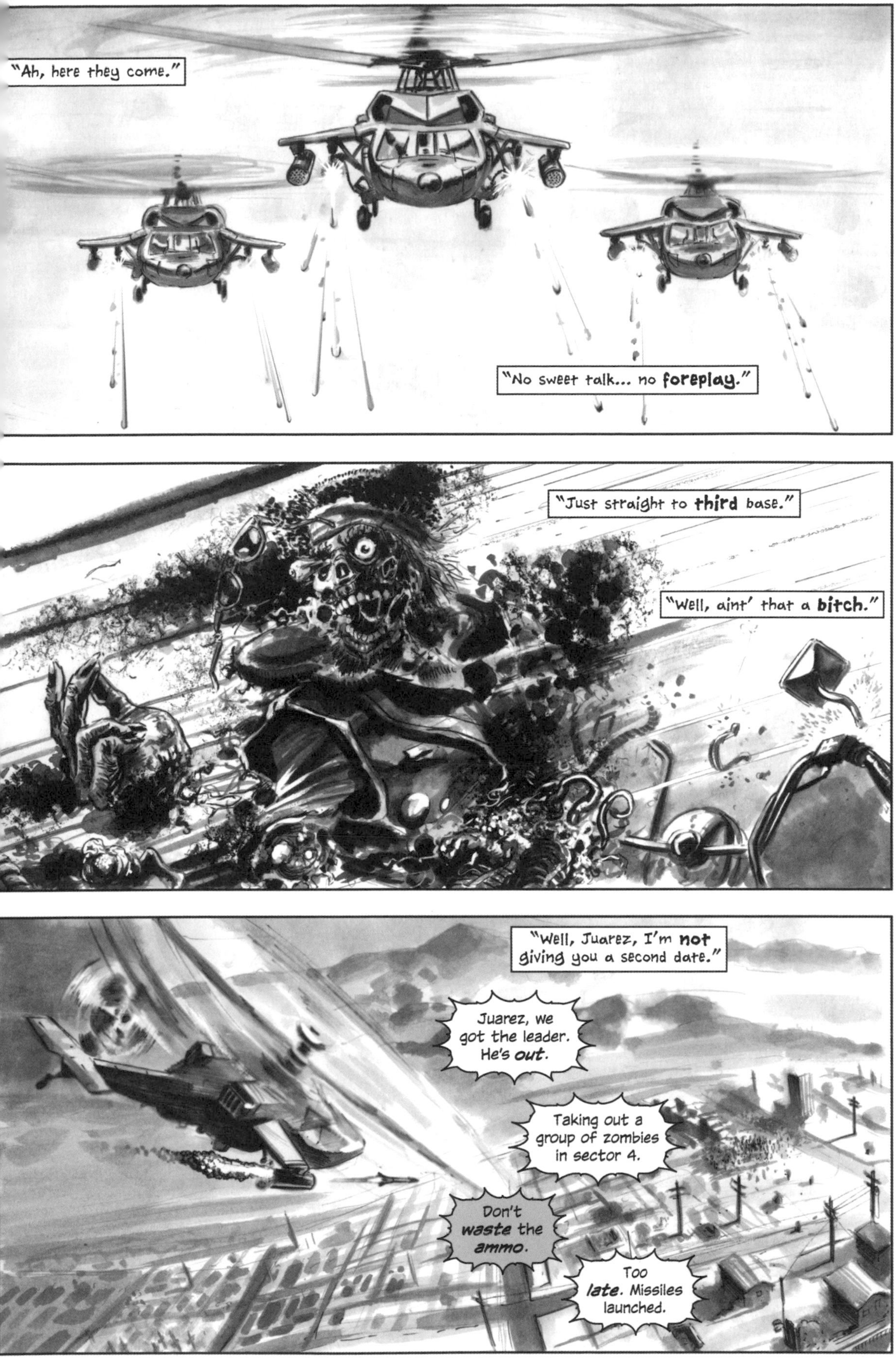
"Ah, here they come."
"No sweet talk... no **foreplay**."
"Just straight to **third** base."
"Well, aint' that a **bitch**."
"Well, Juarez, I'm **not** giving you a second date."
Juarez, we got the leader. He's *out*.
Taking out a group of zombies in sector 4.
Don't *waste* the *ammo*.
Too *late*. Missiles launched.

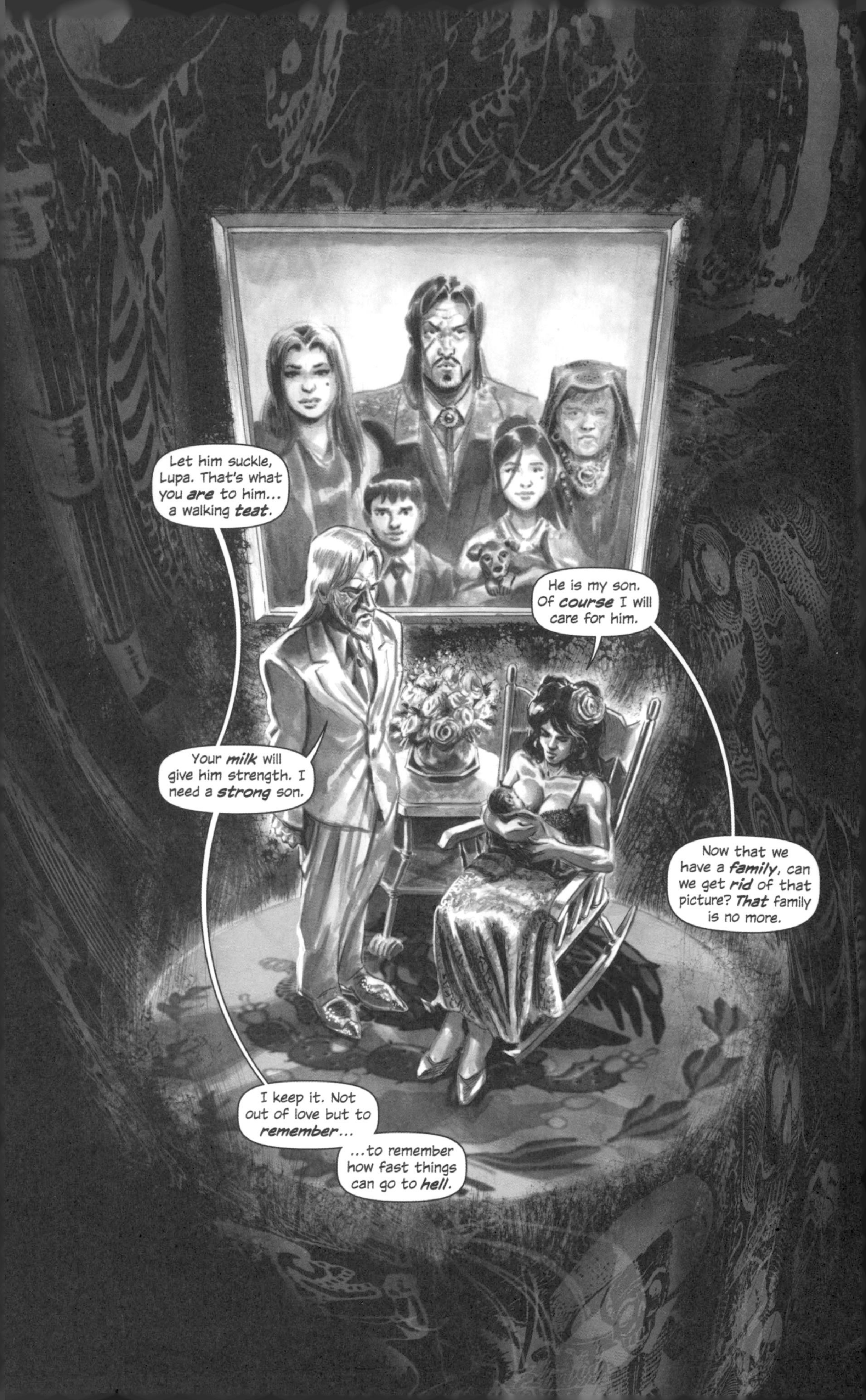

Let him suckle, Lupa. That's what you **are** to him... a walking **teat**.
He is my son. Of **course** I will care for him.
Your **milk** will give him strength. I need a **strong** son.
Now that we have a **family**, can we get **rid** of that picture? **That** family is no more.
I keep it. Not out of love but to **remember**...
...to remember how fast things can go to **hell**.

Chapter one

the DESERT

Chapter one

the DESERT

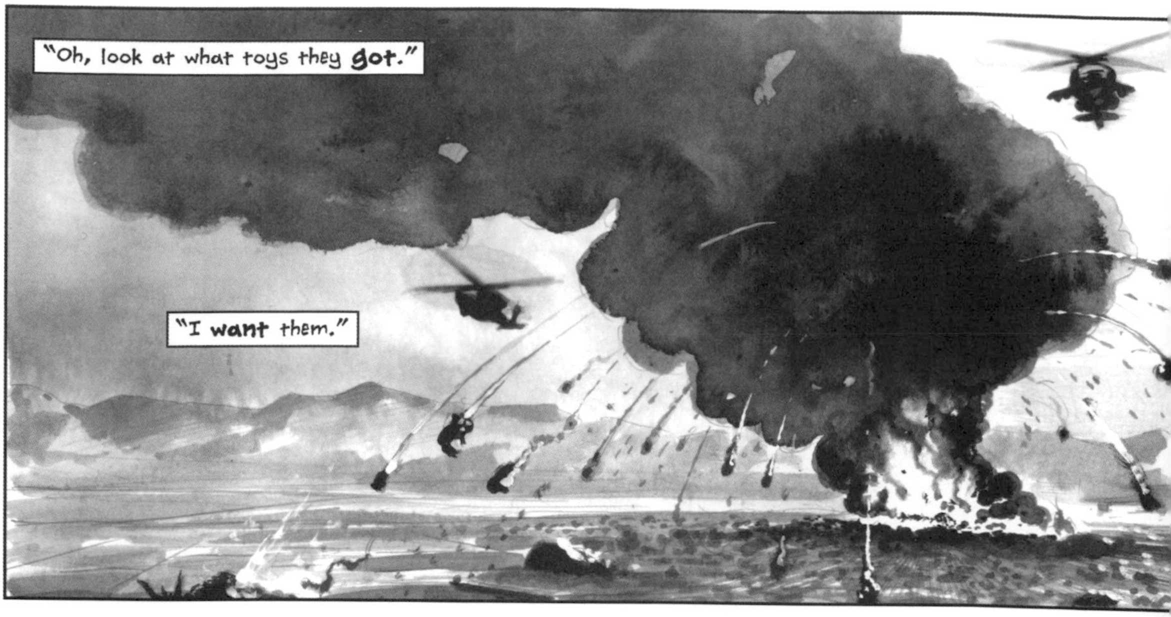
"Oh, look at what toys they got."
"I want them."

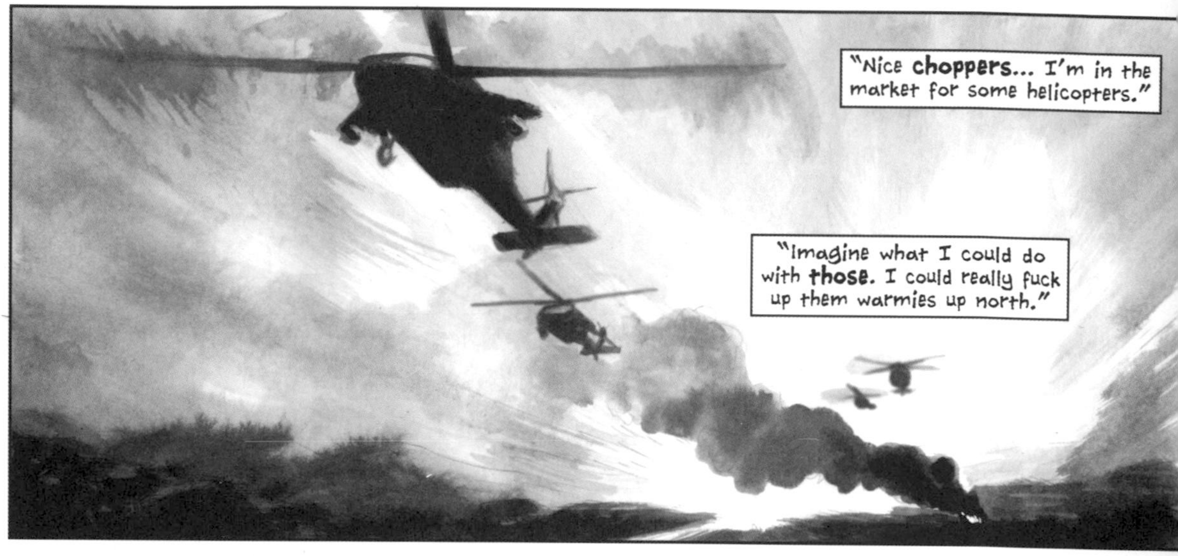
"Nice choppers... I'm in the market for some helicopters."
"Imagine what I could do with those. I could really fuck up them warmies up north."

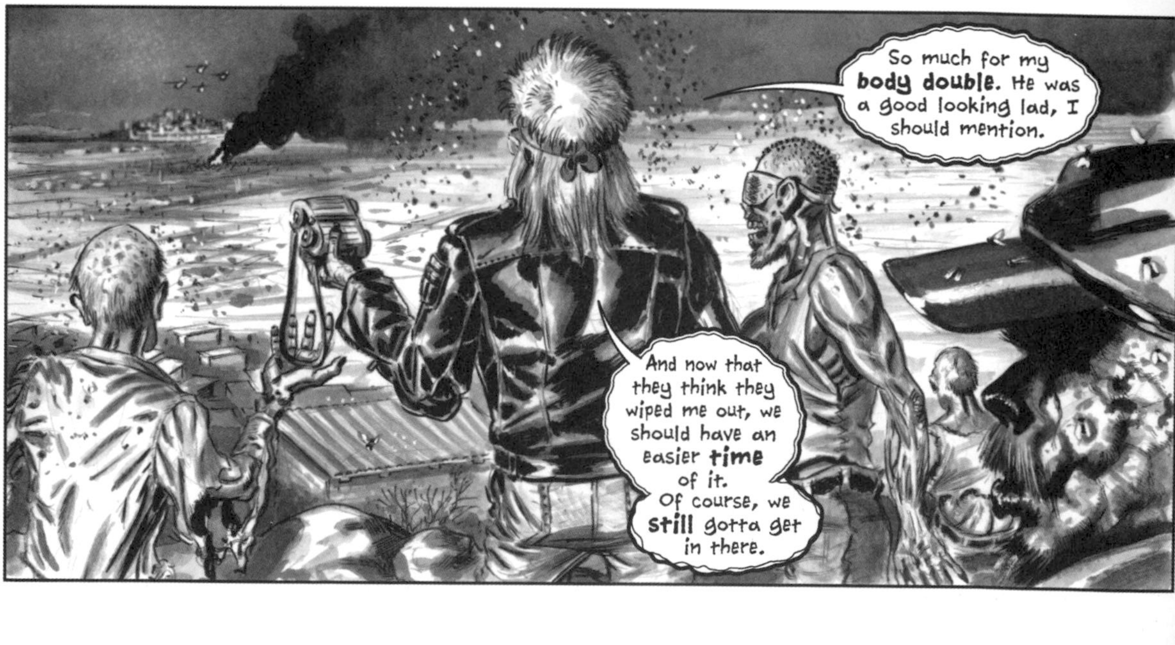
So much for my body double. He was a good looking lad, I should mention.
And now that they think they wiped me out, we should have an easier time of it. Of course, we still gotta get in there.

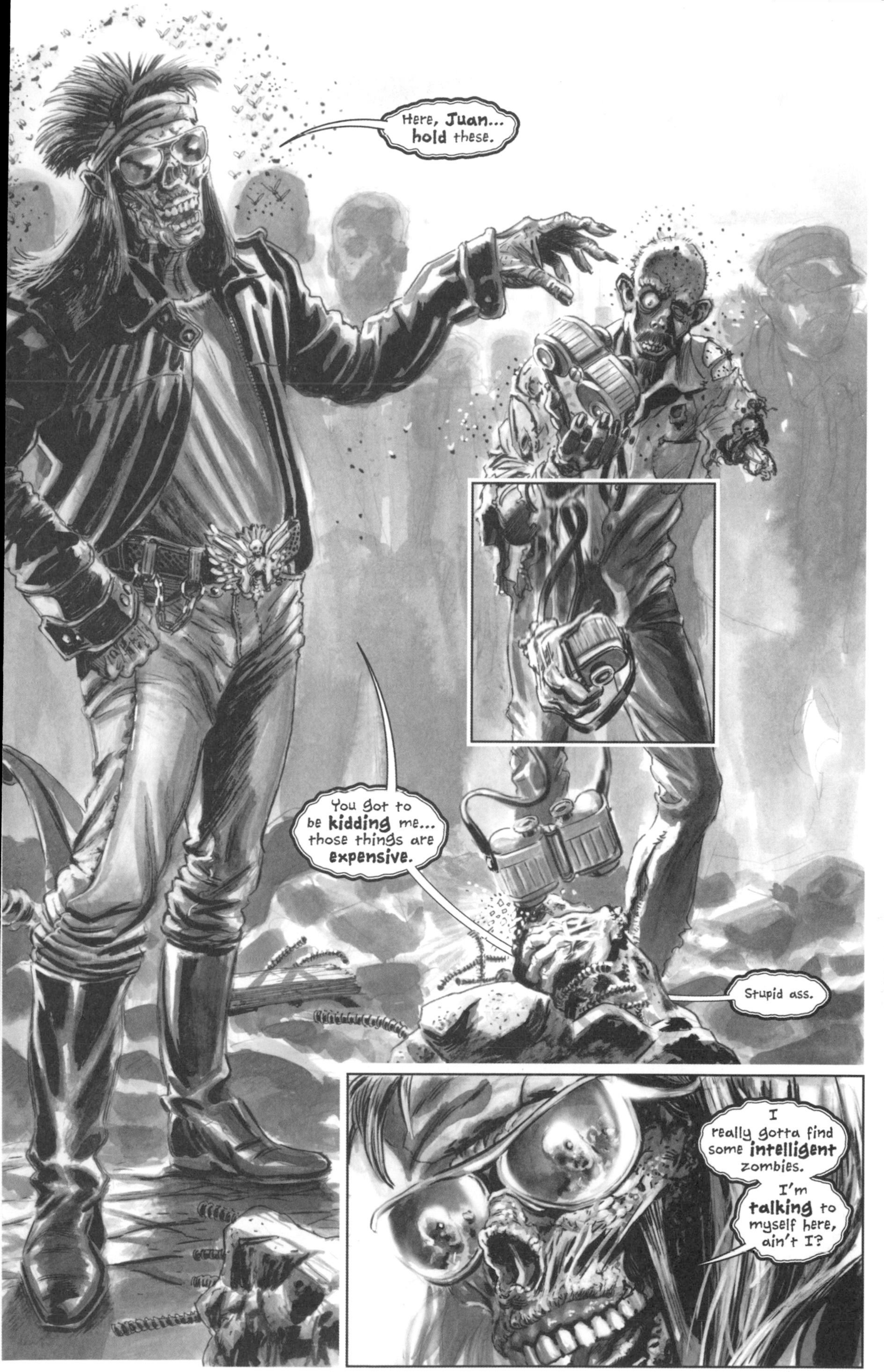
Here, Juan... hold these.
You got to be kidding me... those things are expensive.
Stupid ass.
I really gotta find some intelligent zombies.
I'm talking to myself here, ain't I?

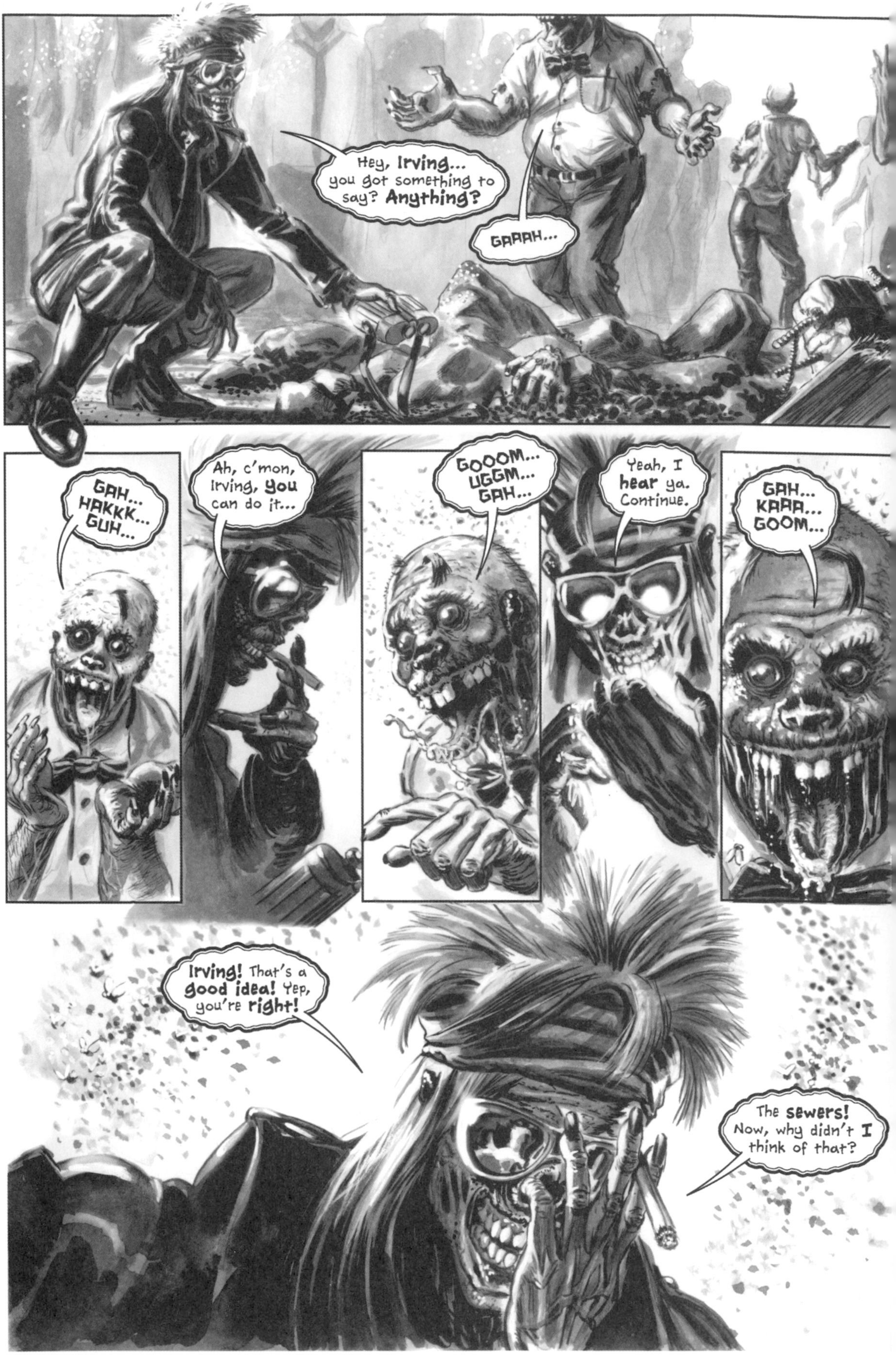
Hey, Irving... you got something to say? Anything?
GAAAH...
GAH... HAKKK... GUH...
Ah, c'mon, Irving, you can do it...
GOOOM... UGGM... GAH...
Yeah, I hear ya. Continue.
GAH... KAAA... GOOM...
Irving! That's a good idea! Yep, you're right!
The sewers! Now, why didn't I think of that?

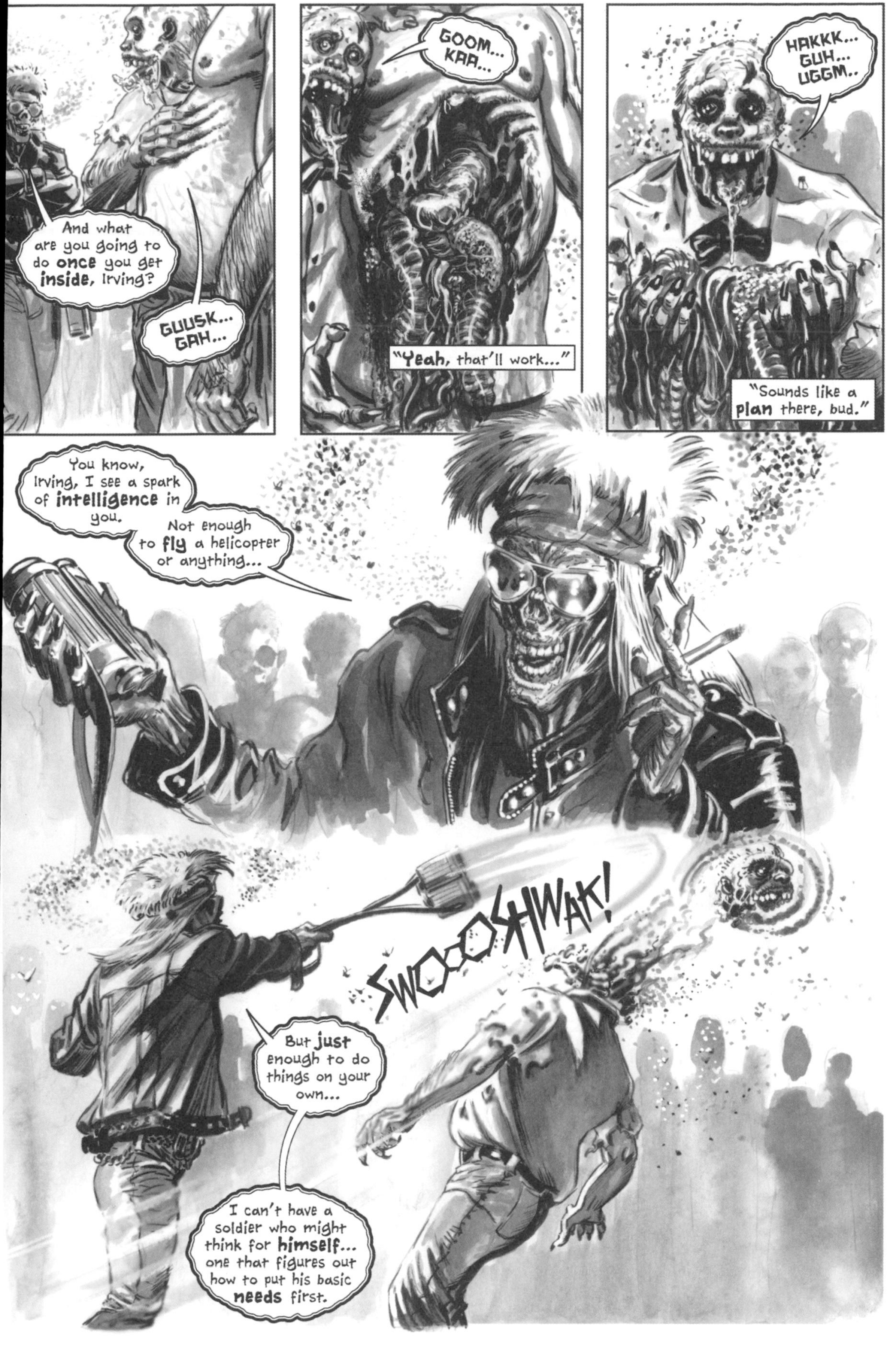

And what are you going to do once you get inside, Irving?
GUUSK... GAH...
GOOM... KAA...
"Yeah, that'll work..."
HAKKK... GUH... UGGM..
"Sounds like a plan there, bud."
You know, Irving, I see a spark of intelligence in you.
Not enough to fly a helicopter or anything...
SWOOOSHWAK!
But just enough to do things on your own...
I can't have a soldier who might think for himself... one that figures out how to put his basic needs first.

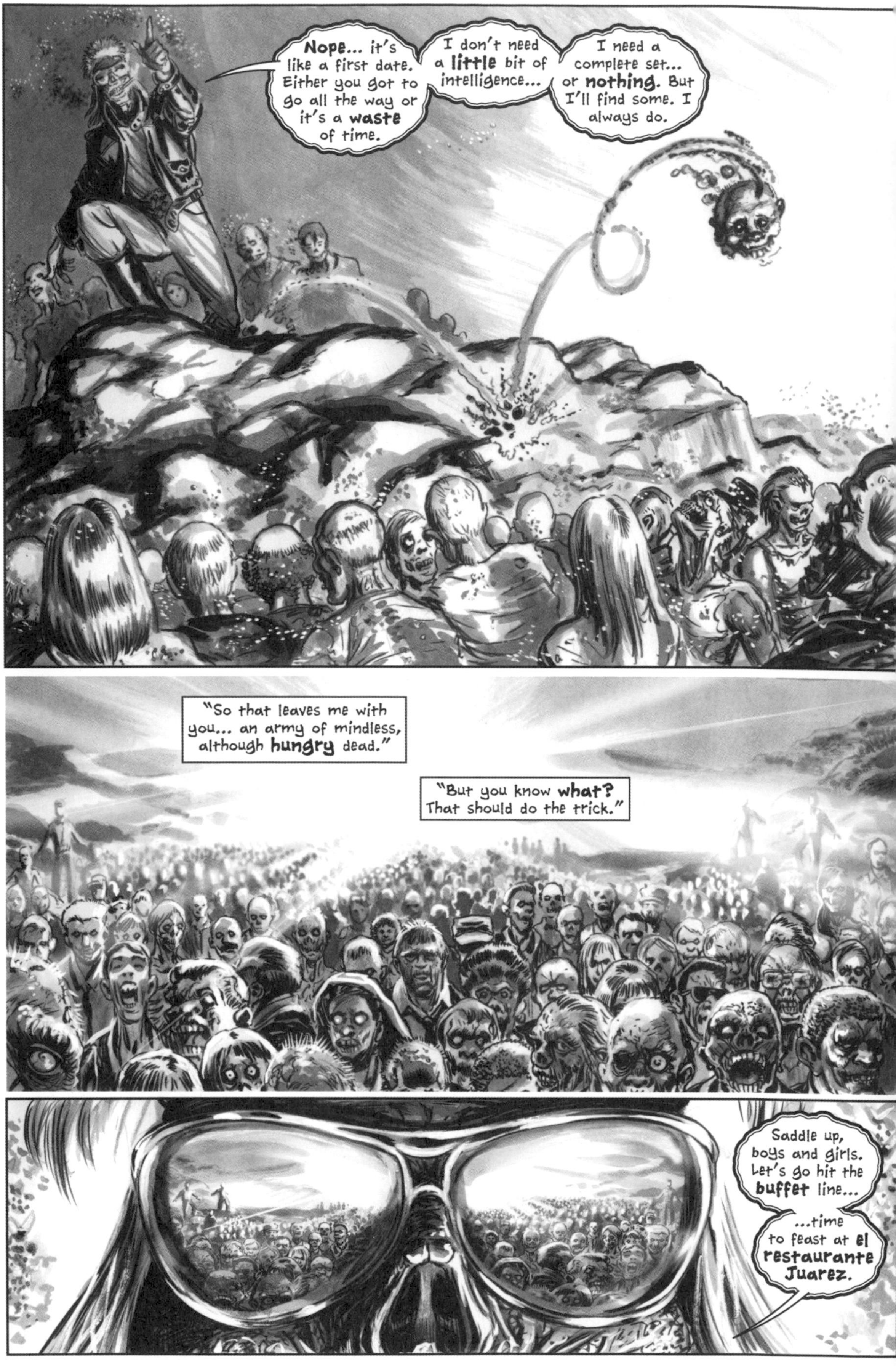
Nope... it's like a first date. Either you got to go all the way or it's a waste of time.
I don't need a little bit of intelligence...
I need a complete set... or nothing. But I'll find some. I always do.
"So that leaves me with you... an army of mindless, although hungry dead."
"But you know what? That should do the trick."
Saddle up, boys and girls. Let's go hit the buffet line...
...time to feast at el restaurante Juarez.

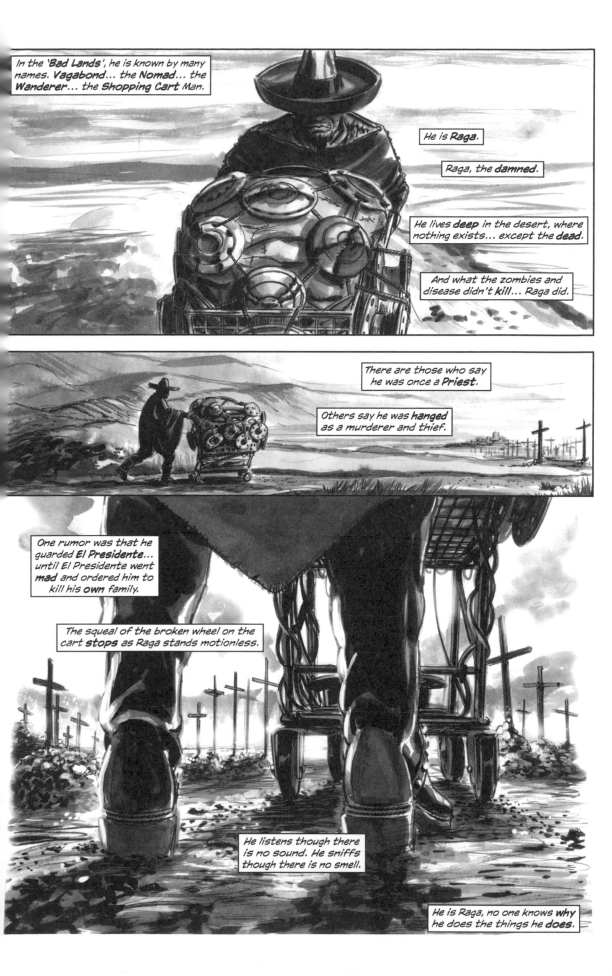

In the 'Bad Lands', he is known by many names. *Vagabond*... the *Nomad*... the *Wanderer*... the *Shopping Cart* Man.

He is *Raga*.

Raga, the *damned*.

He lives *deep* in the desert, where nothing exists... except the *dead*.

And what the zombies and disease didn't *kill*... Raga did.

There are those who say he was once a *Priest*.

Others say he was *hanged* as a murderer and thief.

One rumor was that he guarded *El Presidente*... until El Presidente went *mad* and ordered him to kill his *own* family.

The squeal of the broken wheel on the cart *stops* as Raga stands motionless.

He listens though there is no sound. He sniffs though there is no smell.

He is Raga, no one knows *why* he does the things he *does*.

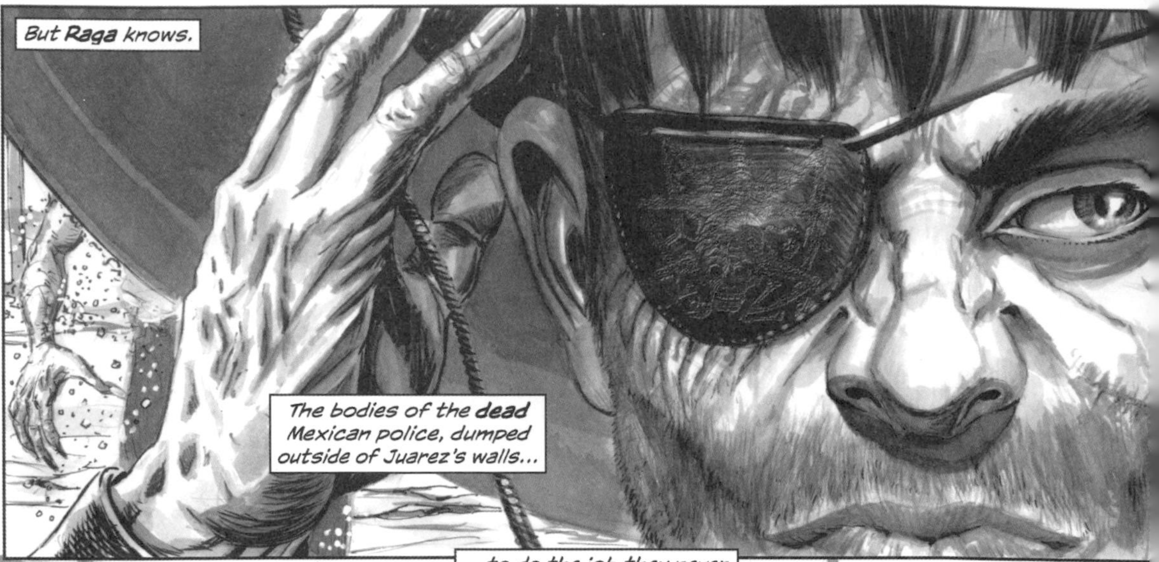
But Raga knows.
The bodies of the dead Mexican police, dumped outside of Juarez's walls...

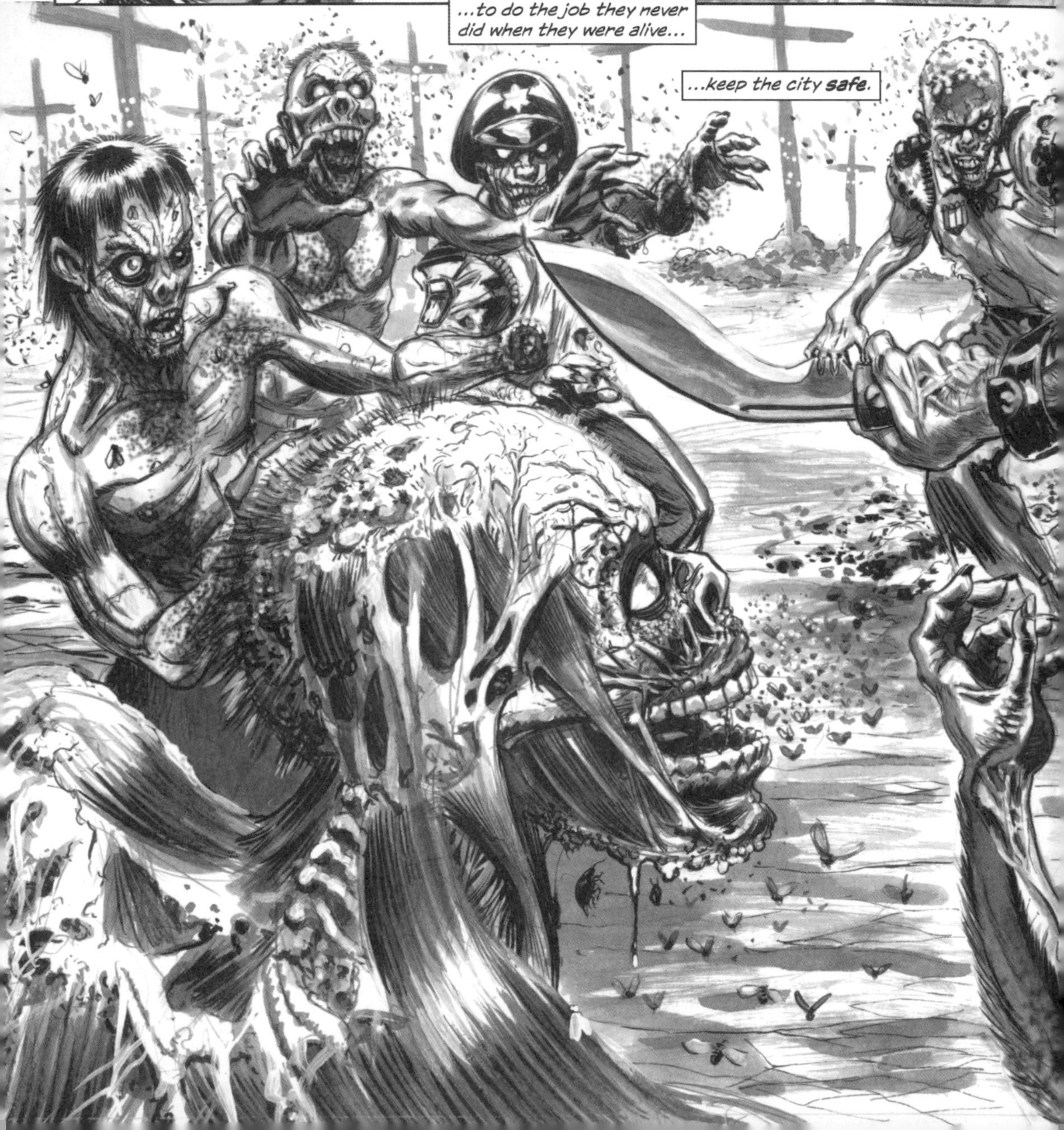
...to do the job they never did when they were alive...
...keep the city safe.

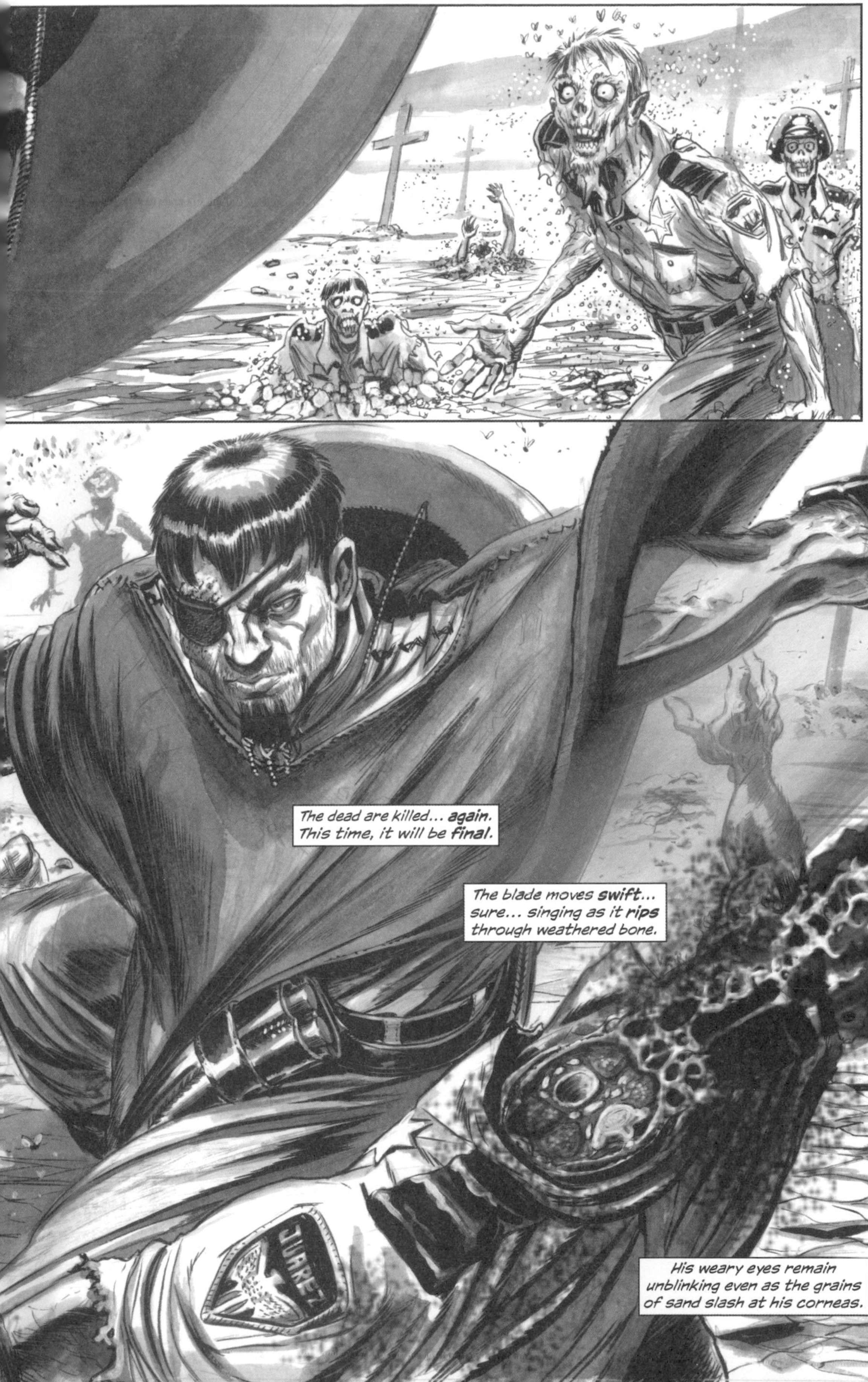
The dead are killed... **again**. This time, it will be **final**.
The blade moves **swift**... sure... singing as it **rips** through weathered bone.
JUAREZ
His weary eyes remain unblinking even as the grains of sand slash at his corneas.

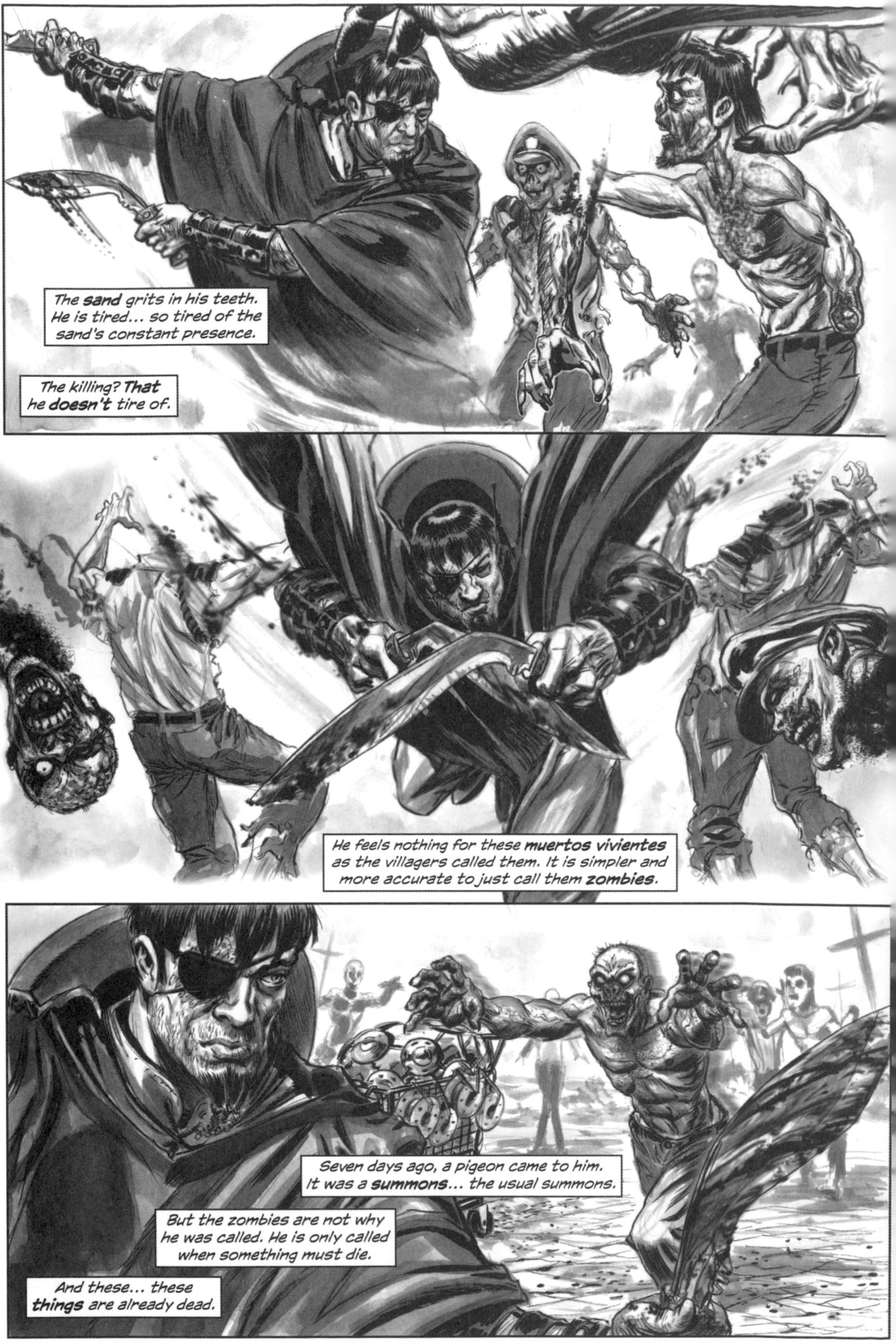
The sand grits in his teeth. He is tired... so tired of the sand's constant presence.
The killing? That he doesn't tire of.
He feels nothing for these muertos vivientes as the villagers called them. It is simpler and more accurate to just call them zombies.
Seven days ago, a pigeon came to him. It was a summons... the usual summons.
But the zombies are not why he was called. He is only called when something must die.
And these... these things are already dead.

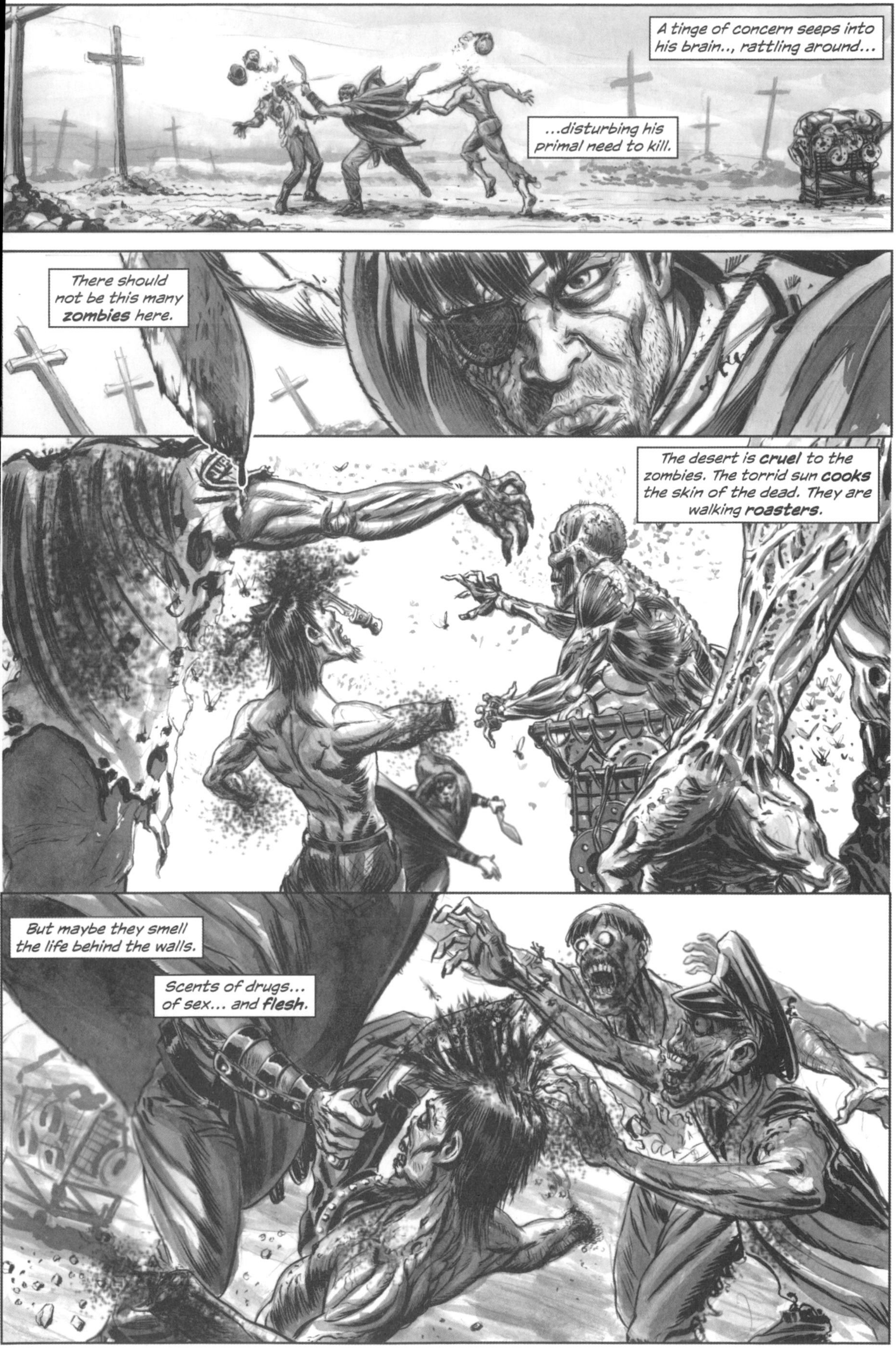
A tinge of concern seeps into his brain.., rattling around...
...disturbing his primal need to kill.
There should not be this many **zombies** here.
The desert is **cruel** to the zombies. The torrid sun **cooks** the skin of the dead. They are walking **roasters**.
But maybe they smell the life behind the walls.
Scents of drugs... of sex... and **flesh**.

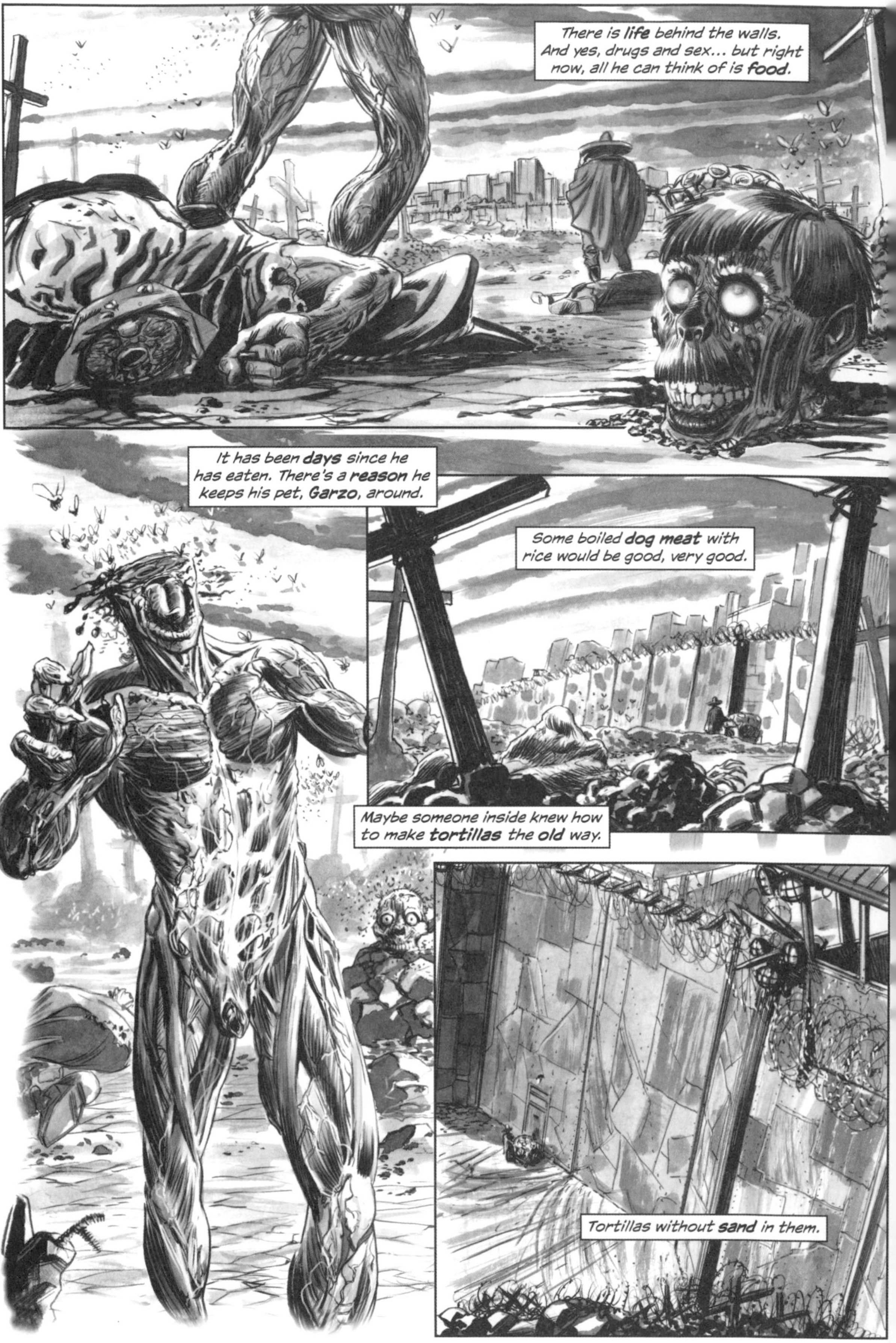
There is life behind the walls. And yes, drugs and sex... but right now, all he can think of is food.
It has been days since he has eaten. There's a reason he keeps his pet, Garzo, around.
Some boiled dog meat with rice would be good, very good.
Maybe someone inside knew how to make tortillas the old way.
Tortillas without sand in them.

Chapter two

the

CITY

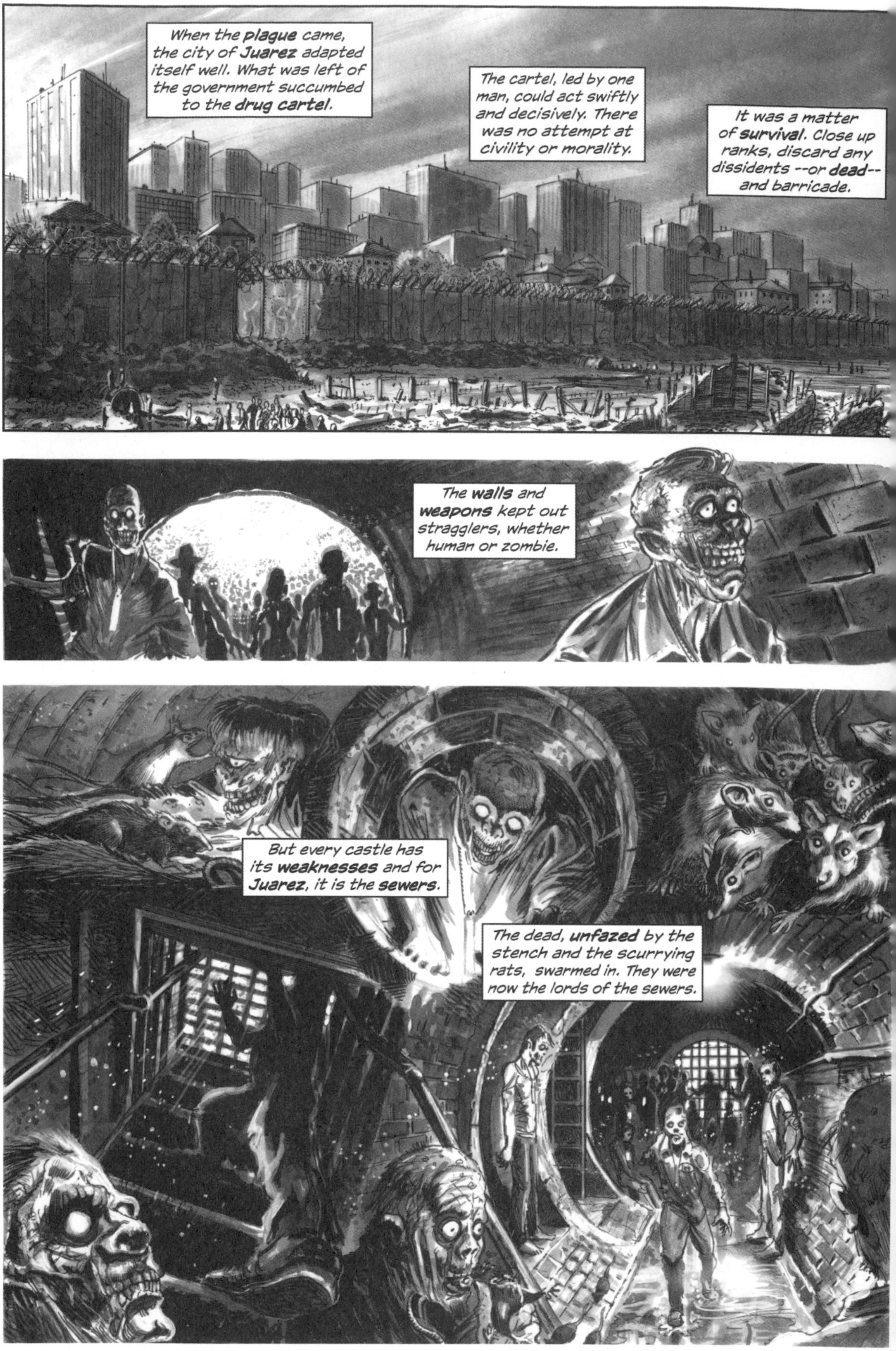
When the **plague** came, the city of **Juarez** adapted itself well. What was left of the government succumbed to the **drug cartel**.
The cartel, led by one man, could act swiftly and decisively. There was no attempt at civility or morality.
It was a matter of **survival**. Close up ranks, discard any dissidents --or **dead**-- and barricade.
The **walls** and **weapons** kept out stragglers, whether human or zombie.
But every castle has its **weaknesses** and for **Juarez**, it is the **sewers**.
The dead, **unfazed** by the stench and the scurrying rats, swarmed in. They were now the lords of the sewers.

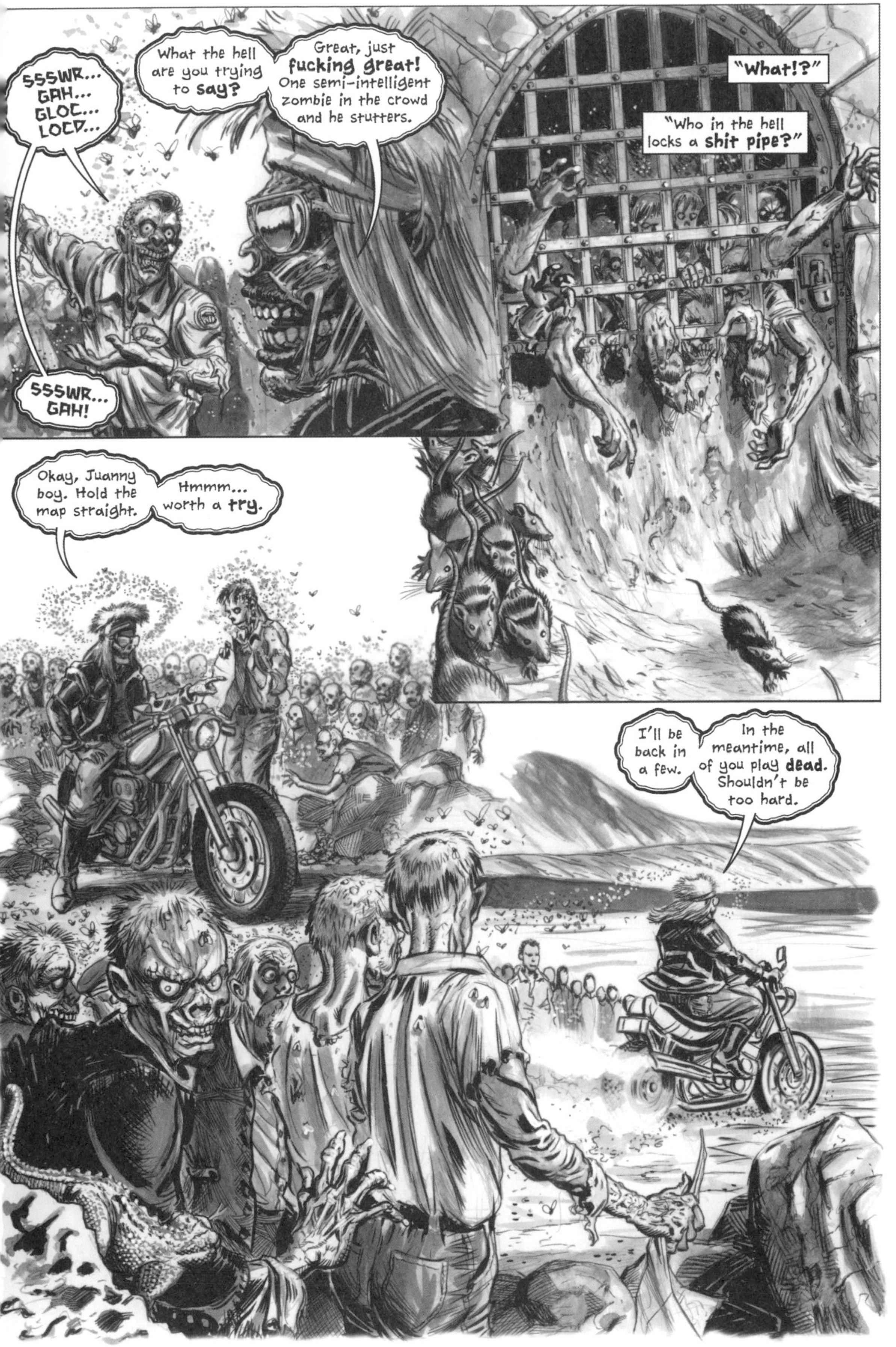
SSSWR... GAH... GLOC... LOCD...
What the hell are you trying to say?
Great, just fucking great! One semi-intelligent zombie in the crowd and he stutters.
SSSWR... GAH!
"What!?"
"Who in the hell locks a shit pipe?"
Okay, Juanny boy. Hold the map straight.
Hmmm... worth a try.
I'll be back in a few.
In the meantime, all of you play dead. Shouldn't be too hard.

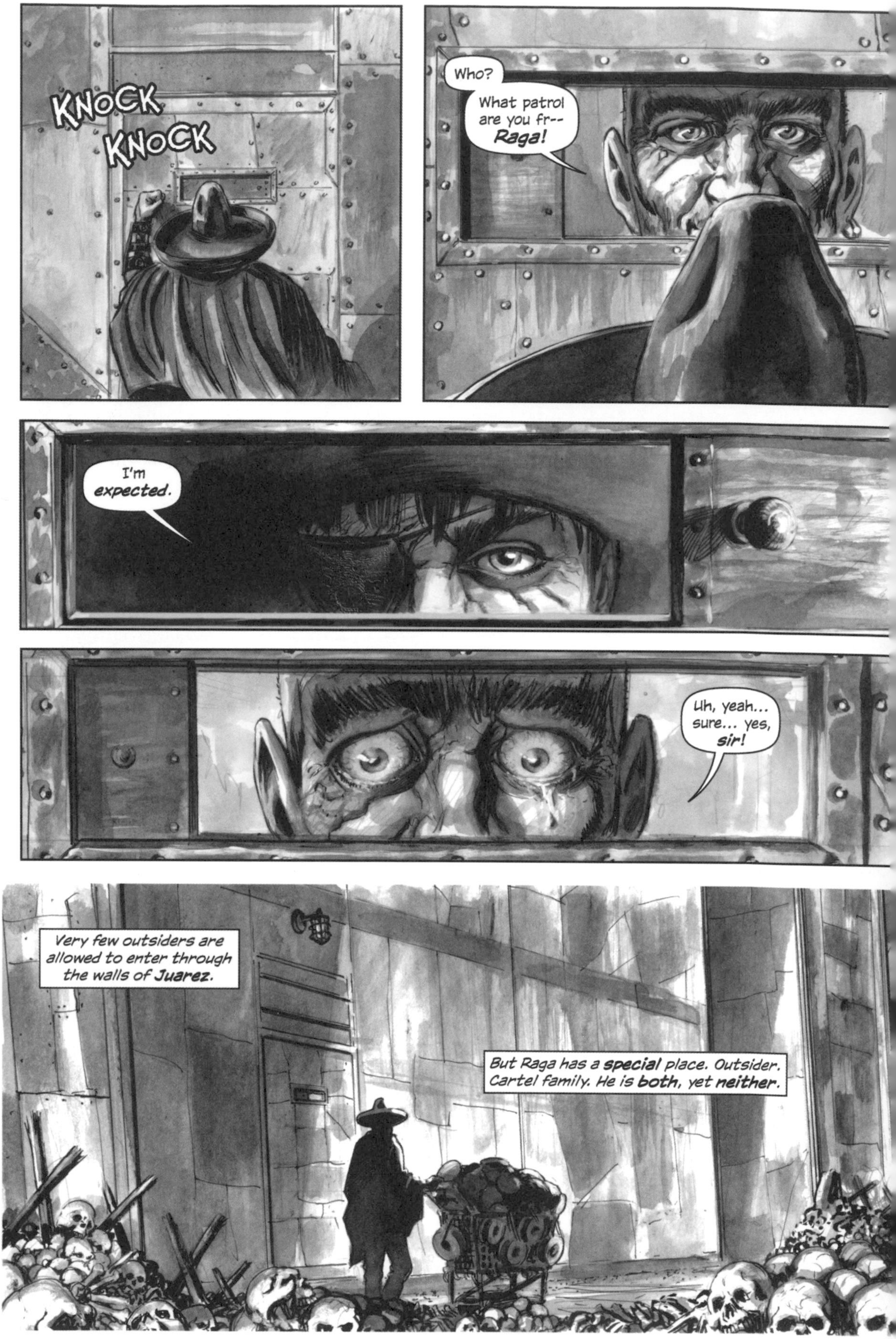
KNOCK
KNOCK
Who?
What patrol are you fr-- Raga!
I'm expected.
Uh, yeah... sure... yes, sir!
Very few outsiders are allowed to enter through the walls of Juarez.
But Raga has a special place. Outsider. Cartel family. He is both, yet neither.

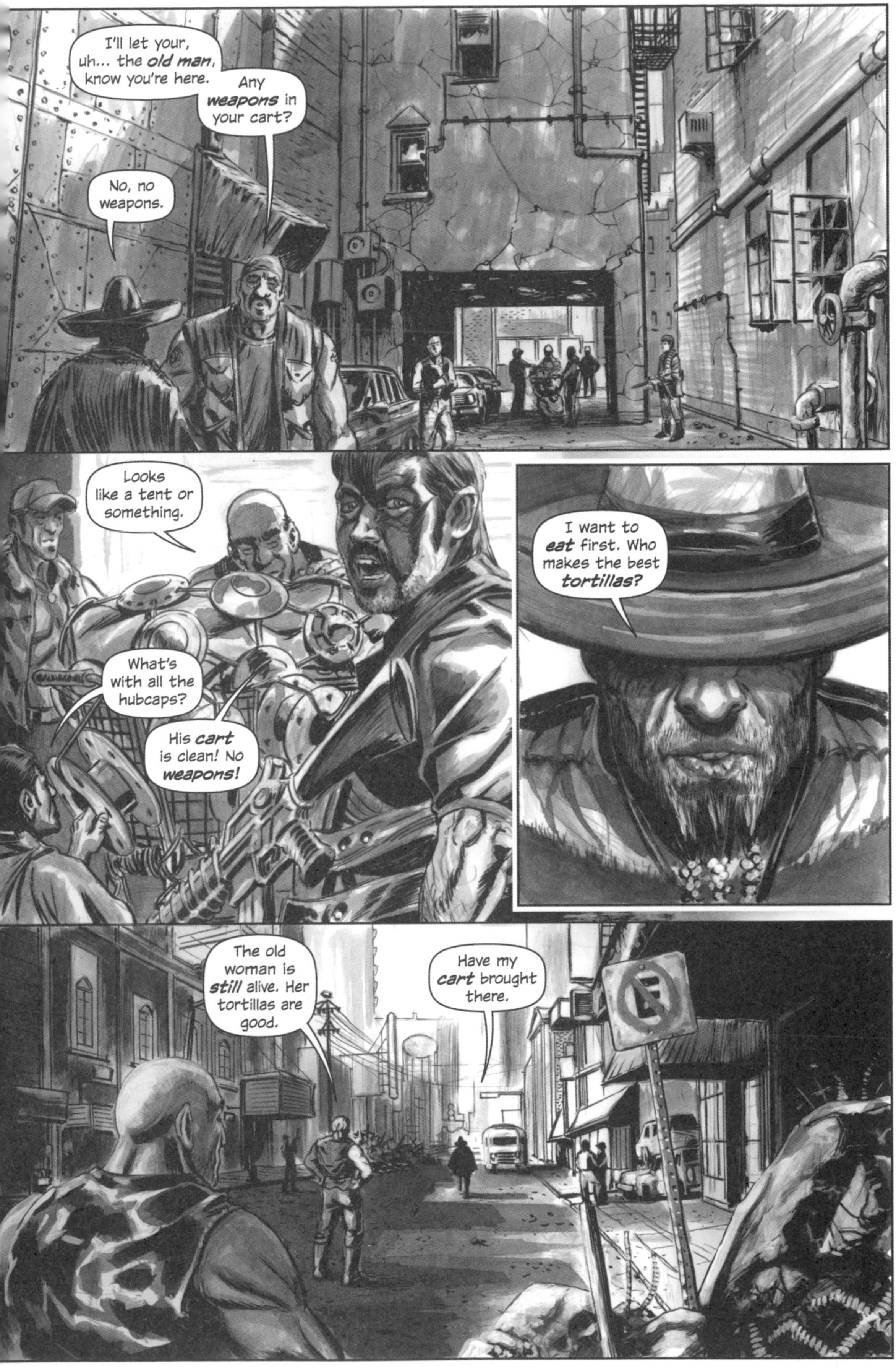

I'll let your, uh... the old man, know you're here.
Any weapons in your cart?
No, no weapons.
Looks like a tent or something.
What's with all the hubcaps?
His cart is clean! No weapons!
I want to eat first. Who makes the best tortillas?
The old woman is still alive. Her tortillas are good.
Have my cart brought there.

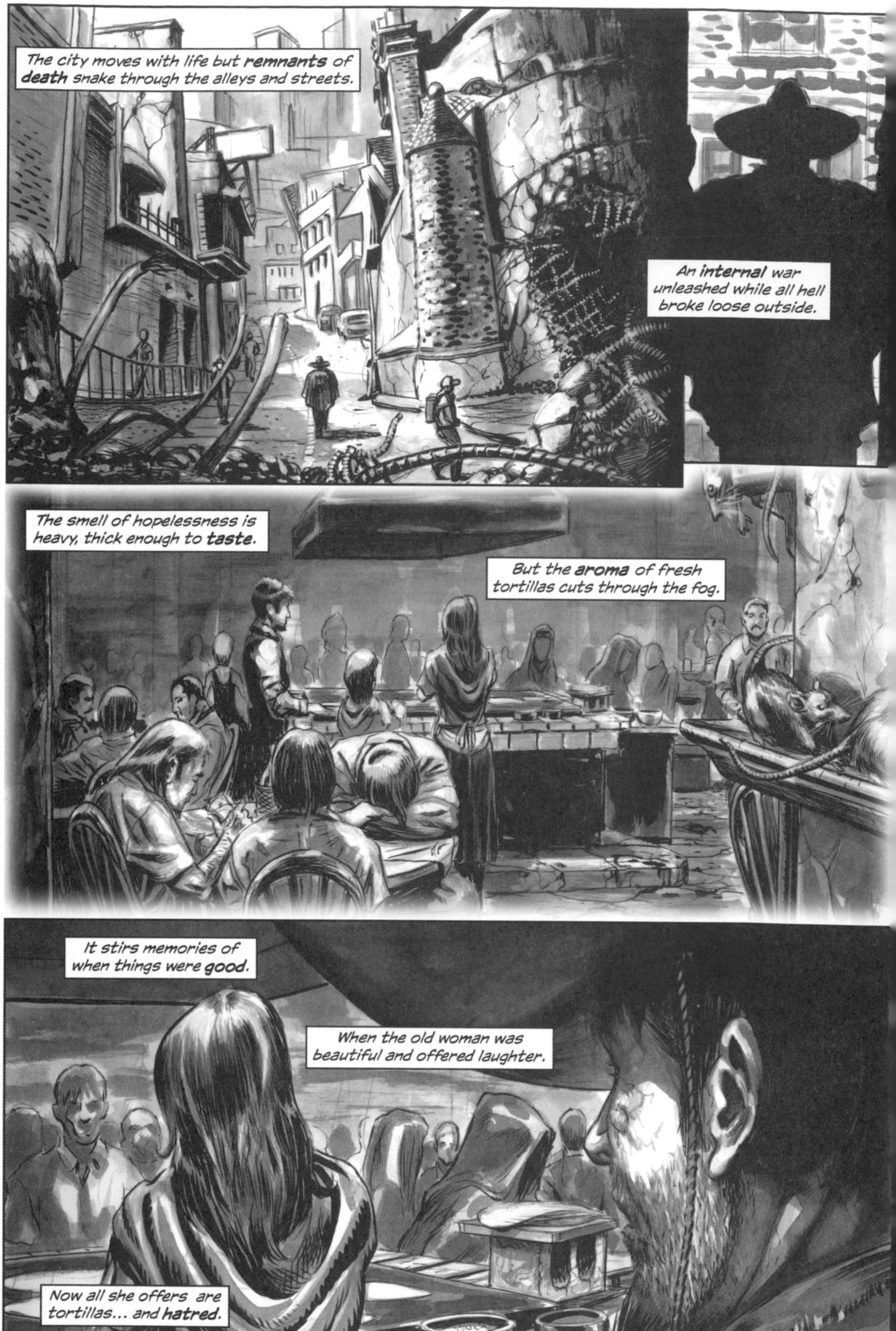
The city moves with life but **remnants** of **death** snake through the alleys and streets.
An **internal** war unleashed while all hell broke loose outside.
The smell of hopelessness is heavy, thick enough to **taste**.
But the **aroma** of fresh tortillas cuts through the fog.
It stirs memories of when things were **good**.
When the old woman was beautiful and offered laughter.
Now all she offers are tortillas... and **hatred**.

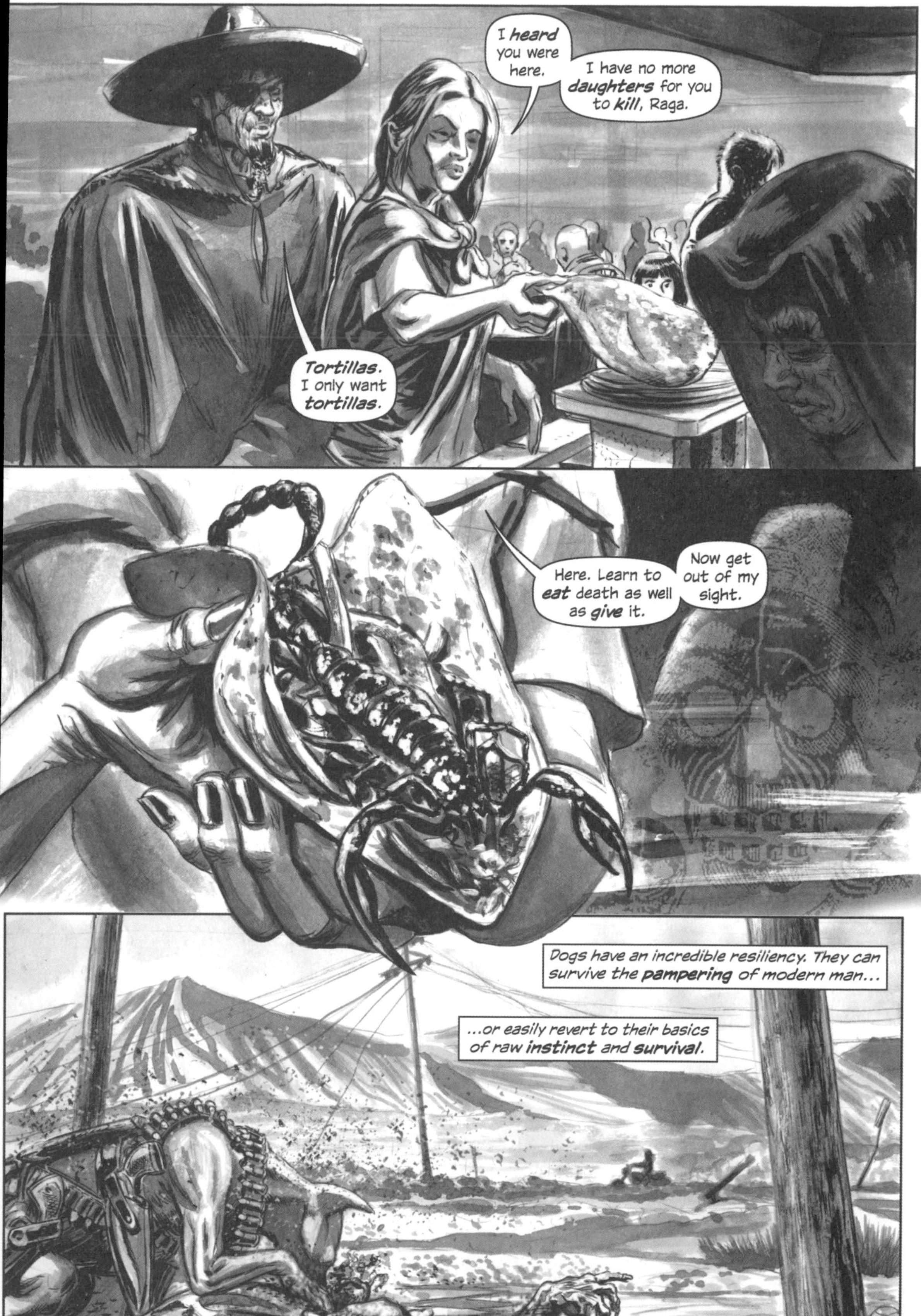

I heard you were here.
I have no more daughters for you to kill, Raga.
Tortillas. I only want tortillas.
Here. Learn to eat death as well as give it.
Now get out of my sight.
Dogs have an incredible resiliency. They can survive the pampering of modern man...
...or easily revert to their basics of raw instinct and survival.

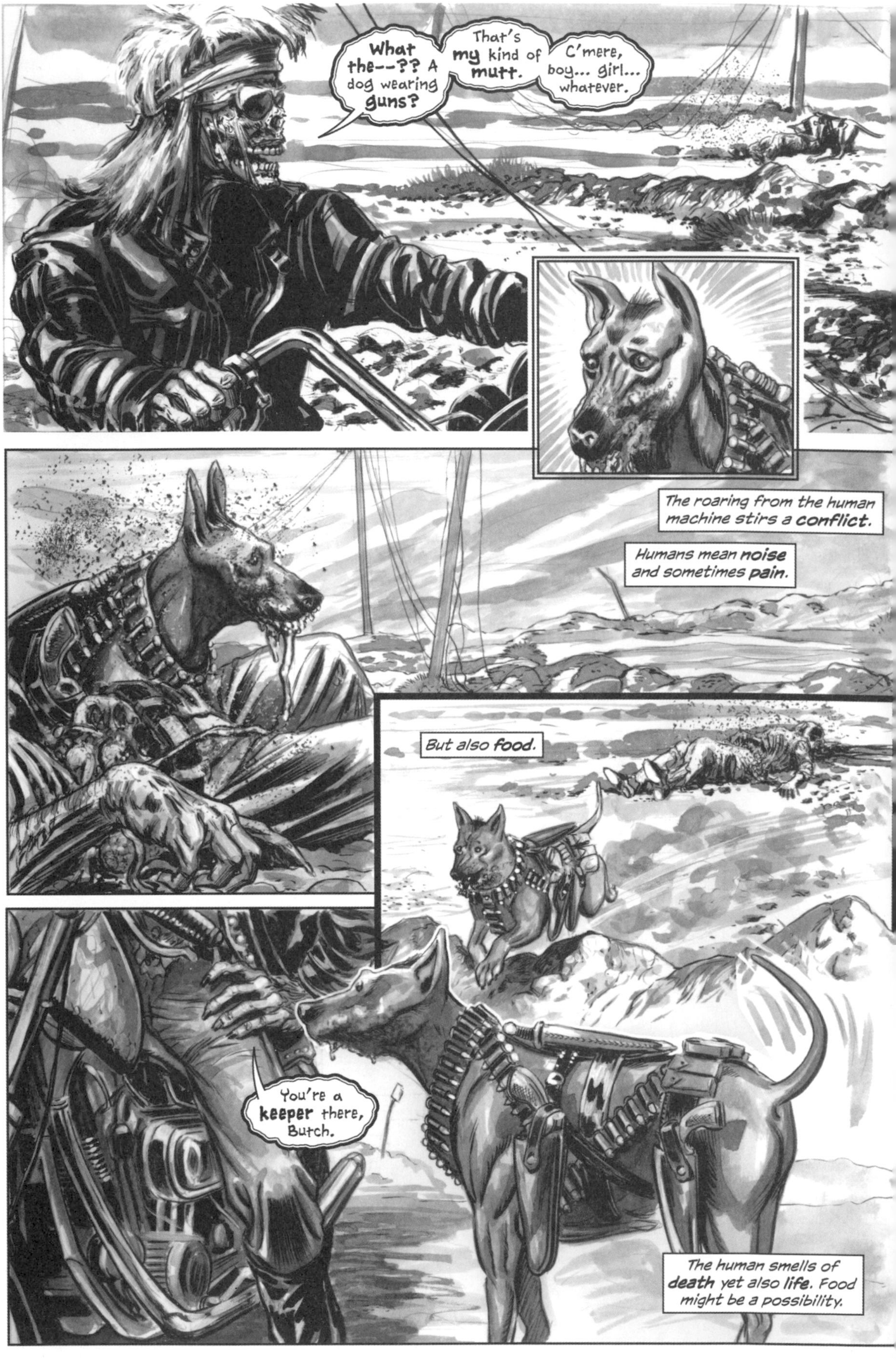
What the--?? A dog wearing guns?
That's my kind of mutt.
C'mere, boy... girl... whatever.
The roaring from the human machine stirs a conflict.
Humans mean noise and sometimes pain.
But also food.
You're a keeper there, Butch.
The human smells of death yet also life. Food might be a possibility.

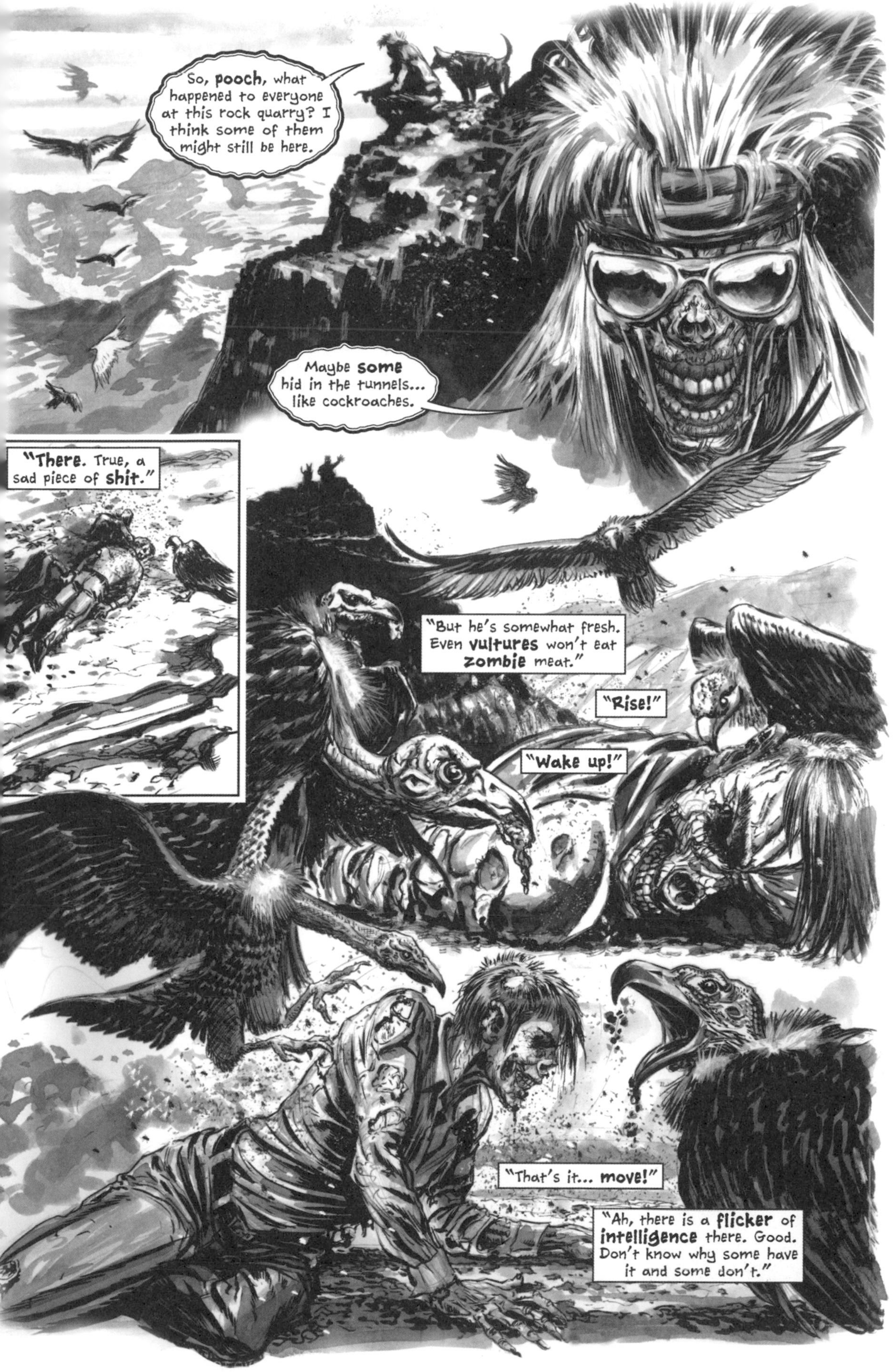
So, pooch, what happened to everyone at this rock quarry? I think some of them might still be here.
Maybe some hid in the tunnels... like cockroaches.
"There. True, a sad piece of shit."
"But he's somewhat fresh. Even vultures won't eat zombie meat."
"Rise!"
"Wake up!"
"That's it... move!"
"Ah, there is a flicker of intelligence there. Good. Don't know why some have it and some don't."

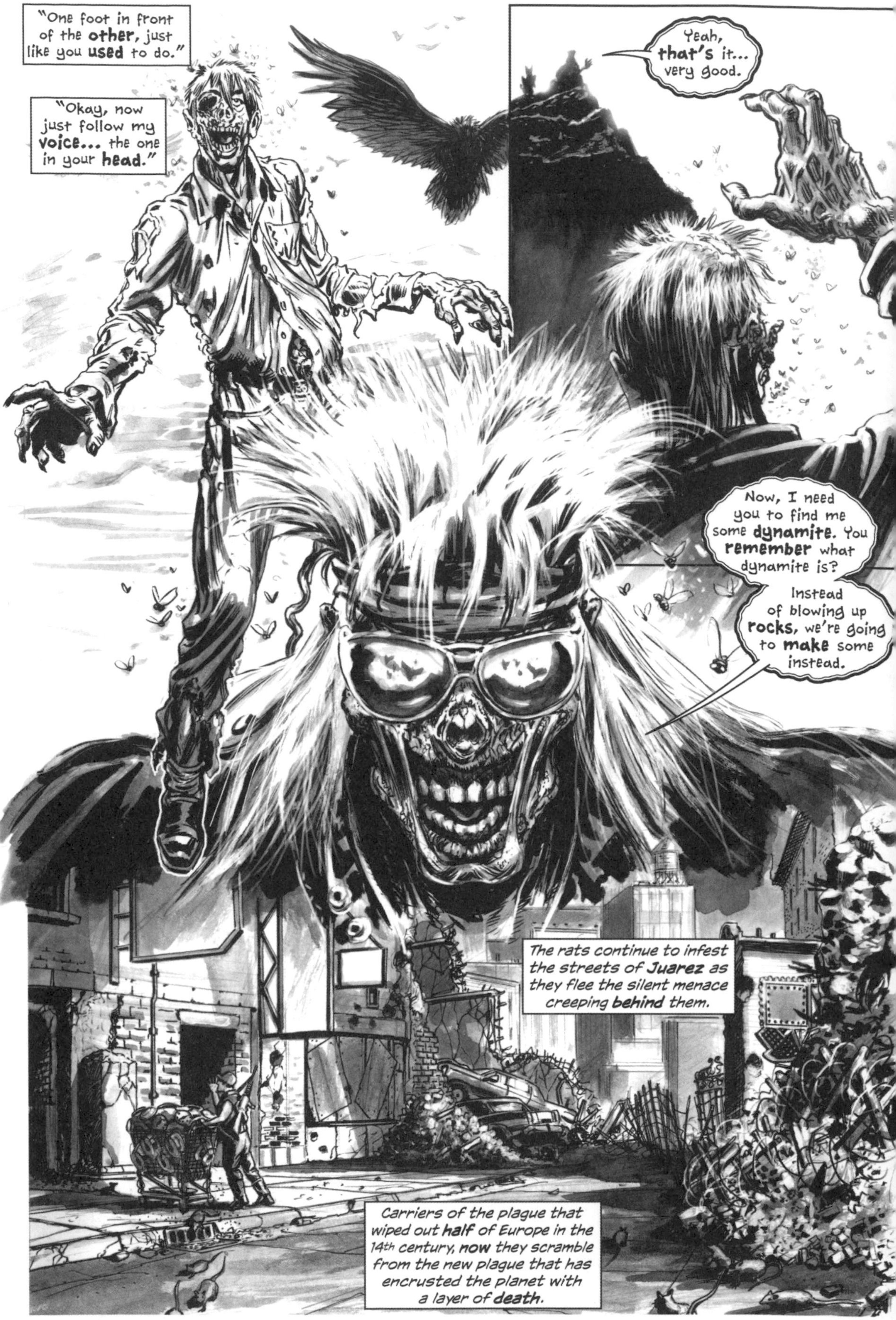
"One foot in front of the other, just like you used to do."
"Okay, now just follow my voice... the one in your head."
Yeah, that's it... very good.
Now, I need you to find me some dynamite. You remember what dynamite is?
Instead of blowing up rocks, we're going to make some instead.
The rats continue to infest the streets of Juarez as they flee the silent menace creeping behind them.
Carriers of the plague that wiped out half of Europe in the 14th century, now they scramble from the new plague that has encrusted the planet with a layer of death.

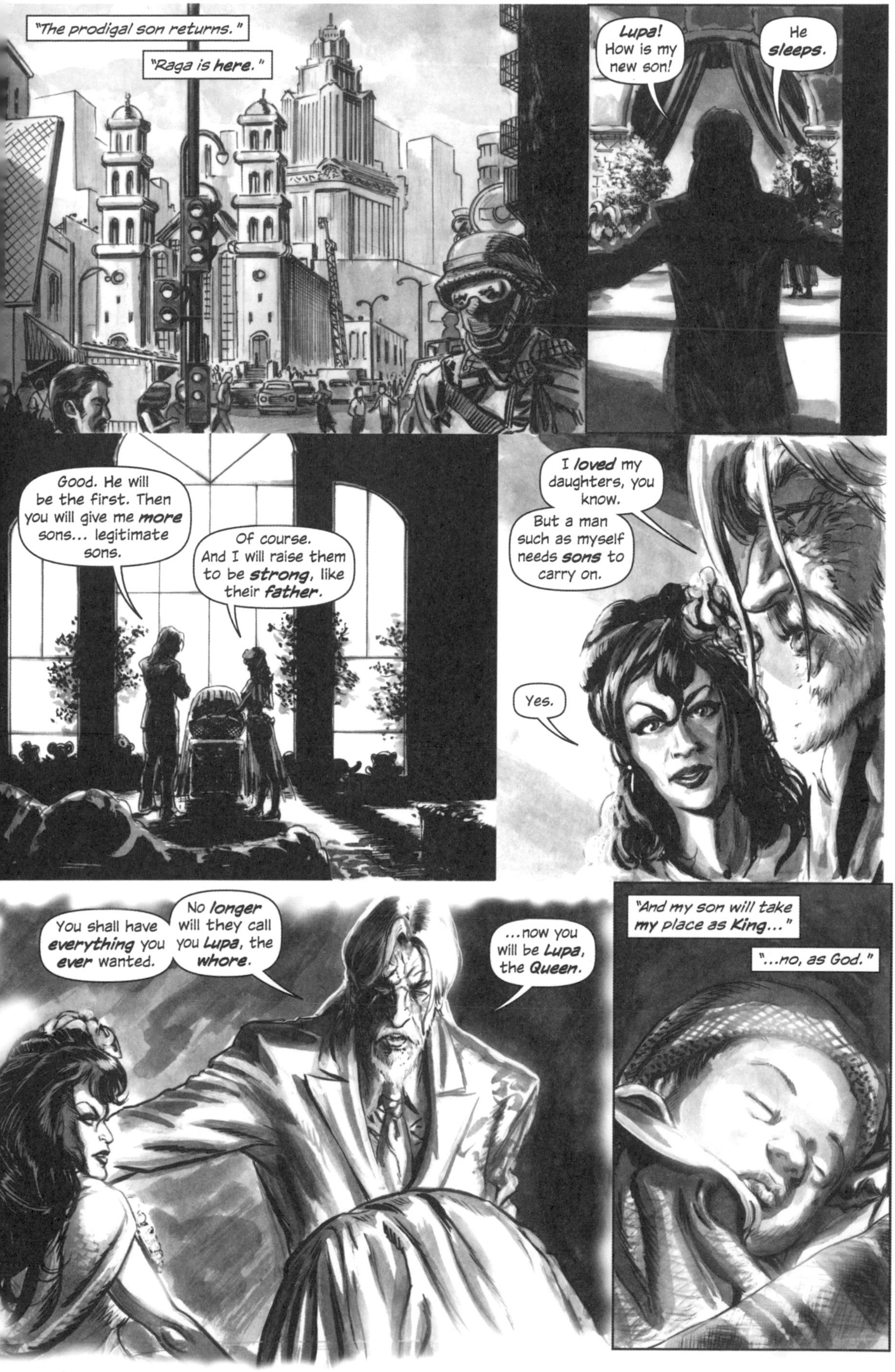
"The prodigal son returns."
"Raga is here."
Lupa! How is my new son!
He sleeps.
Good. He will be the first. Then you will give me more sons... legitimate sons.
Of course. And I will raise them to be strong, like their father.
I loved my daughters, you know.
But a man such as myself needs sons to carry on.
Yes.
You shall have everything you ever wanted.
No longer will they call you Lupa, the whore.
...now you will be Lupa, the Queen.
"And my son will take my place as King..."
"...no, as God."

Chapter three

the SINS

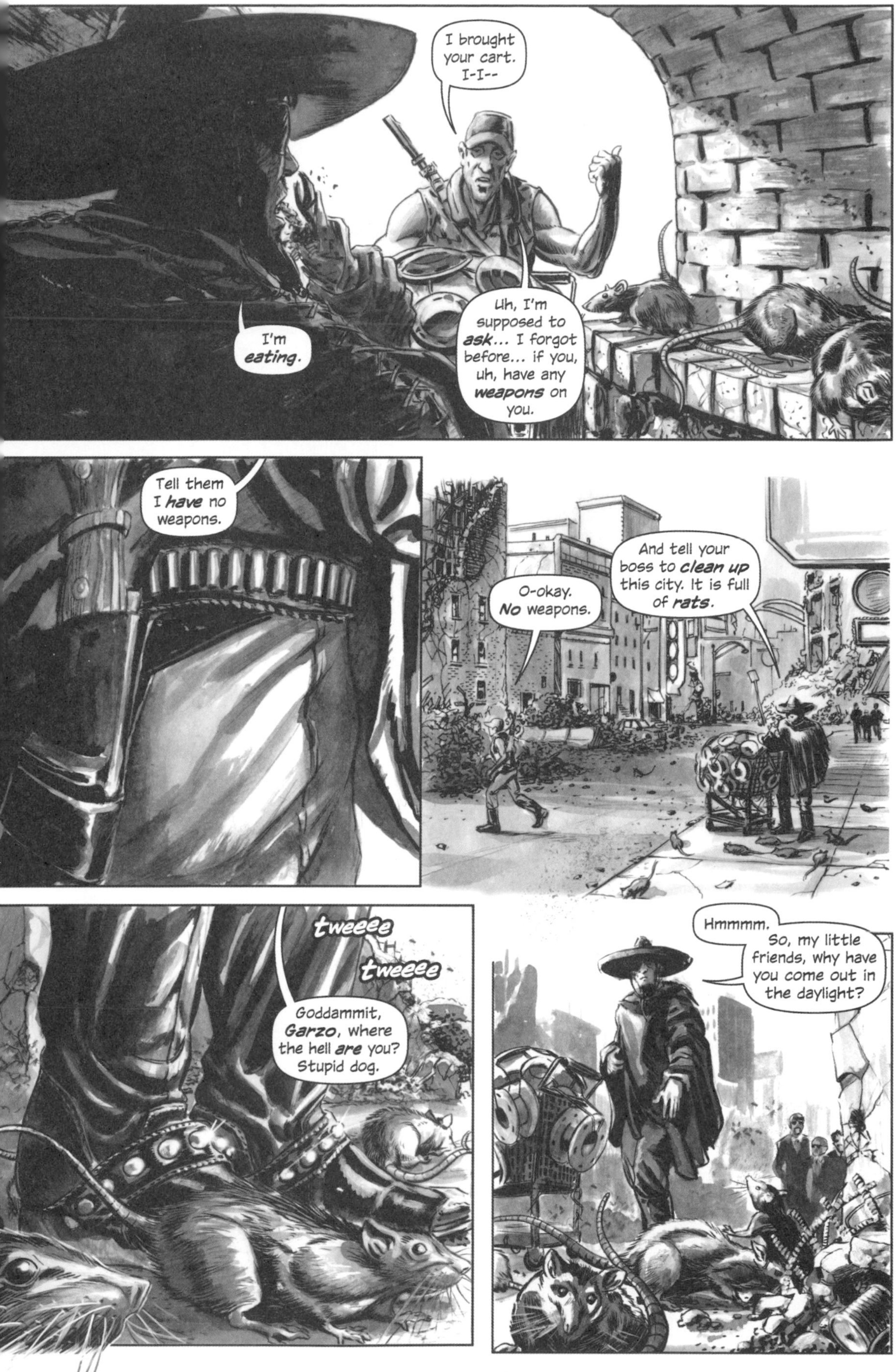

I brought your cart. I-I--
I'm *eating*.
Uh, I'm supposed to *ask*... I forgot before... if you, uh, have any *weapons* on you.
Tell them I *have* no weapons.
O-okay. *No* weapons.
And tell your boss to *clean up* this city. It is full of *rats*.
tweeee
tweeee
Goddammit, *Garzo*, where the hell *are* you? Stupid dog.
Hmmmm.
So, my little friends, why have you come out in the daylight?

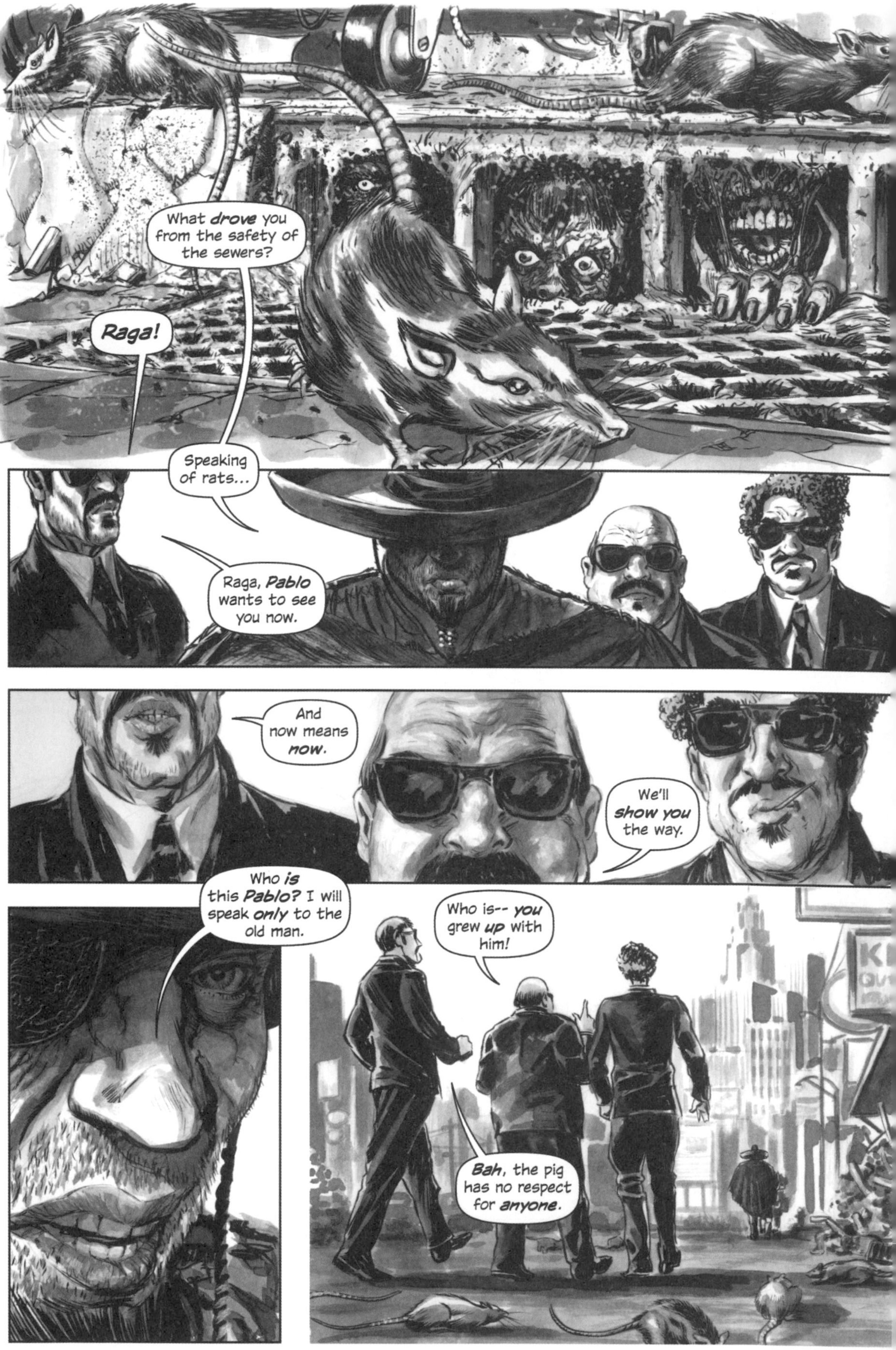
What drove you from the safety of the sewers?
Raga!
Speaking of rats...
Raga, Pablo wants to see you now.
And now means now.
We'll show you the way.
Who is this Pablo? I will speak only to the old man.
Who is-- you grew up with him!
Bah, the pig has no respect for anyone.

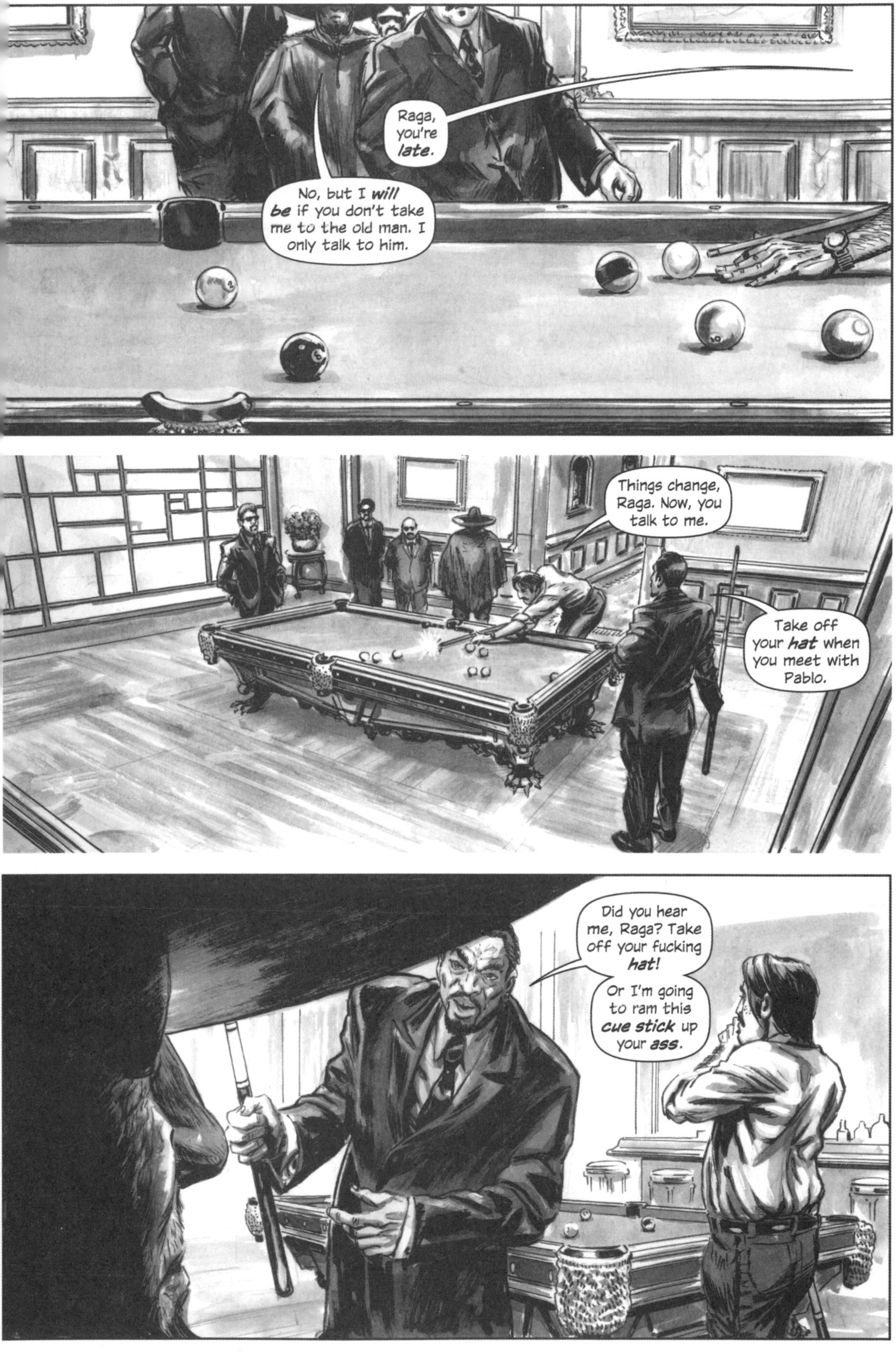
Raga, you're *late*.
No, but I *will be* if you don't take me to the old man. I only talk to him.
Things change, Raga. Now, you talk to me.
Take off your *hat* when you meet with Pablo.
Did you hear me, Raga? Take off your fucking *hat!*
Or I'm going to ram this *cue stick* up your *ass*.

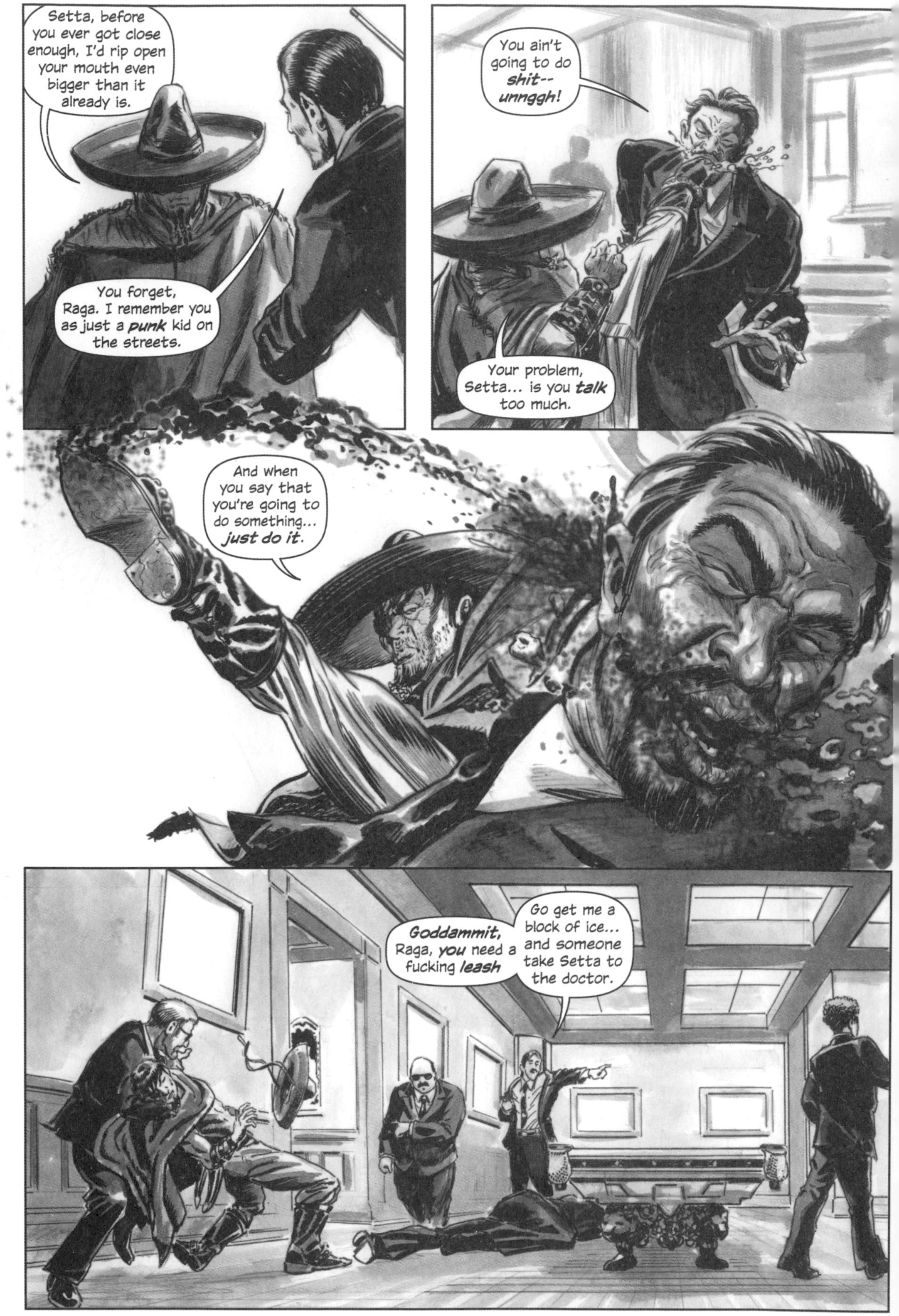
Setta, before you ever got close enough, I'd rip open your mouth even bigger than it already is.
You forget, Raga. I remember you as just a punk kid on the streets.
You ain't going to do shit-- unnggh!
Your problem, Setta... is you talk too much.
And when you say that you're going to do something... just do it.
Goddammit, Raga, you need a fucking leash
Go get me a block of ice... and someone take Setta to the doctor.

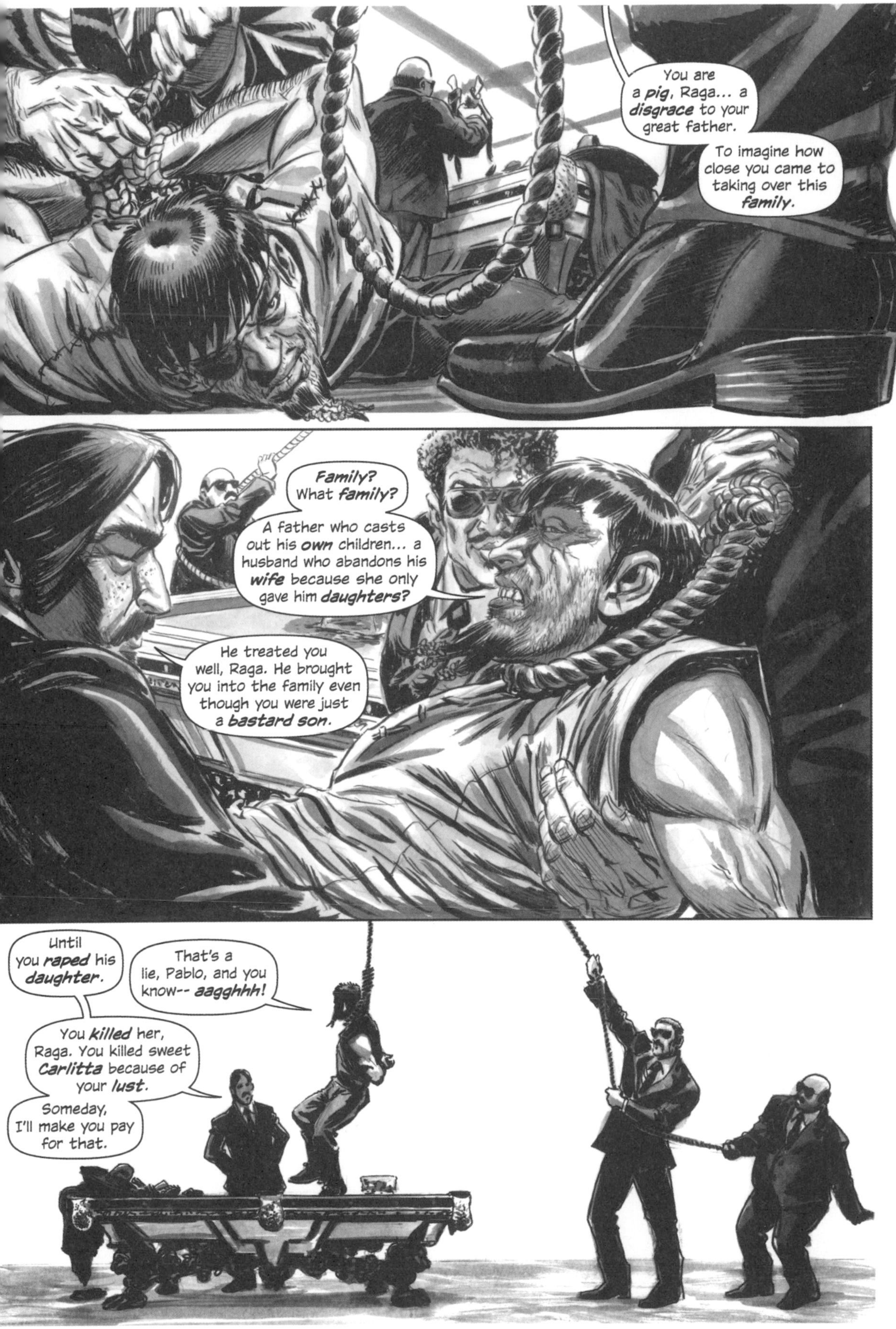
You are a pig, Raga... a disgrace to your great father.
To imagine how close you came to taking over this family.
Family? What family?
A father who casts out his own children... a husband who abandons his wife because she only gave him daughters?
He treated you well, Raga. He brought you into the family even though you were just a bastard son.
Until you raped his daughter.
That's a lie, Pablo, and you know-- aagghhh!
You killed her, Raga. You killed sweet Carlitta because of your lust.
Someday, I'll make you pay for that.

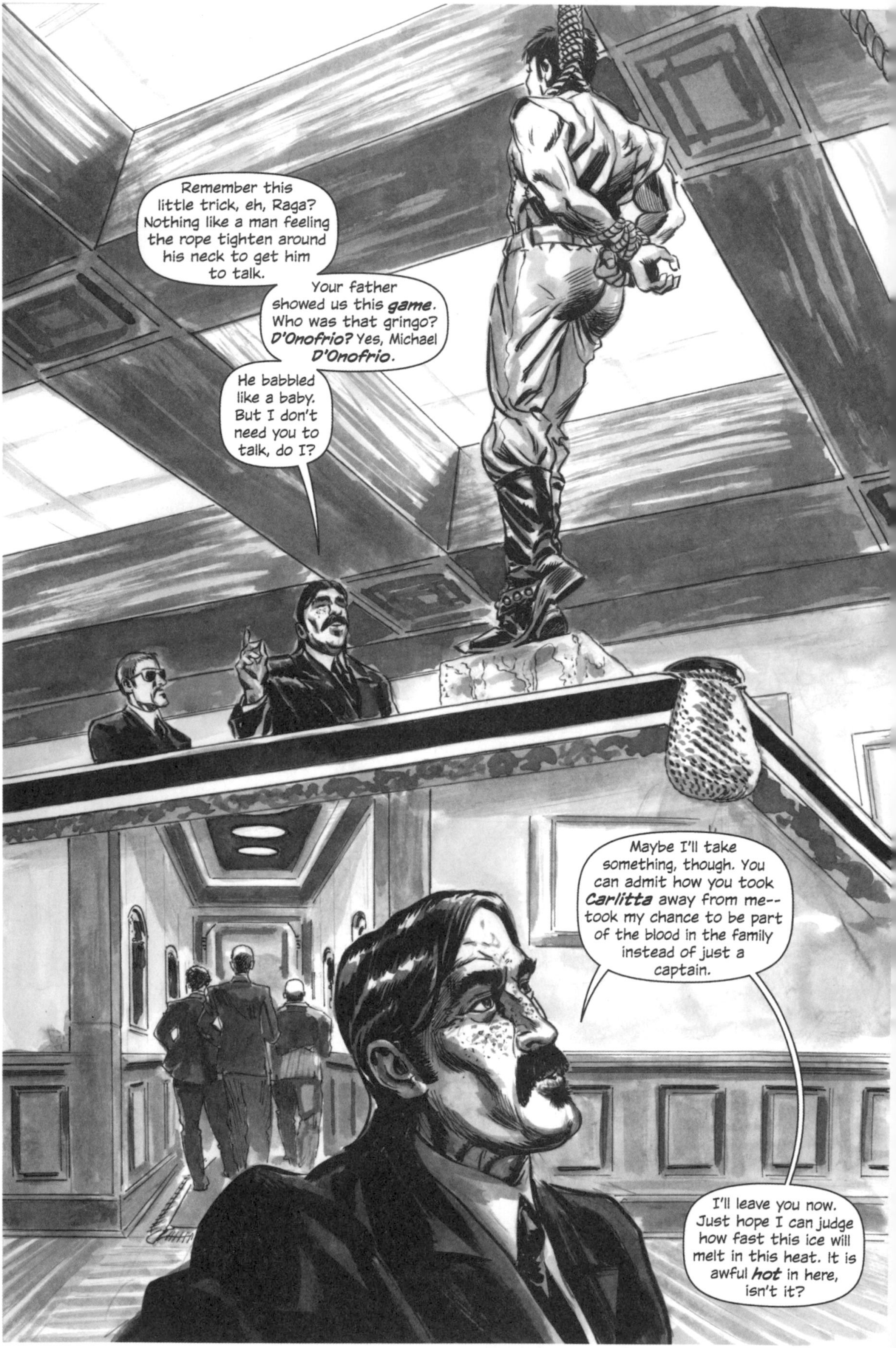
Remember this little trick, eh, Raga? Nothing like a man feeling the rope tighten around his neck to get him to talk.
Your father showed us this **game**. Who was that gringo? **D'Onofrio?** Yes, Michael **D'Onofrio**.
He babbled like a baby. But I don't need you to talk, do I?
Maybe I'll take something, though. You can admit how you took **Carlitta** away from me--took my chance to be part of the blood in the family instead of just a captain.
I'll leave you now. Just hope I can judge how fast this ice will melt in this heat. It is awful **hot** in here, isn't it?

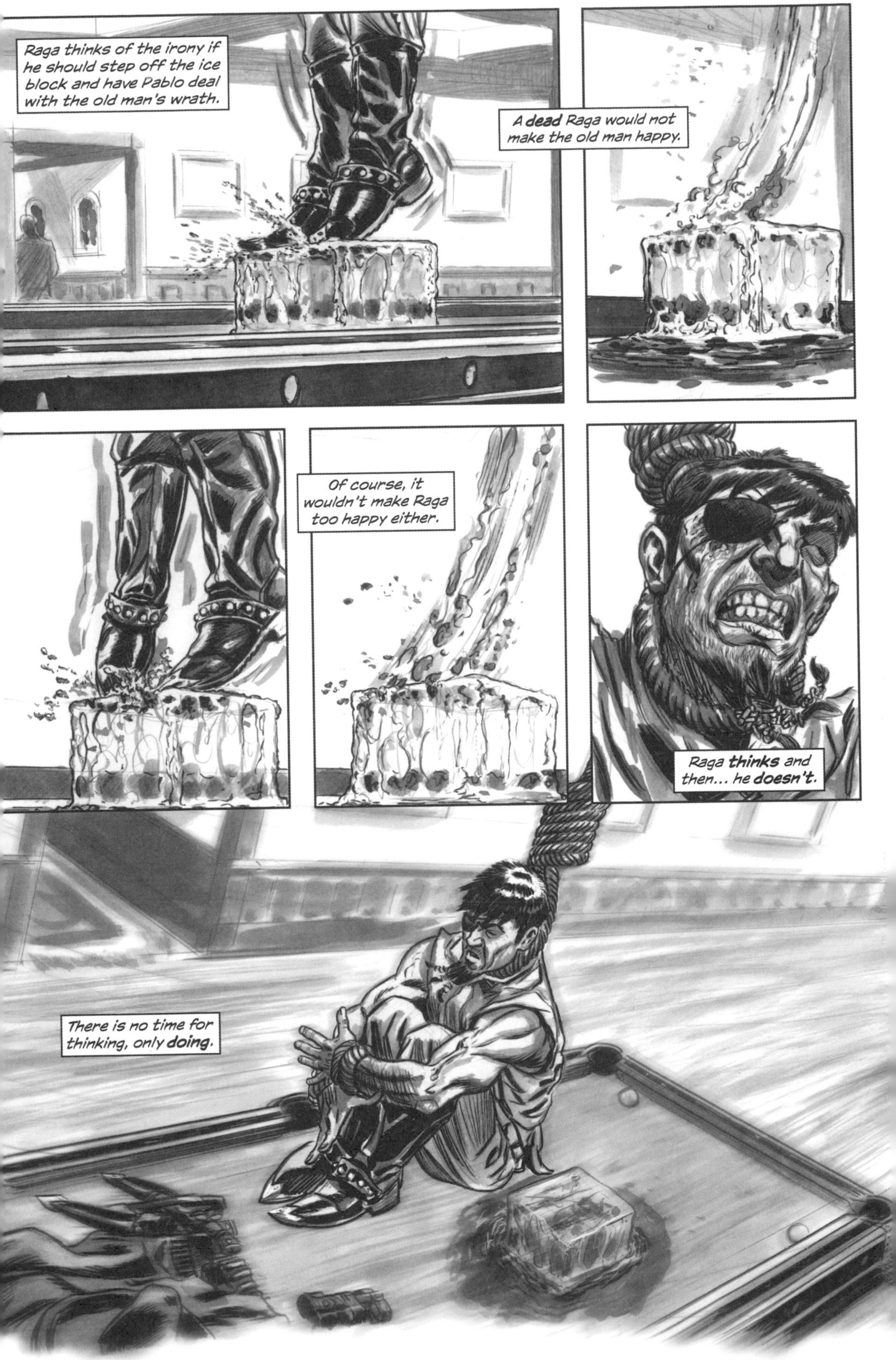
Raga thinks of the irony if he should step off the ice block and have Pablo deal with the old man's wrath.
A **dead** Raga would not make the old man happy.
Of course, it wouldn't make Raga too happy either.
Raga **thinks** and then... he **doesn't**.
There is no time for thinking, only **doing**.

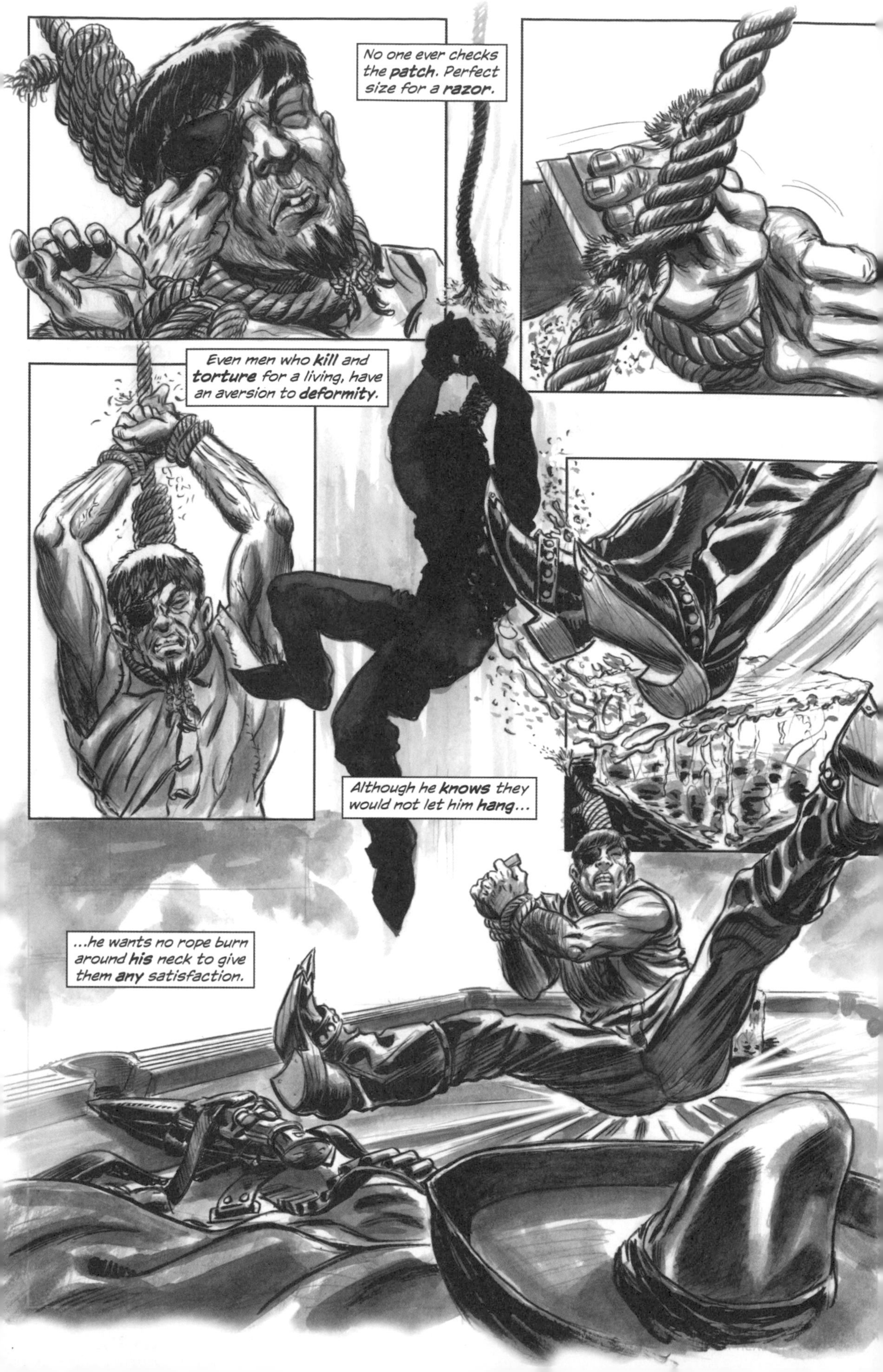
No one ever checks the patch. Perfect size for a razor.
Even men who kill and torture for a living, have an aversion to deformity.
Although he knows they would not let him hang...
...he wants no rope burn around his neck to give them any satisfaction.

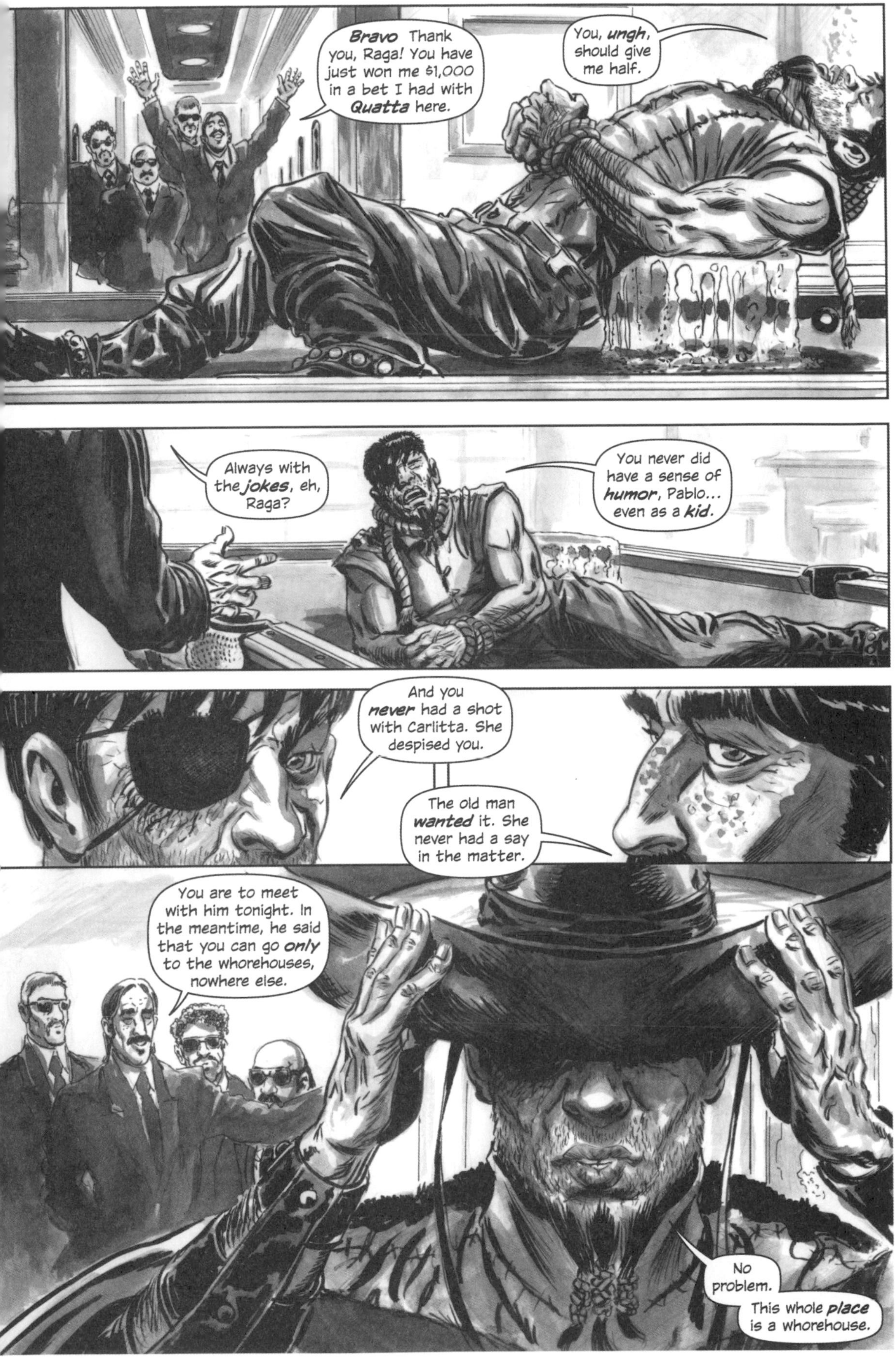

Bravo Thank you, Raga! You have just won me $1,000 in a bet I had with Quatta here.
You, ungh, should give me half.
Always with the jokes, eh, Raga?
You never did have a sense of humor, Pablo... even as a kid.
And you never had a shot with Carlitta. She despised you.
The old man wanted it. She never had a say in the matter.
You are to meet with him tonight. In the meantime, he said that you can go only to the whorehouses, nowhere else.
No problem.
This whole place is a whorehouse.

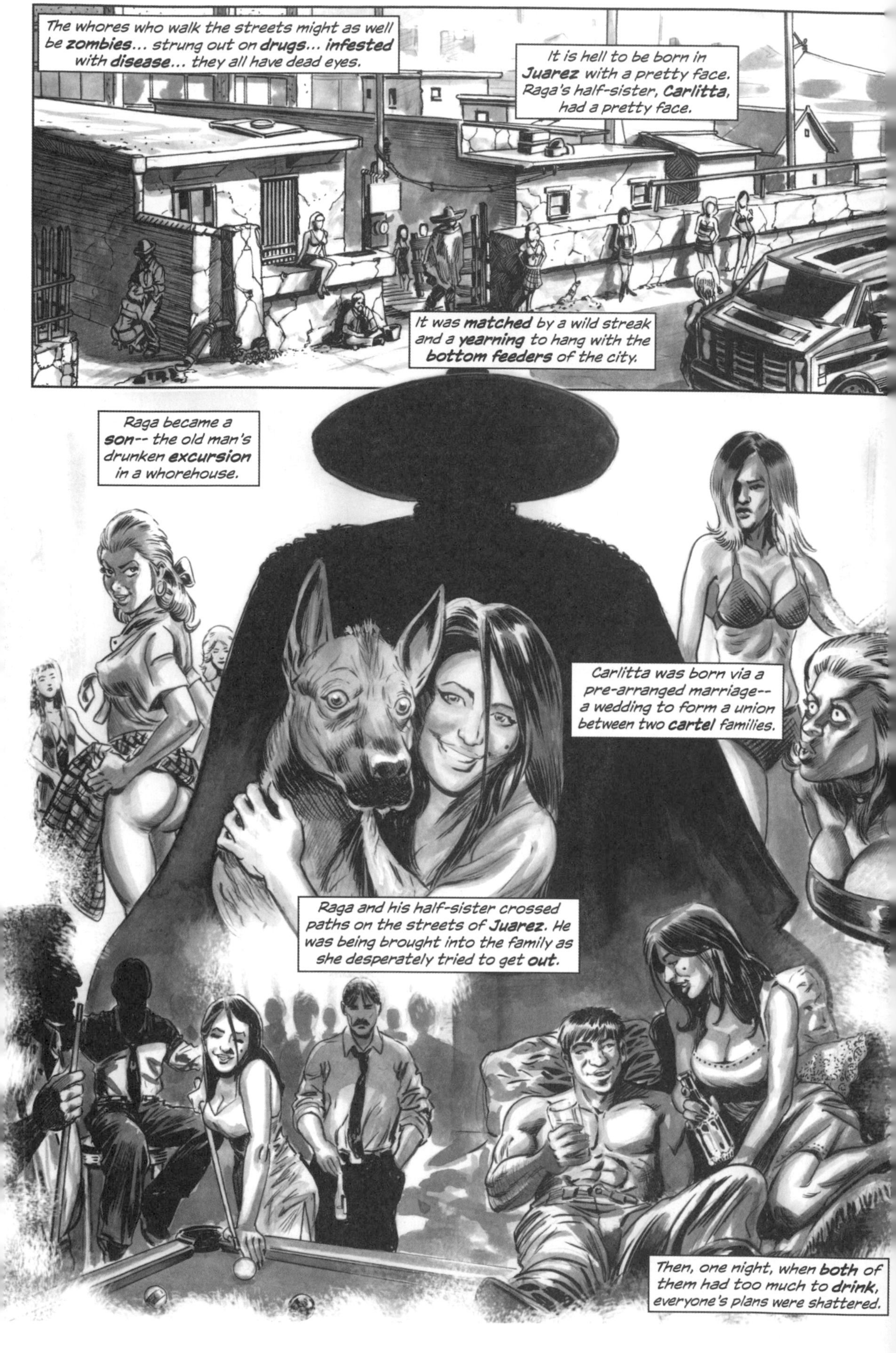

The whores who walk the streets might as well be **zombies**... strung out on **drugs**... **infested** with **disease**... they all have dead eyes.
It is hell to be born in **Juarez** with a pretty face. Raga's half-sister, **Carlitta**, had a pretty face.
It was **matched** by a wild streak and a **yearning** to hang with the **bottom feeders** of the city.
Raga became a **son**-- the old man's drunken **excursion** in a whorehouse.
Carlitta was born via a pre-arranged marriage-- a wedding to form a union between two **cartel** families.
Raga and his half-sister crossed paths on the streets of **Juarez**. He was being brought into the family as she desperately tried to get **out**.
Then, one night, when **both** of them had too much to **drink**, everyone's plans were shattered.

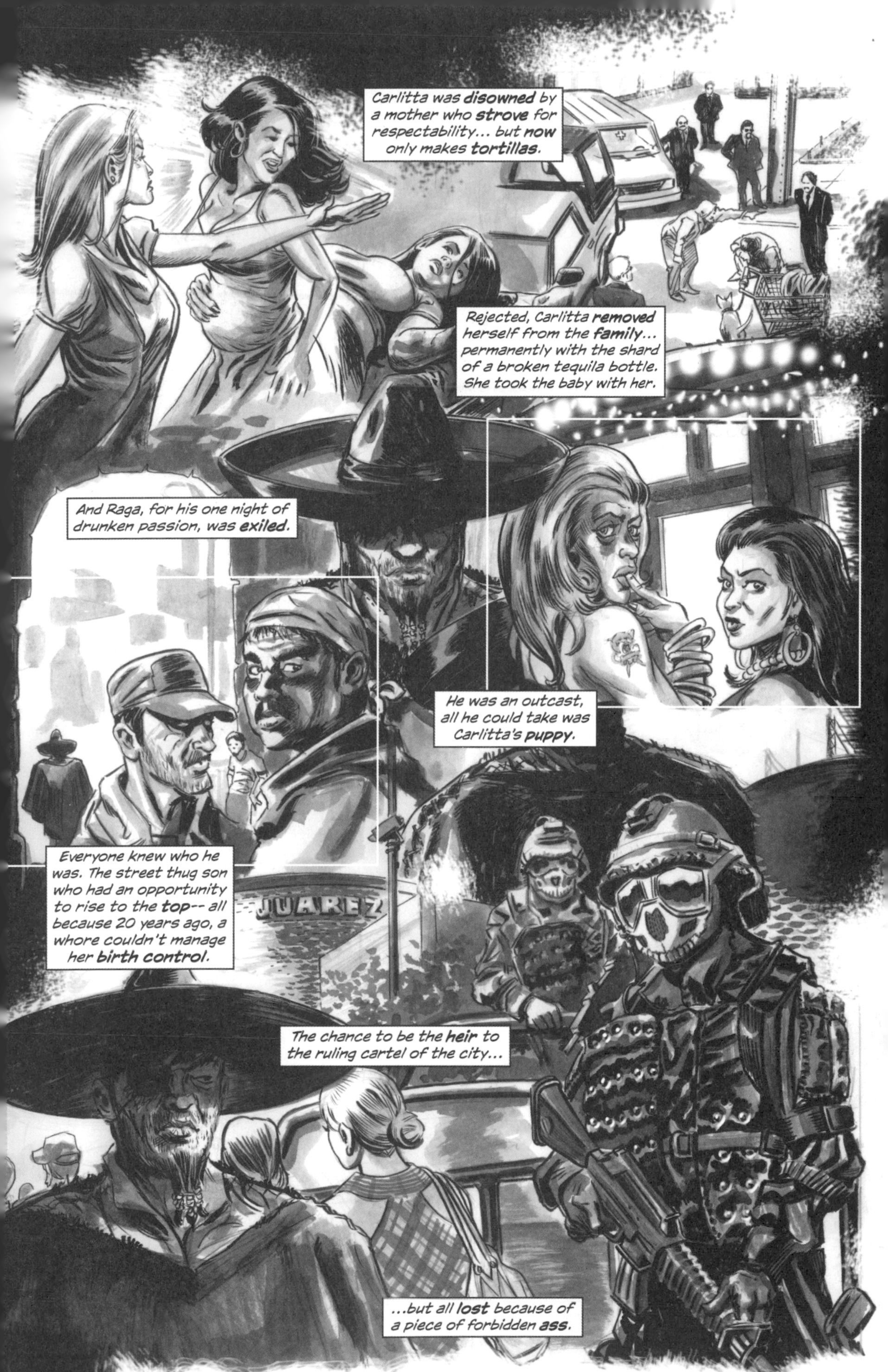
Carlitta was disowned by a mother who strove for respectability... but now only makes tortillas.
Rejected, Carlitta removed herself from the family... permanently with the shard of a broken tequila bottle. She took the baby with her.
And Raga, for his one night of drunken passion, was exiled.
He was an outcast, all he could take was Carlitta's puppy.
Everyone knew who he was. The street thug son who had an opportunity to rise to the top-- all because 20 years ago, a whore couldn't manage her birth control.
JUAREZ
The chance to be the heir to the ruling cartel of the city...
...but all lost because of a piece of forbidden ass.

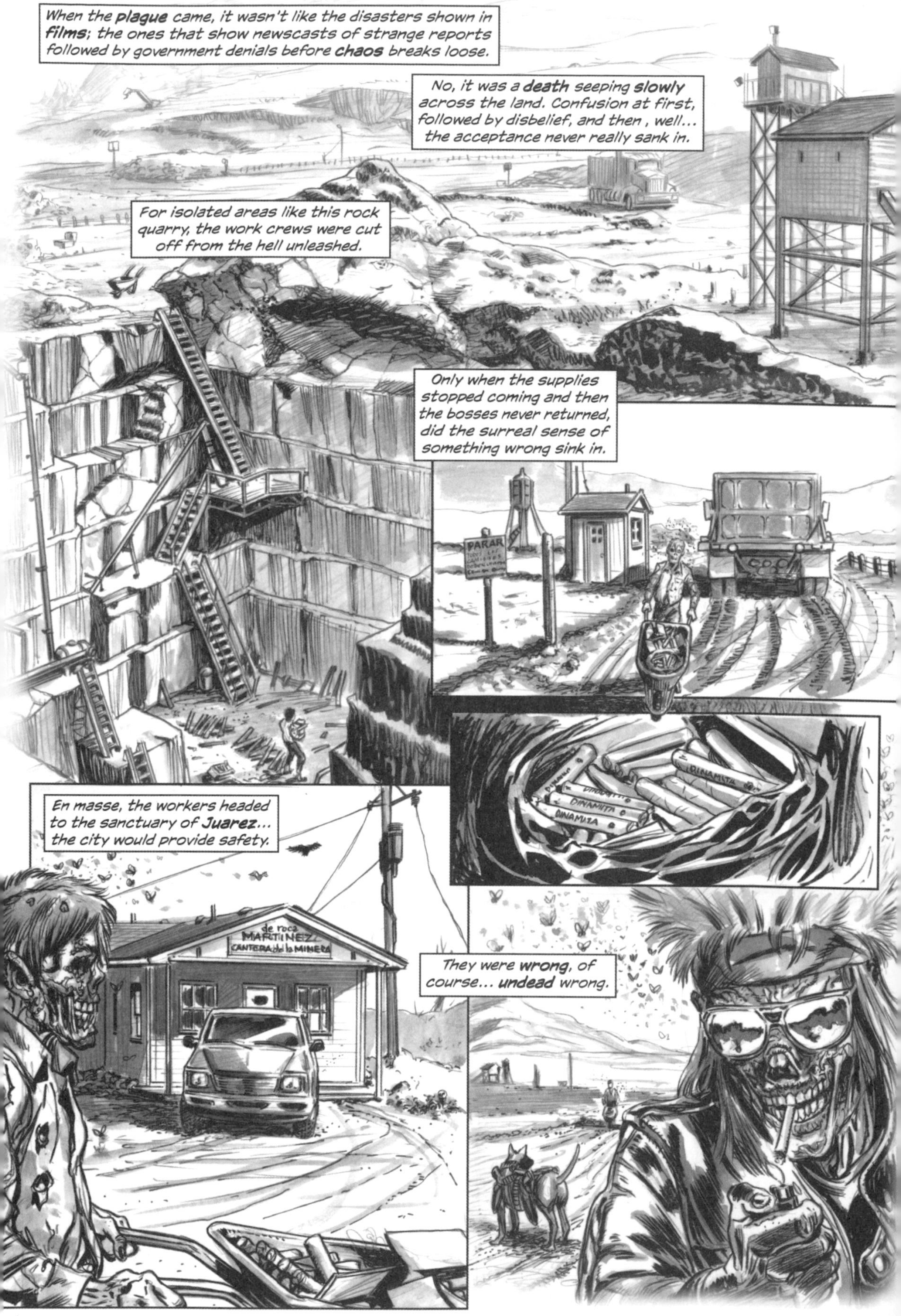
When the **plague** came, it wasn't like the disasters shown in **films**; the ones that show newscasts of strange reports followed by government denials before **chaos** breaks loose.
No, it was a **death** seeping **slowly** across the land. Confusion at first, followed by disbelief, and then , well... the acceptance never really sank in.
For isolated areas like this rock quarry, the work crews were cut off from the hell unleashed.
Only when the supplies stopped coming and then the bosses never returned, did the surreal sense of something wrong sink in.
PARAR
DINAMITA
DINAMITA
DINAMITA
DINAMITA
En masse, the workers headed to the sanctuary of **Juarez**... the city would provide safety.
de roca
MARTINEZ
CANTERA de la MINERA
They were **wrong**, of course... **undead** wrong.

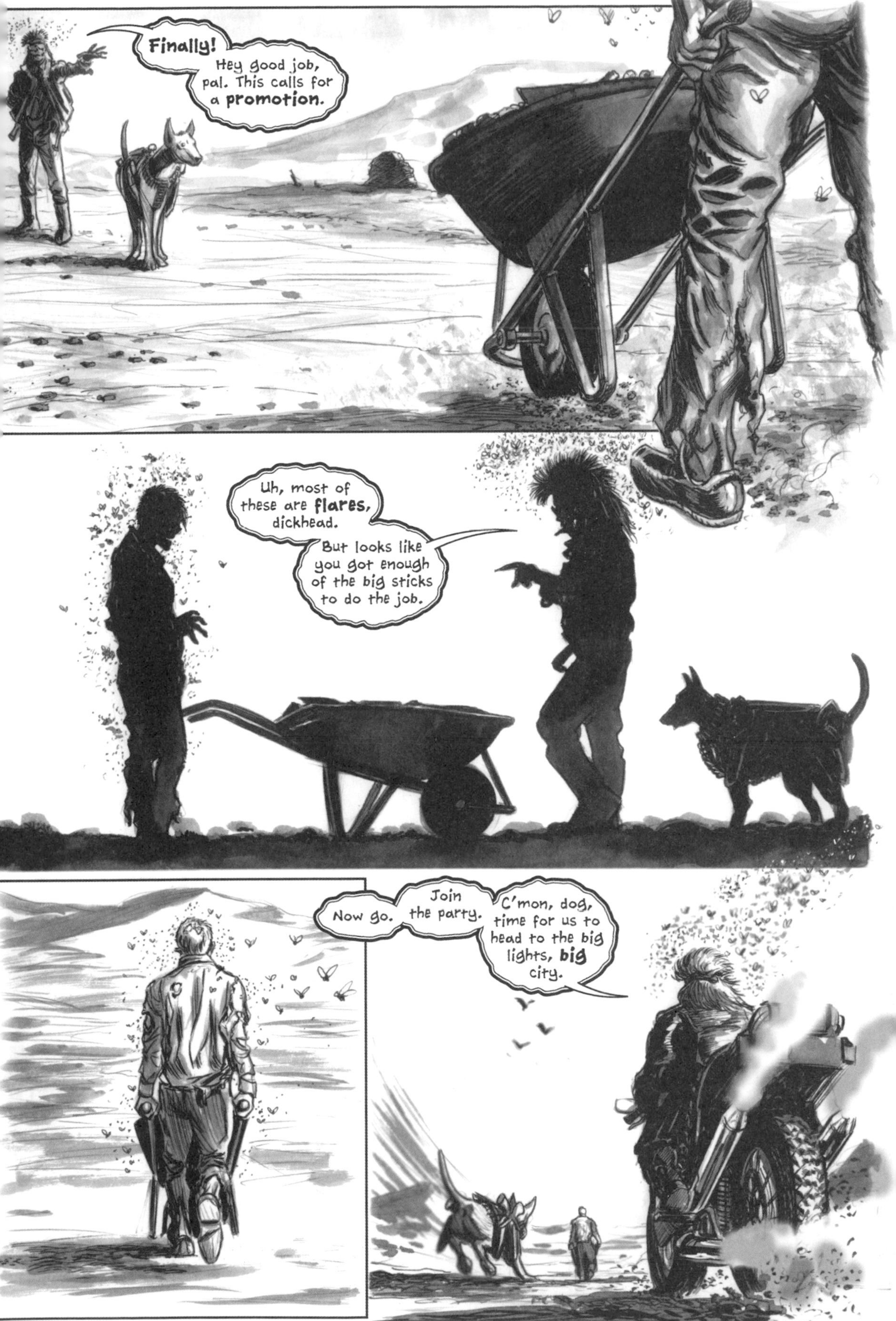
Finally!
Hey good job, pal. This calls for a **promotion**.
Uh, most of these are **flares**, dickhead.
But looks like you got enough of the big sticks to do the job.
Now go.
Join the party.
C'mon, dog, time for us to head to the big lights, **big** city.

Chapter four

the

PLANS

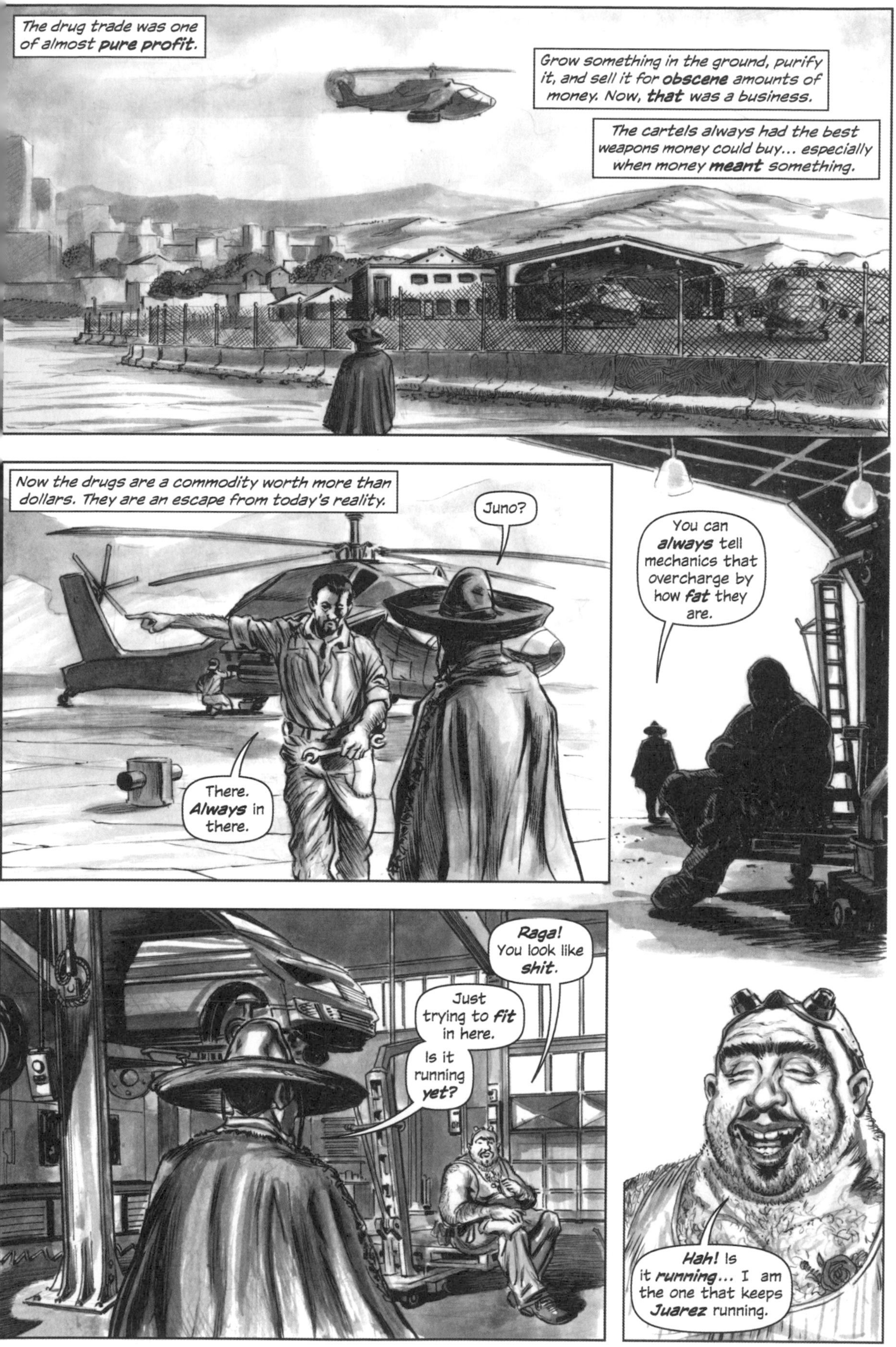
The drug trade was one of almost **pure profit**.
Grow something in the ground, purify it, and sell it for **obscene** amounts of money. Now, **that** was a business.
The cartels always had the best weapons money could buy... especially when money **meant** something.
Now the drugs are a commodity worth more than dollars. They are an escape from today's reality.
Juno?
There. **Always** in there.
You can **always** tell mechanics that overcharge by how **fat** they are.
Raga! You look like **shit**.
Just trying to **fit** in here.
Is it running **yet?**
Hah! Is it **running...** I am the one that keeps **Juarez** running.

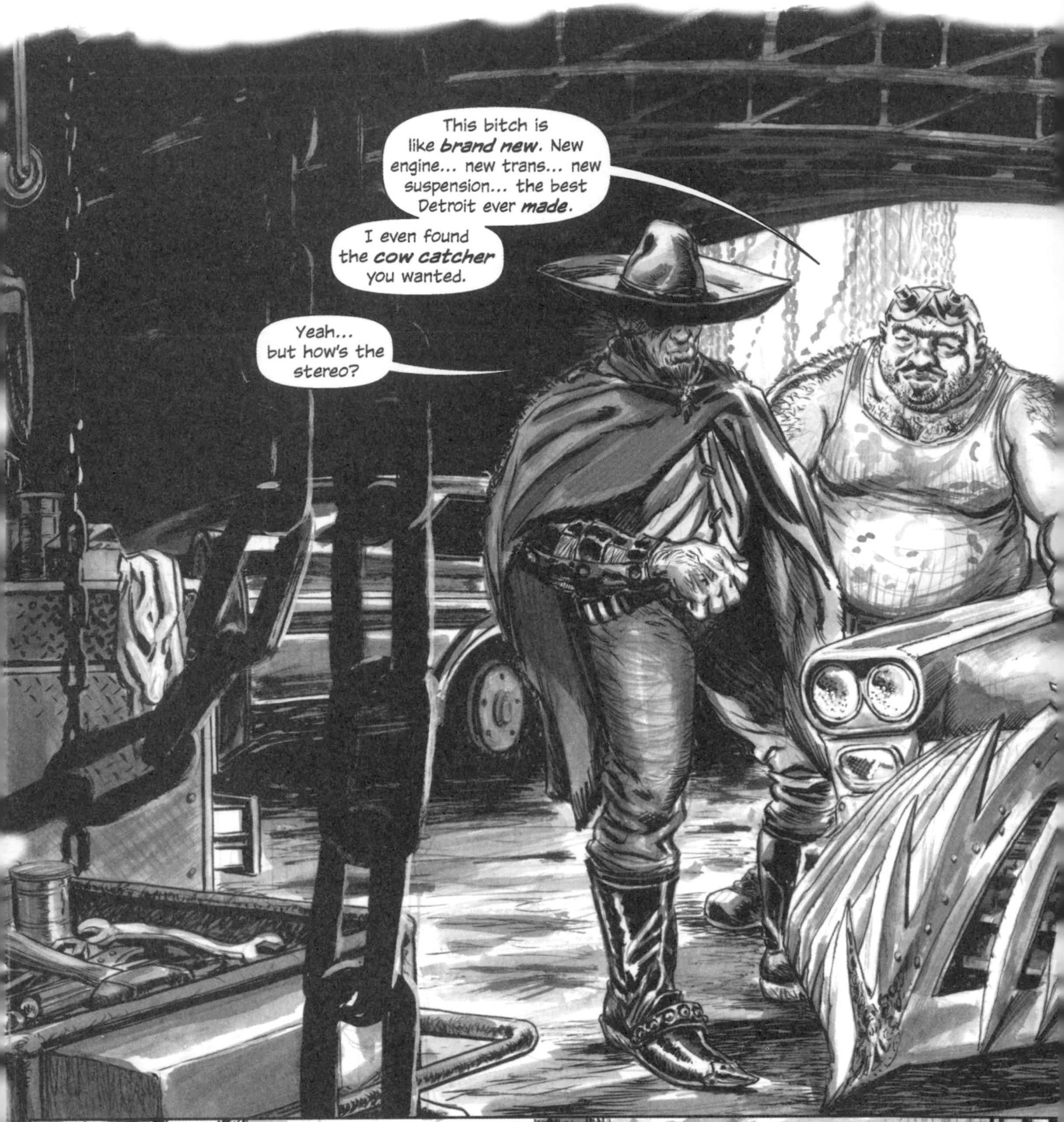
This bitch is like brand new. New engine... new trans... new suspension... the best Detroit ever made.
I even found the cow catcher you wanted.
Yeah... but how's the stereo?

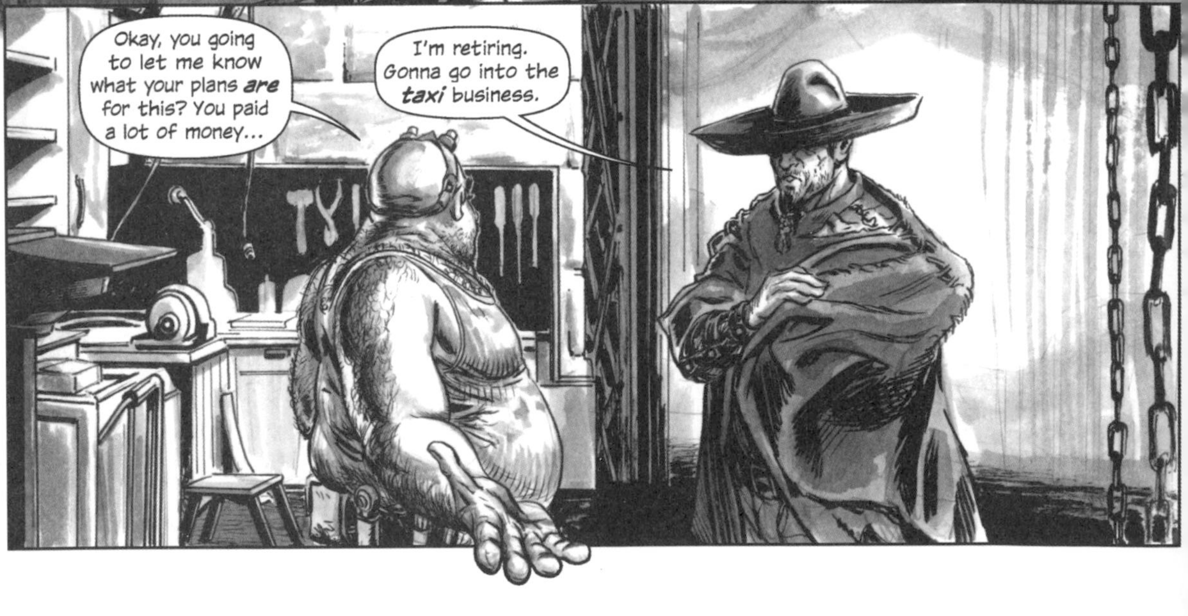
Okay, you going to let me know what your plans are for this? You paid a lot of money...
I'm retiring. Gonna go into the taxi business.

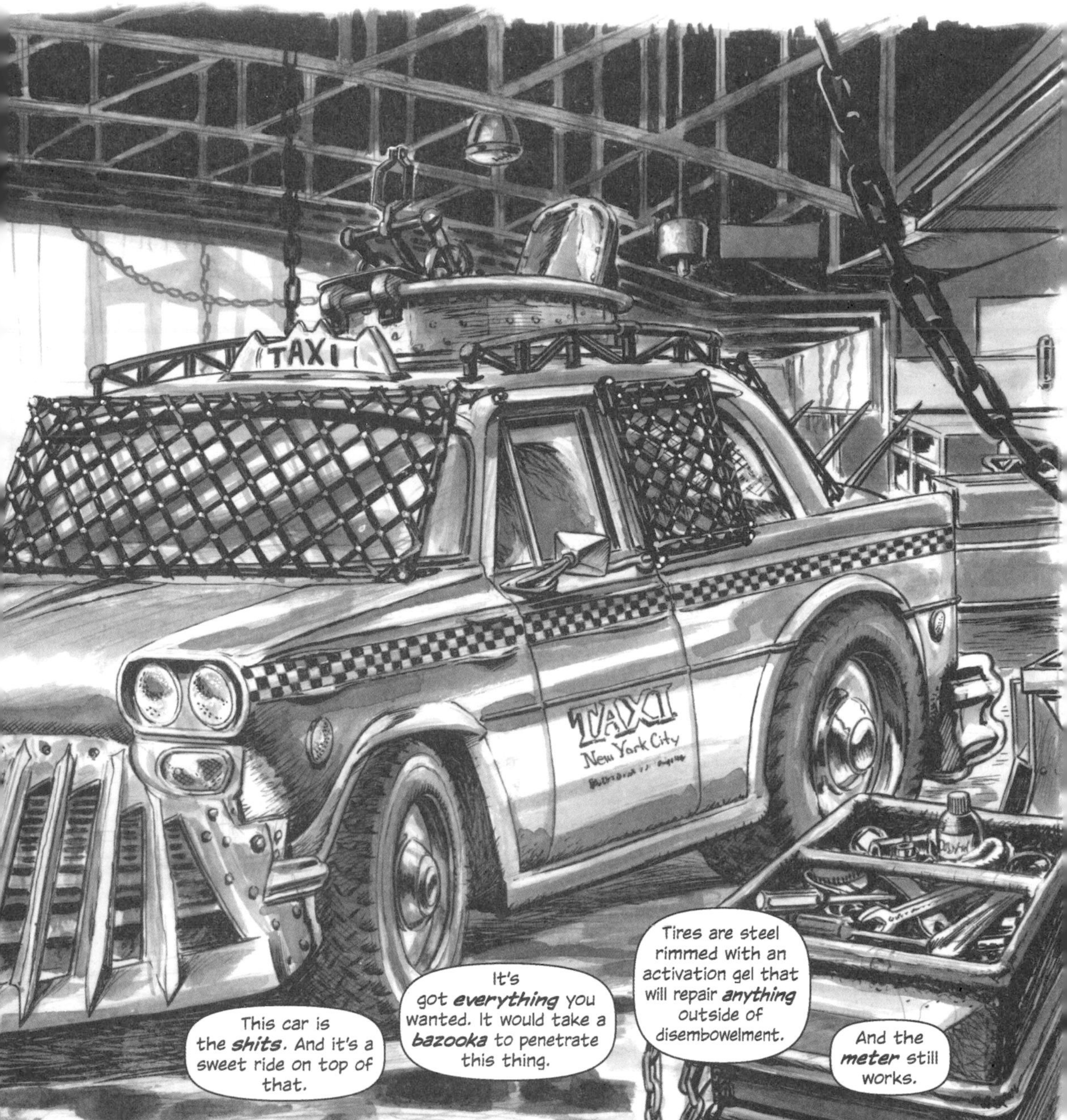
TAXI
TAXI
New York City
This car is the *shits*. And it's a sweet ride on top of that.
It's got *everything* you wanted. It would take a *bazooka* to penetrate this thing.
Tires are steel rimmed with an activation gel that will repair *anything* outside of disembowelment.
And the *meter* still works.

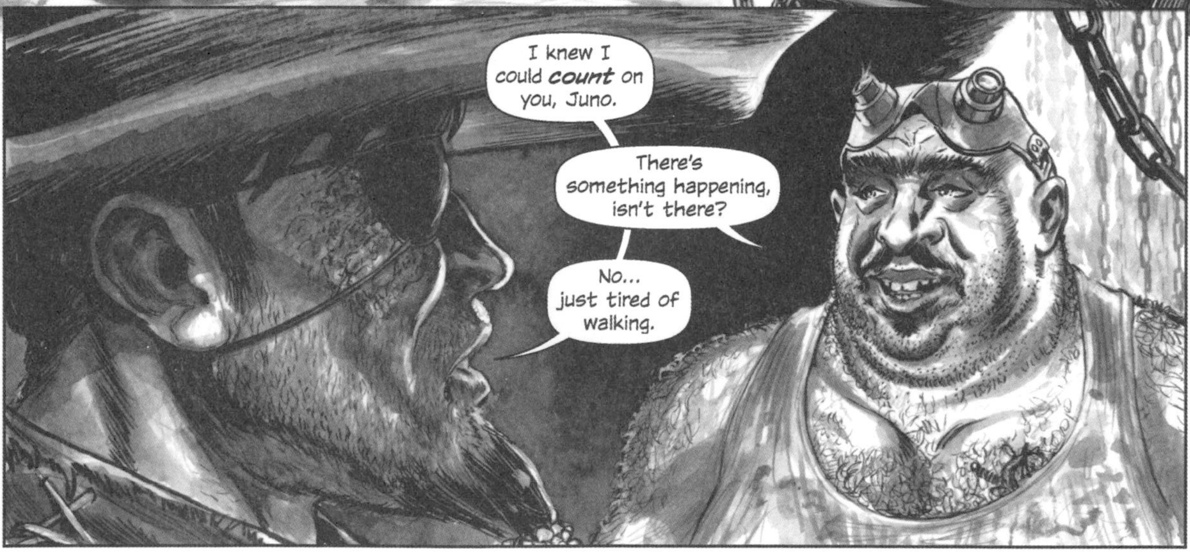
I knew I could *count* on you, Juno.
There's something happening, isn't there?
No... just tired of walking.

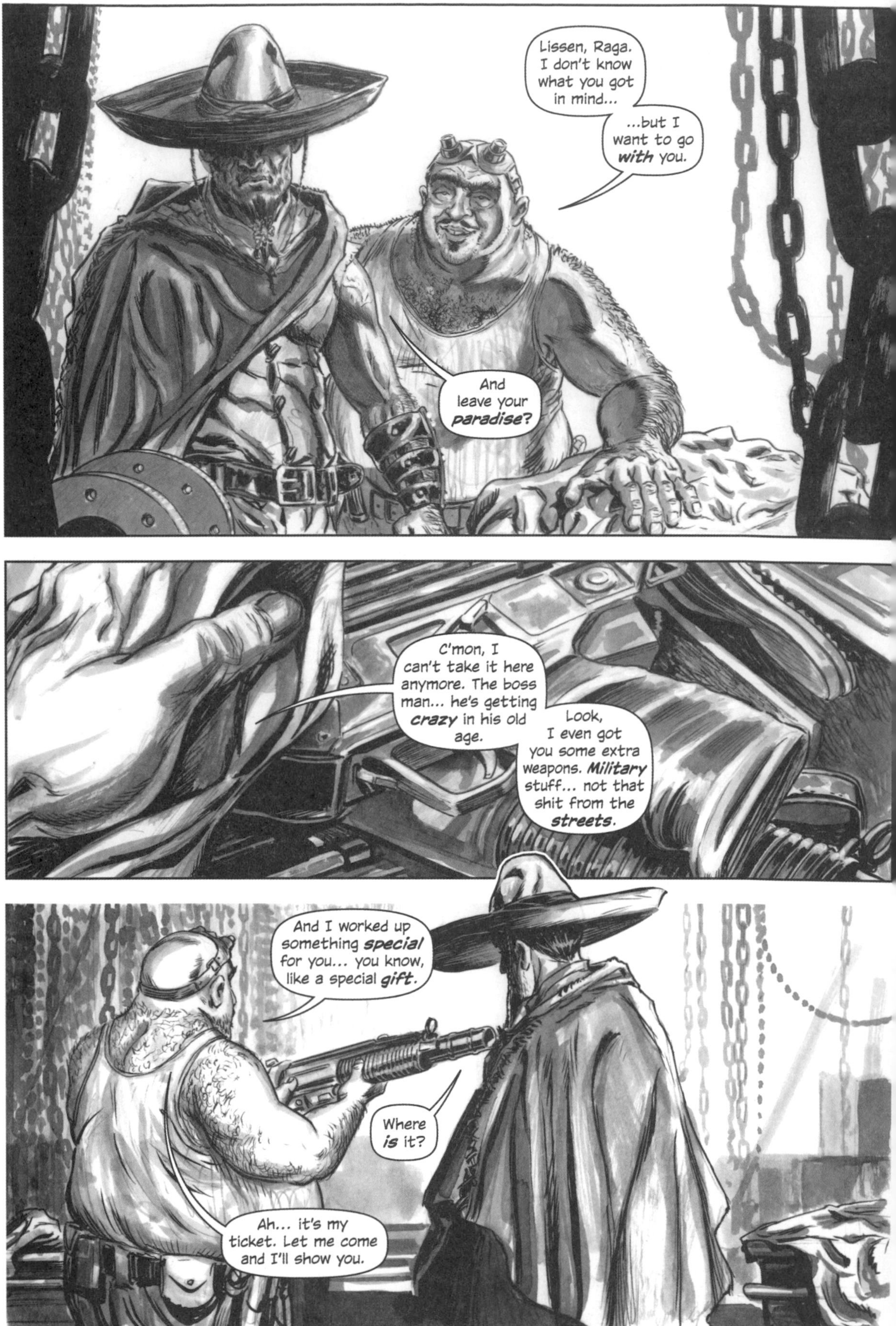
Lissen, Raga. I don't know what you got in mind...
...but I want to go *with* you.
And leave your *paradise?*
C'mon, I can't take it here anymore. The boss man... he's getting *crazy* in his old age.
Look, I even got you some extra weapons. *Military* stuff... not that shit from the *streets*.
And I worked up something *special* for you... you know, like a special *gift*.
Where *is* it?
Ah... it's my ticket. Let me come and I'll show you.

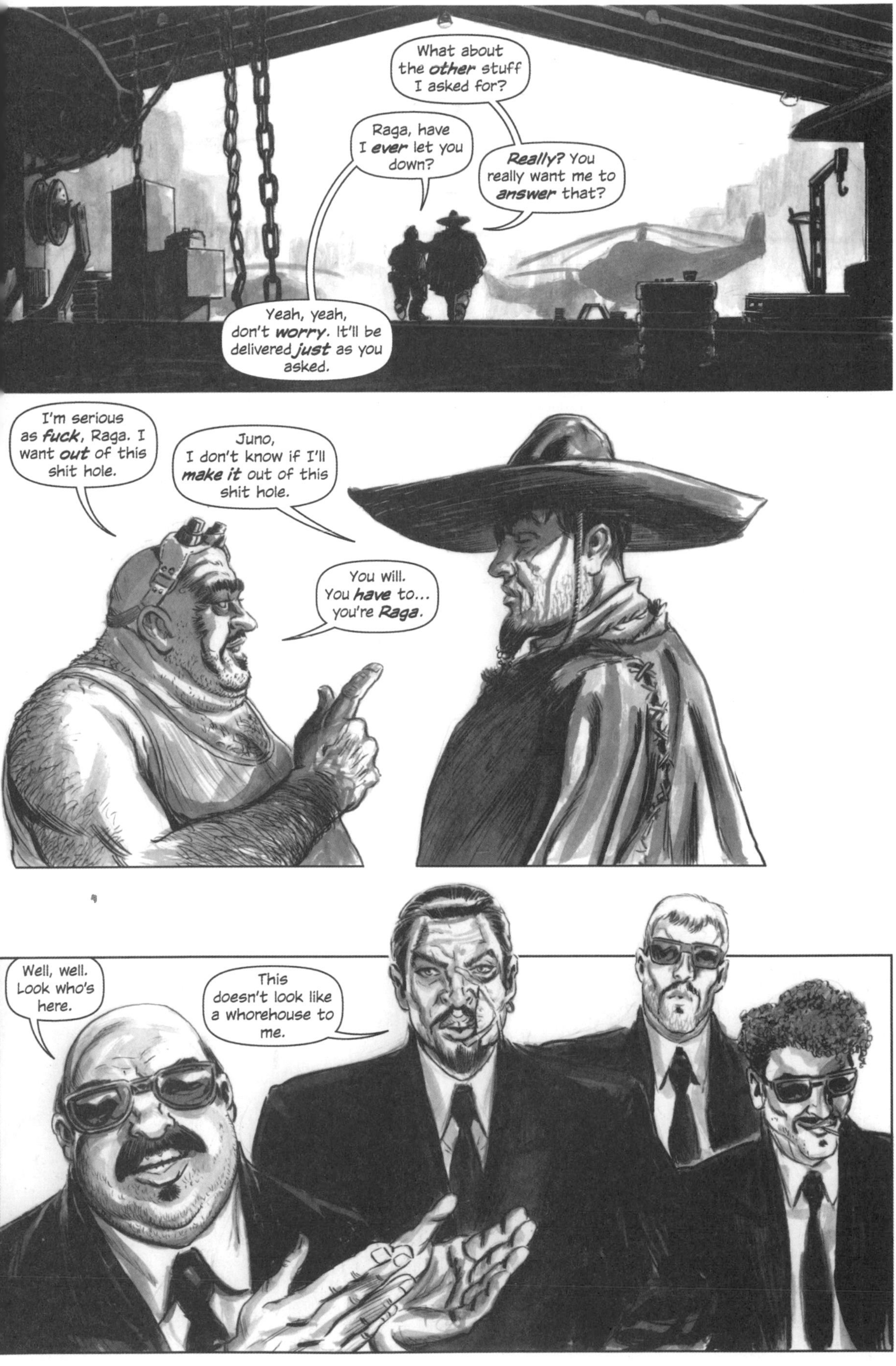
What about the other stuff I asked for?
Raga, have I ever let you down?
Really? You really want me to answer that?
Yeah, yeah, don't worry. It'll be delivered just as you asked.
I'm serious as fuck, Raga. I want out of this shit hole.
Juno, I don't know if I'll make it out of this shit hole.
You will. You have to... you're Raga.
Well, well. Look who's here.
This doesn't look like a whorehouse to me.

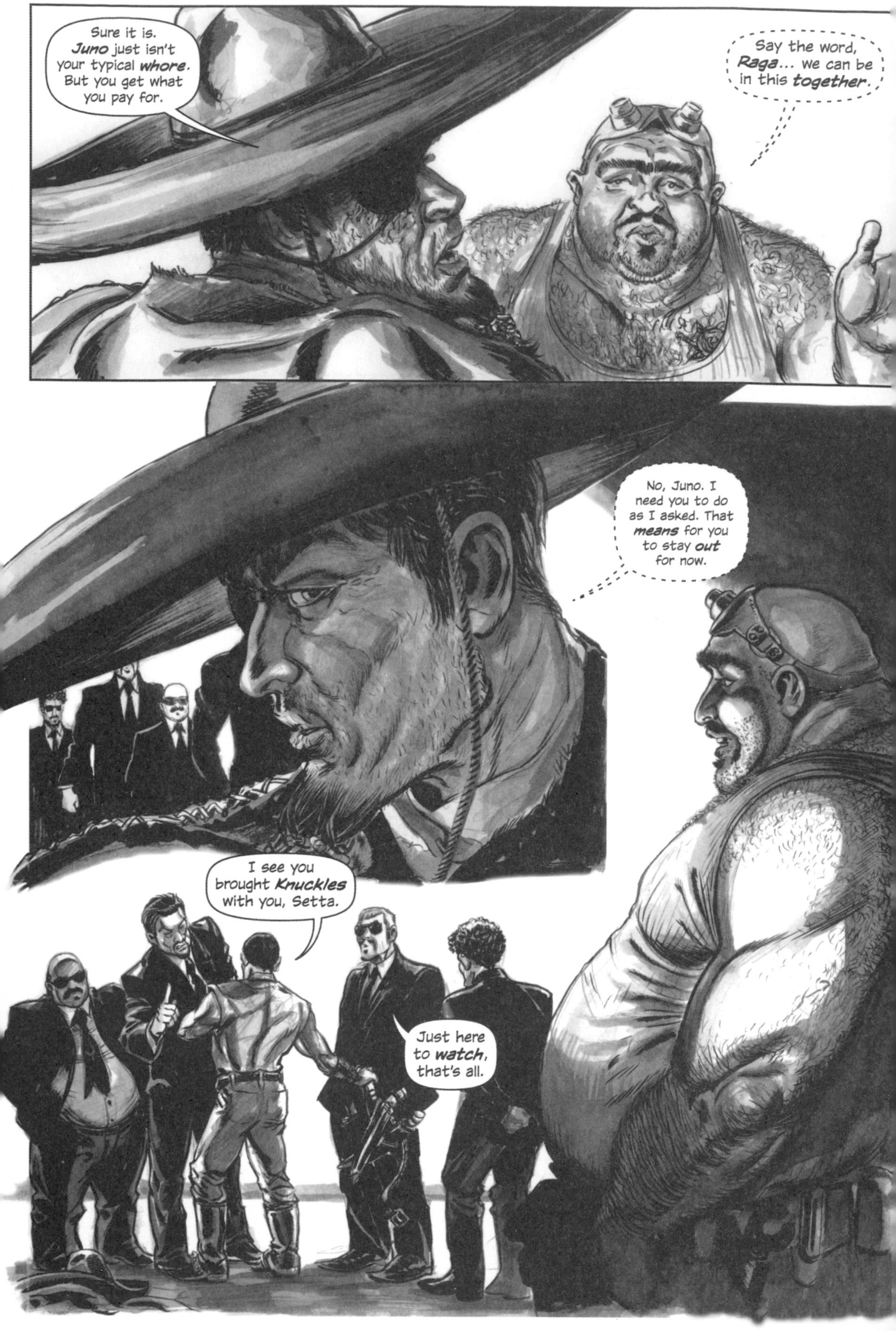
Sure it is. *Juno* just isn't your typical *whore*. But you get what you pay for.
Say the word, *Raga*... we can be in this *together*.
No, Juno. I need you to do as I asked. That *means* for you to stay *out* for now.
I see you brought *Knuckles* with you, Setta.
Just here to *watch*, that's all.

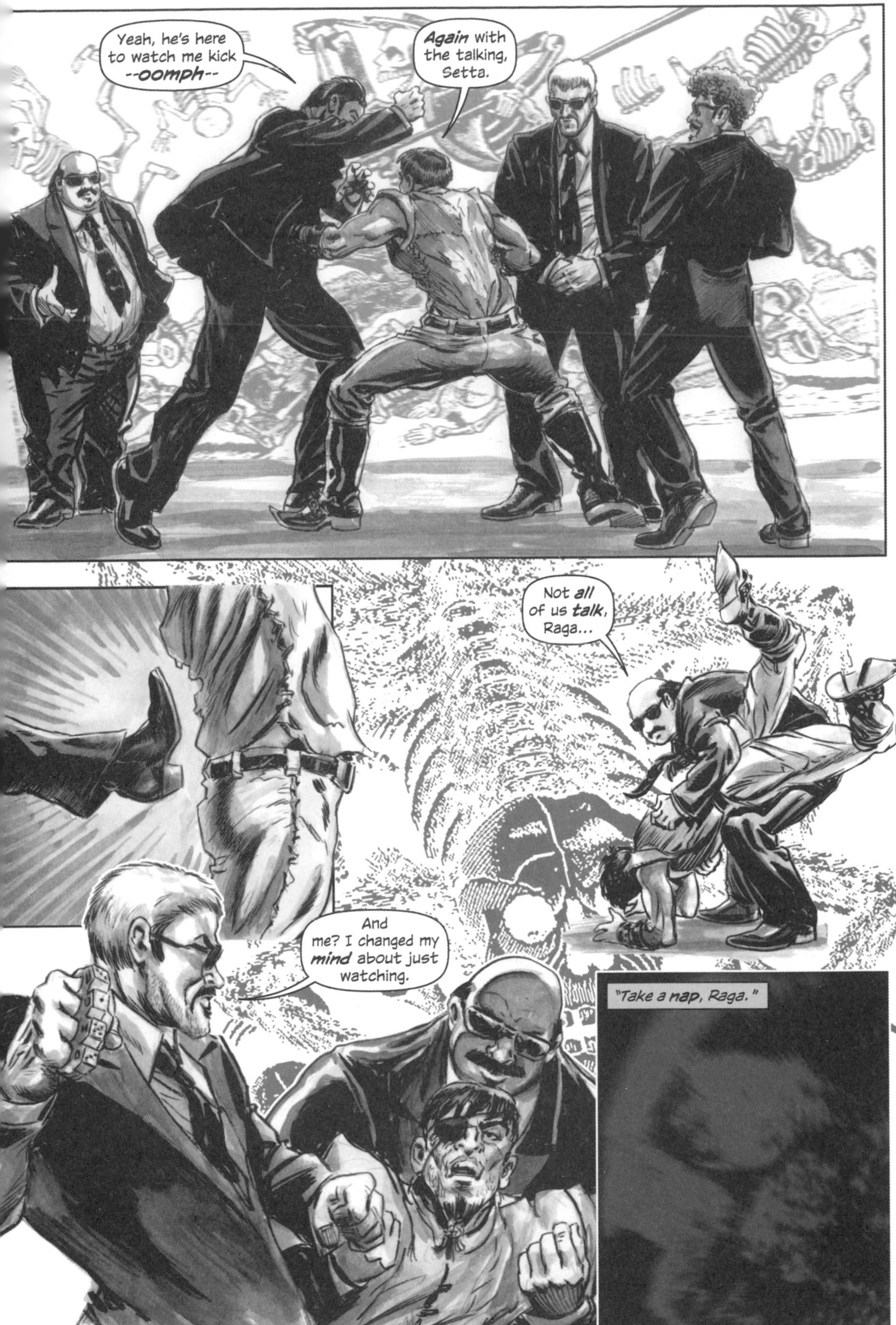
Yeah, he's here to watch me kick --oomph--
Again with the talking, Setta.
Not all of us talk, Raga...
And me? I changed my mind about just watching.
"Take a nap, Raga."

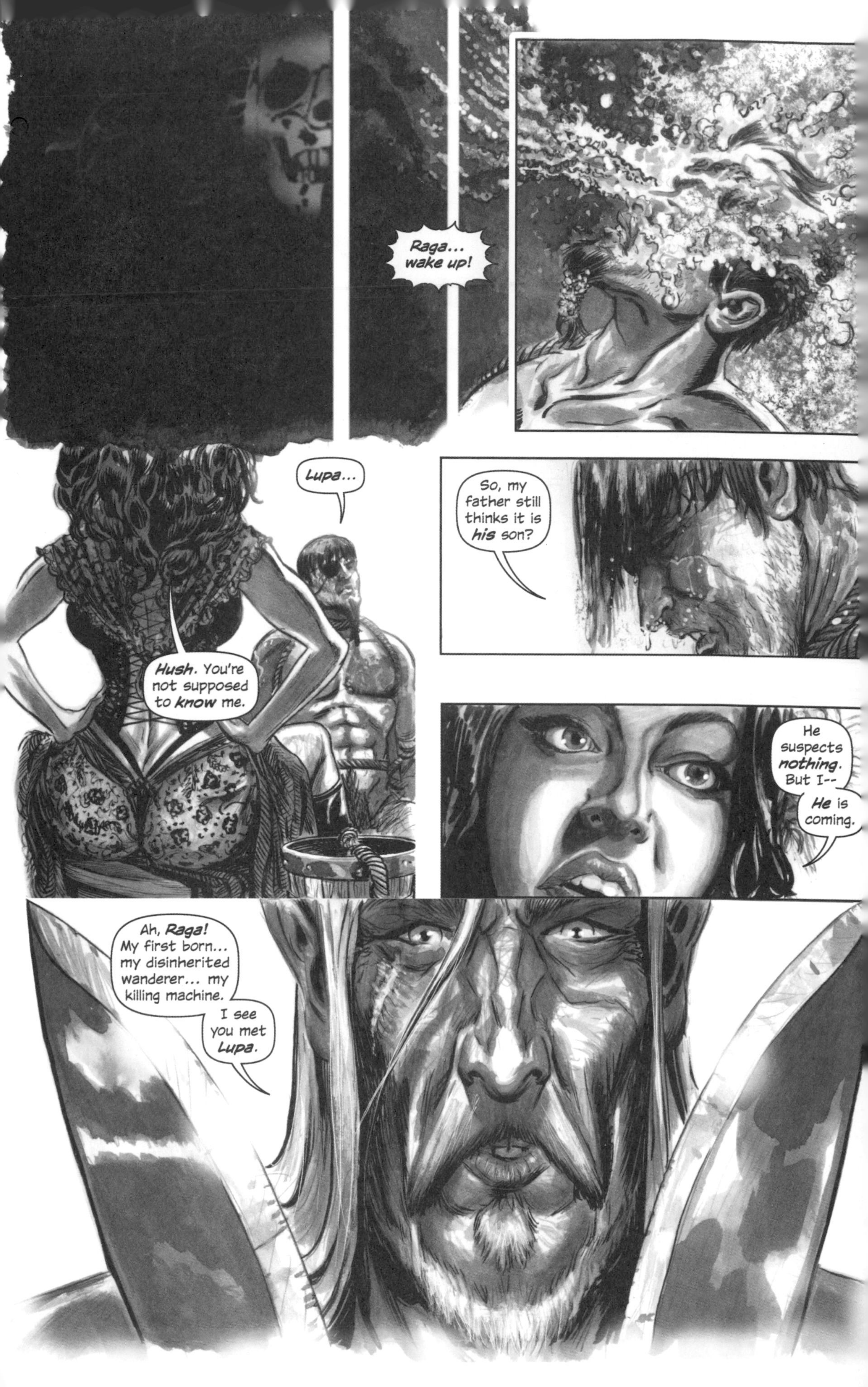
Raga... wake up!
Lupa...
Hush. You're not supposed to know me.
So, my father still thinks it is his son?
He suspects nothing. But I--
He is coming.
Ah, Raga! My first born... my disinherited wanderer... my killing machine.
I see you met Lupa.

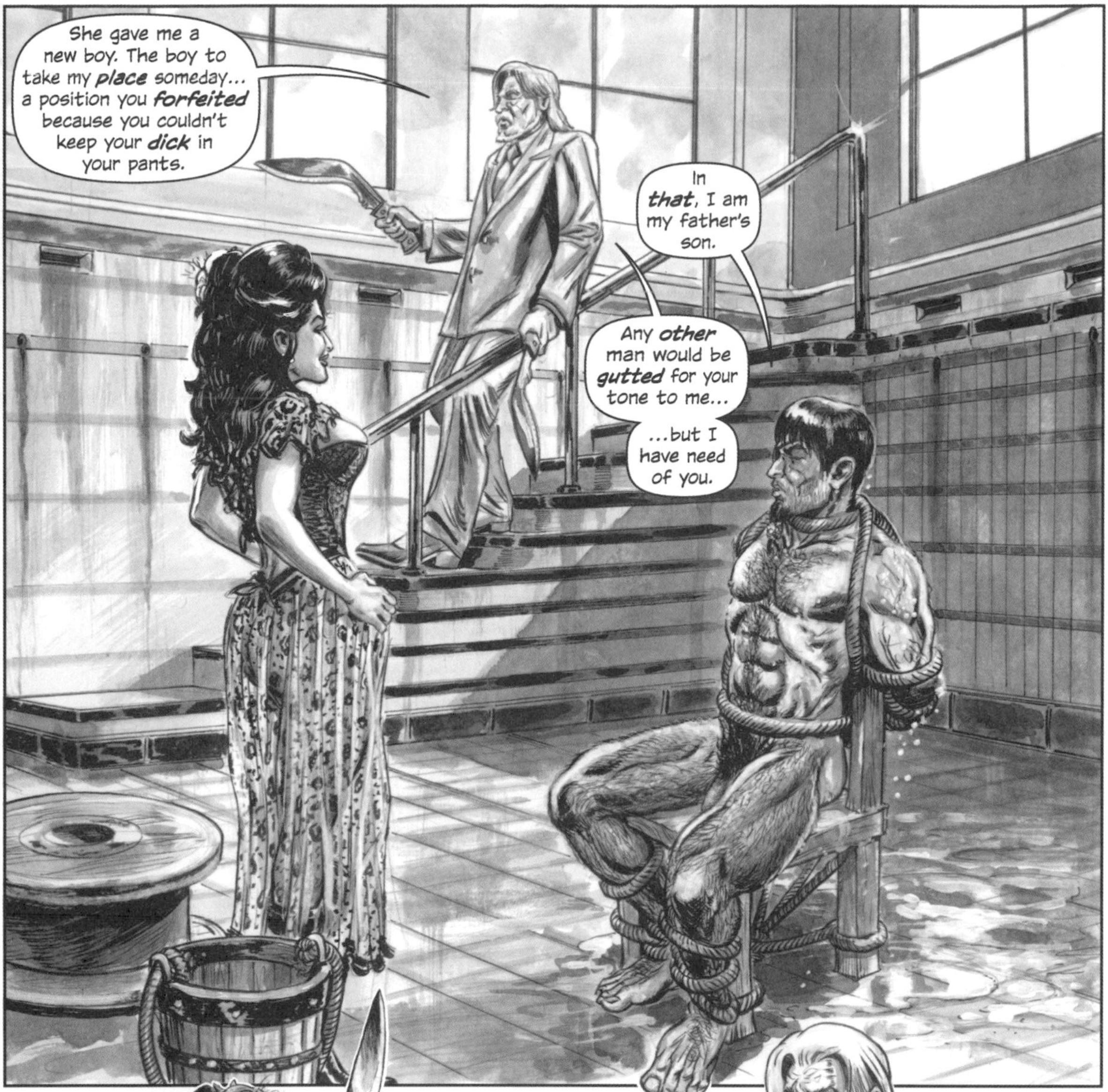
She gave me a new boy. The boy to take my place someday... a position you forfeited because you couldn't keep your dick in your pants.
In that, I am my father's son.
Any other man would be gutted for your tone to me...
...but I have need of you.

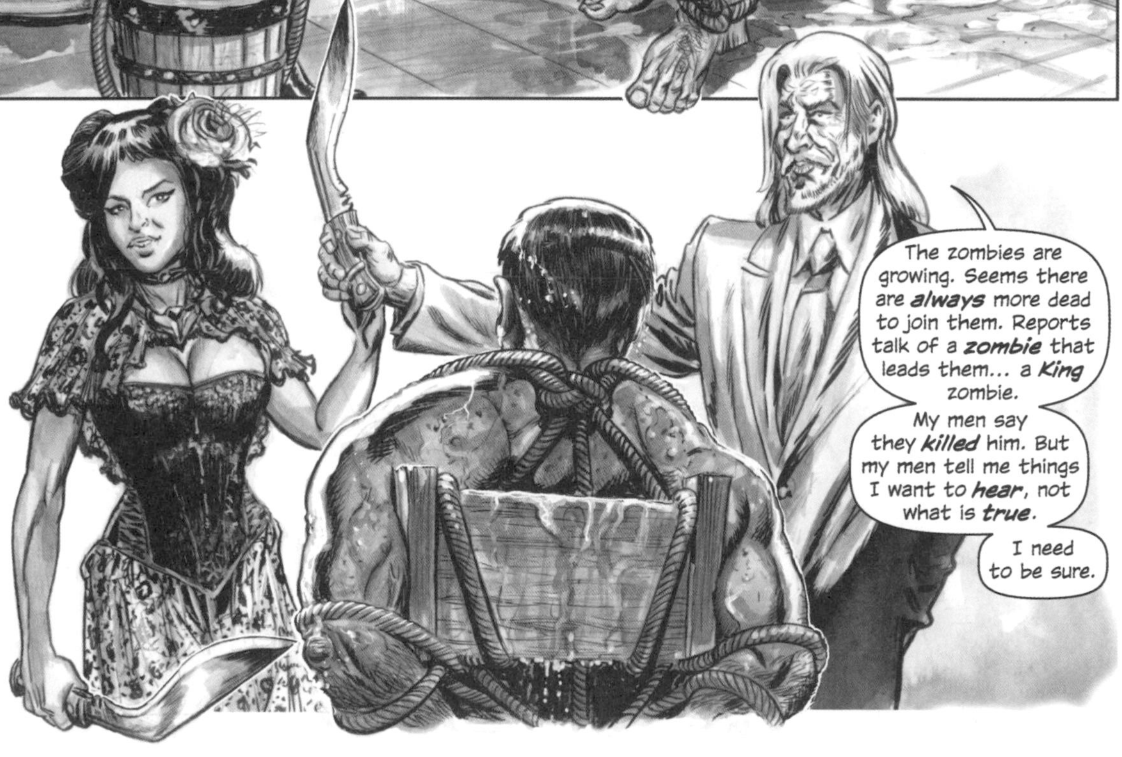
The zombies are growing. Seems there are always more dead to join them. Reports talk of a zombie that leads them... a King zombie.
My men say they killed him. But my men tell me things I want to hear, not what is true.
I need to be sure.

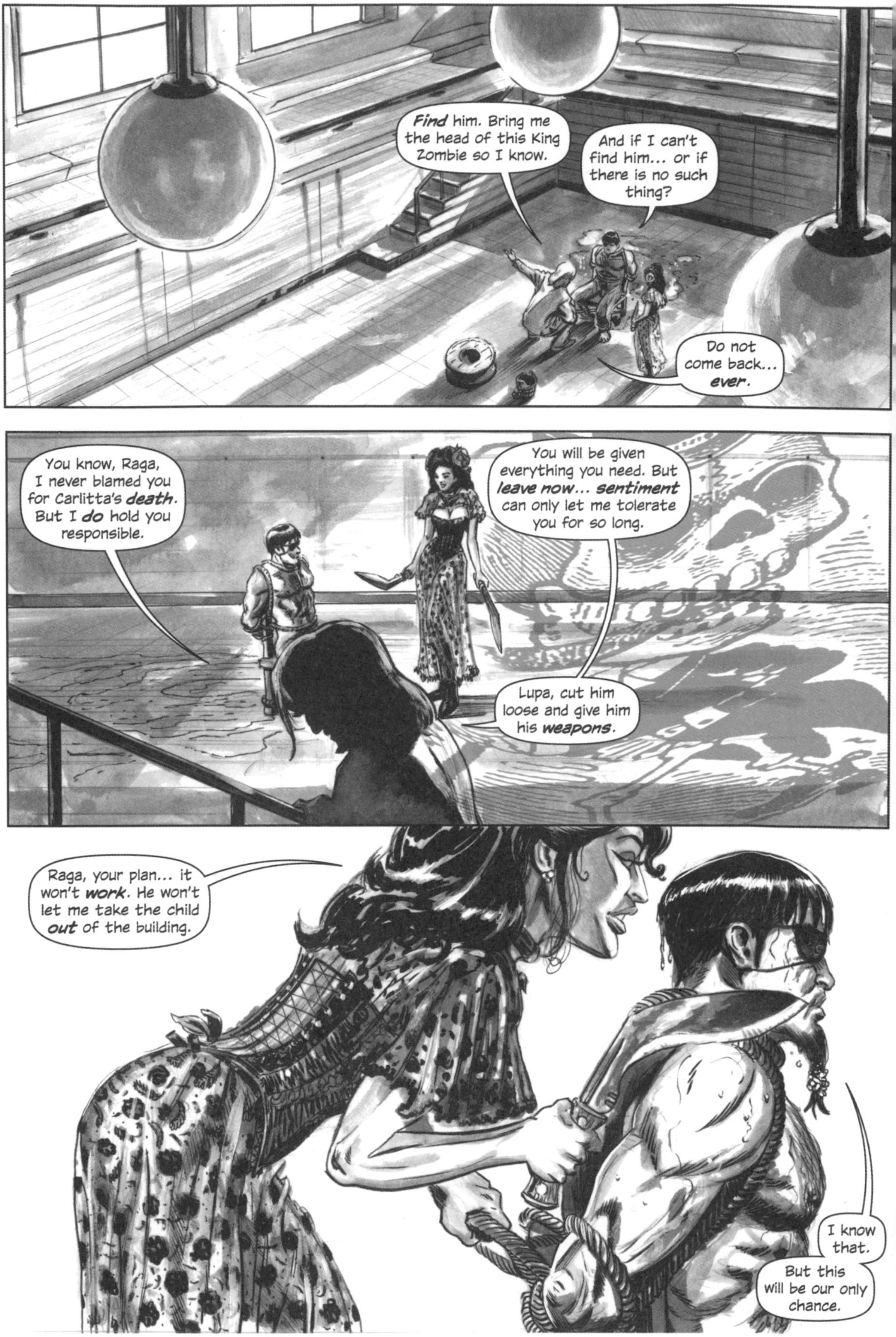

Find him. Bring me the head of this King Zombie so I know.
And if I can't find him... or if there is no such thing?
Do not come back... ever.
You know, Raga, I never blamed you for Carlitta's death. But I do hold you responsible.
You will be given everything you need. But leave now... sentiment can only let me tolerate you for so long.
Lupa, cut him loose and give him his weapons.
Raga, your plan... it won't work. He won't let me take the child out of the building.
I know that.
But this will be our only chance.

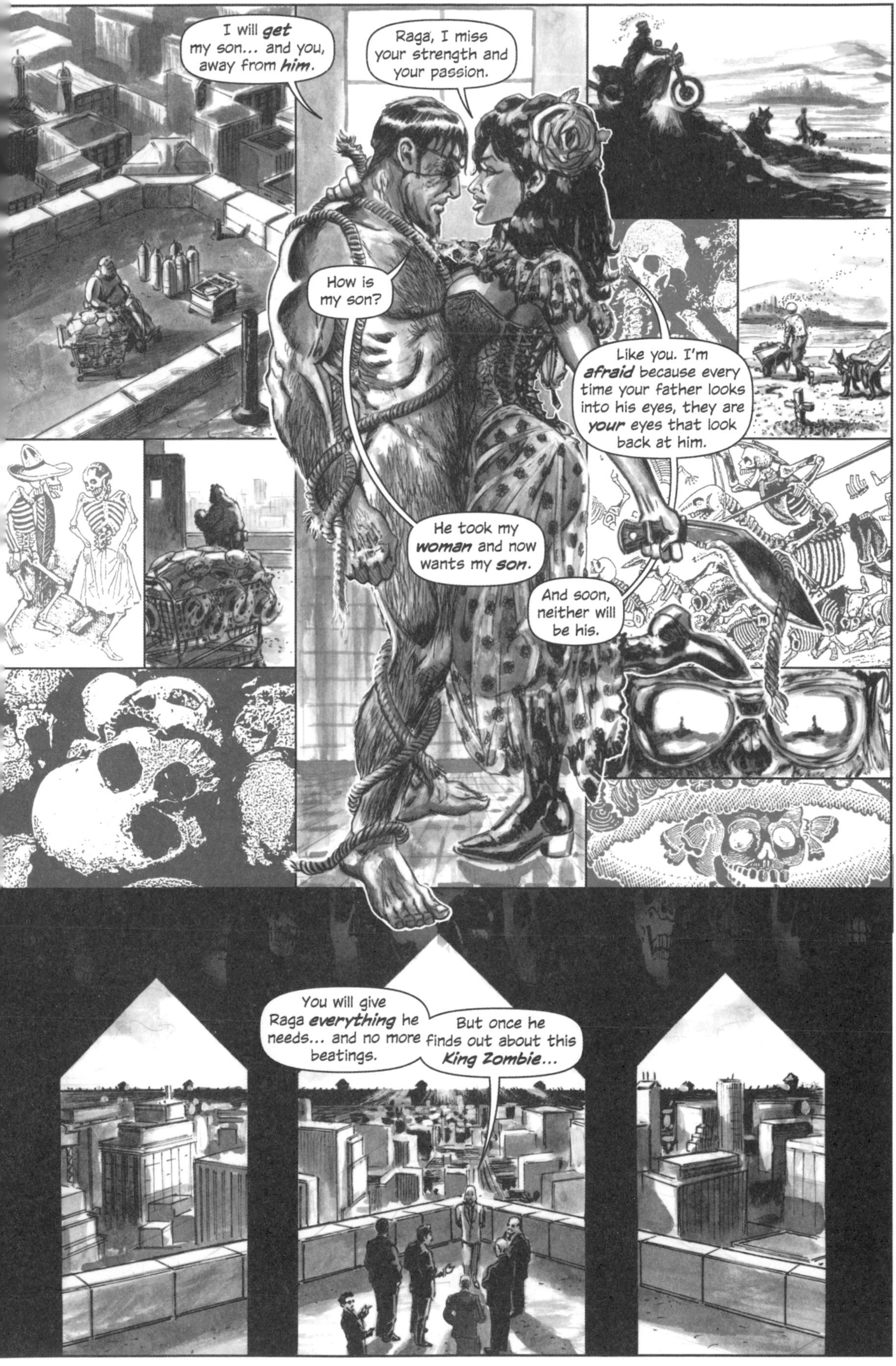
I will get my son... and you, away from him.
Raga, I miss your strength and your passion.
How is my son?
Like you. I'm afraid because every time your father looks into his eyes, they are your eyes that look back at him.
He took my woman and now wants my son.
And soon, neither will be his.
You will give Raga everything he needs... and no more beatings.
But once he finds out about this King Zombie...

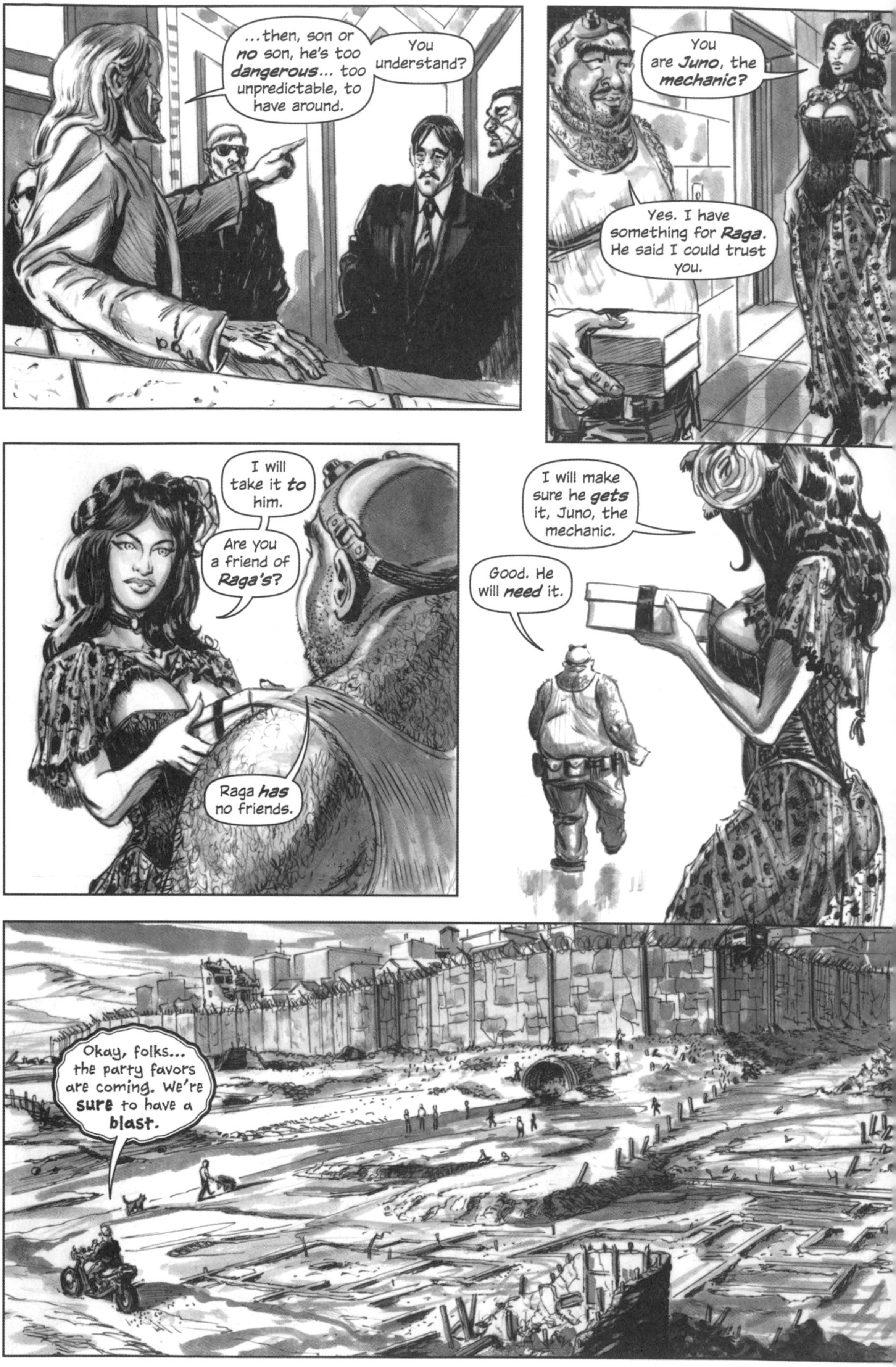
...then, son or no son, he's too dangerous... too unpredictable, to have around.
You understand?
You are Juno, the mechanic?
Yes. I have something for Raga. He said I could trust you.
I will take it to him.
Are you a friend of Raga's?
Raga has no friends.
I will make sure he gets it, Juno, the mechanic.
Good. He will need it.
Okay, folks... the party favors are coming. We're sure to have a blast.

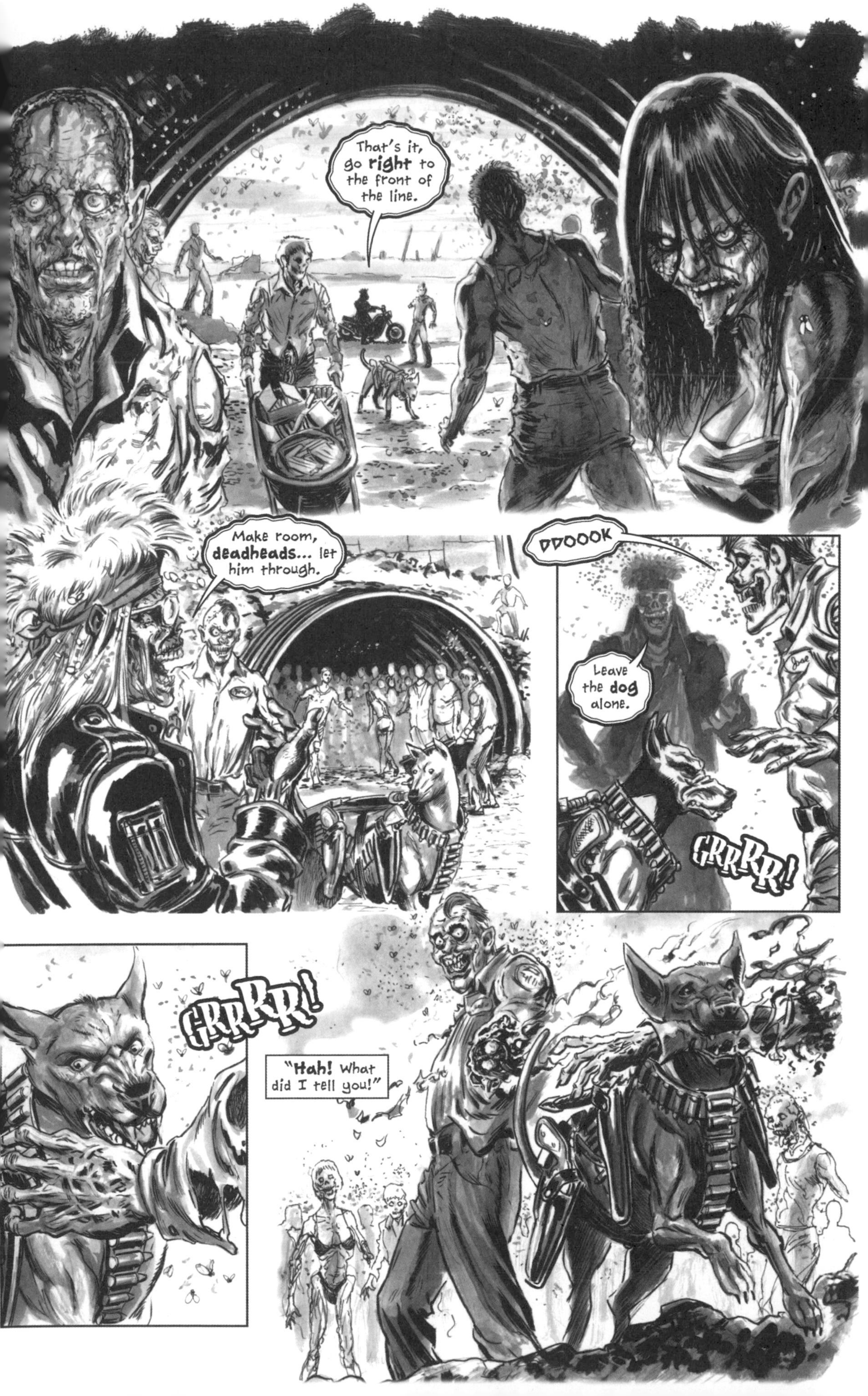
That's it, go **right** to the front of the line.
Make room, **deadheads...** let him through.
DDOOOK
Leave the **dog** alone.
GRRRR!
GRRRR!
"**Hah!** What did I tell you!"

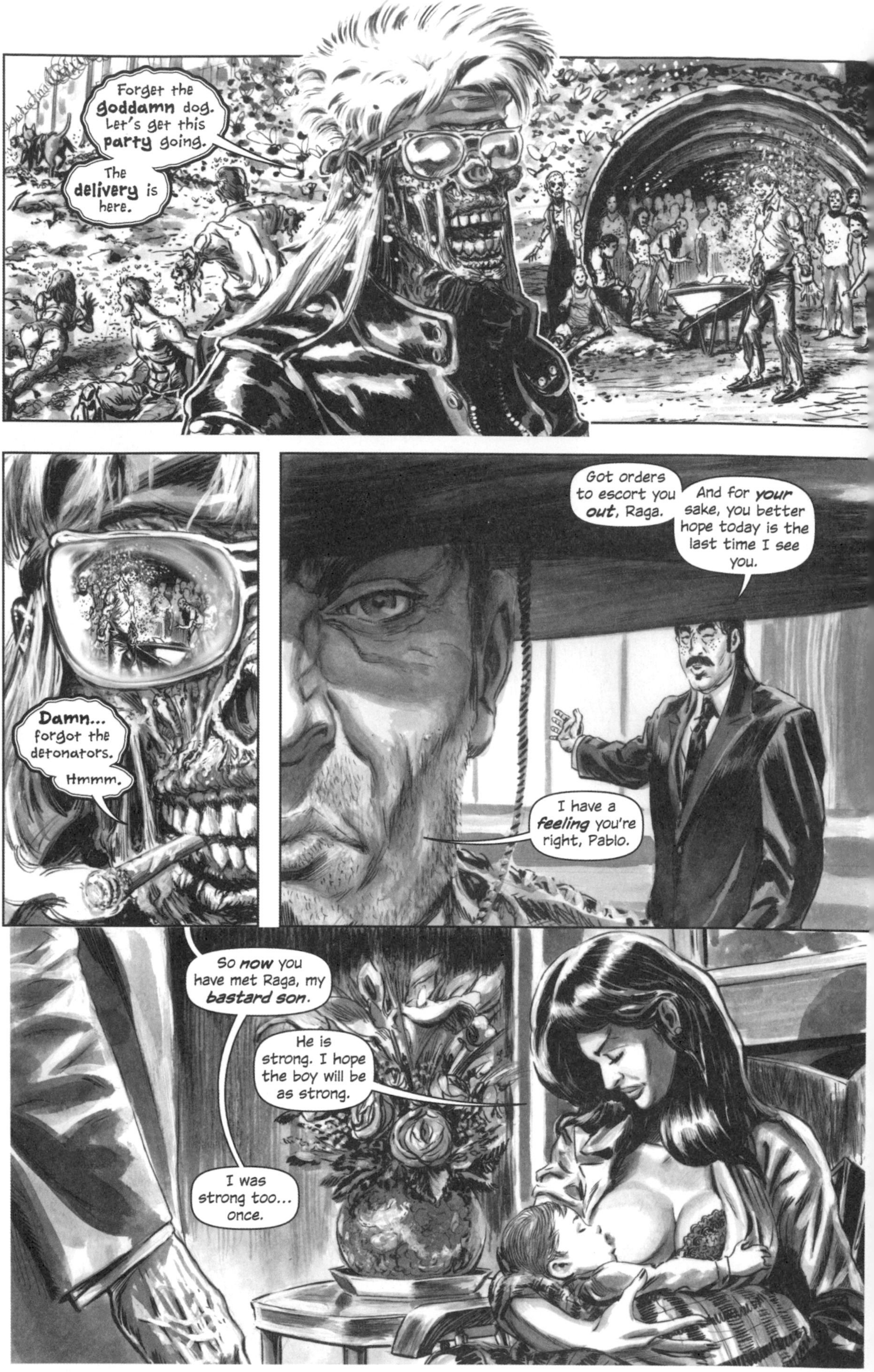

Forget the goddamn dog. Let's get this party going.
The delivery is here.
Damn... forgot the detonators.
Hmmm.
Got orders to escort you out, Raga.
And for your sake, you better hope today is the last time I see you.
I have a feeling you're right, Pablo.
So now you have met Raga, my bastard son.
He is strong. I hope the boy will be as strong.
I was strong too... once.

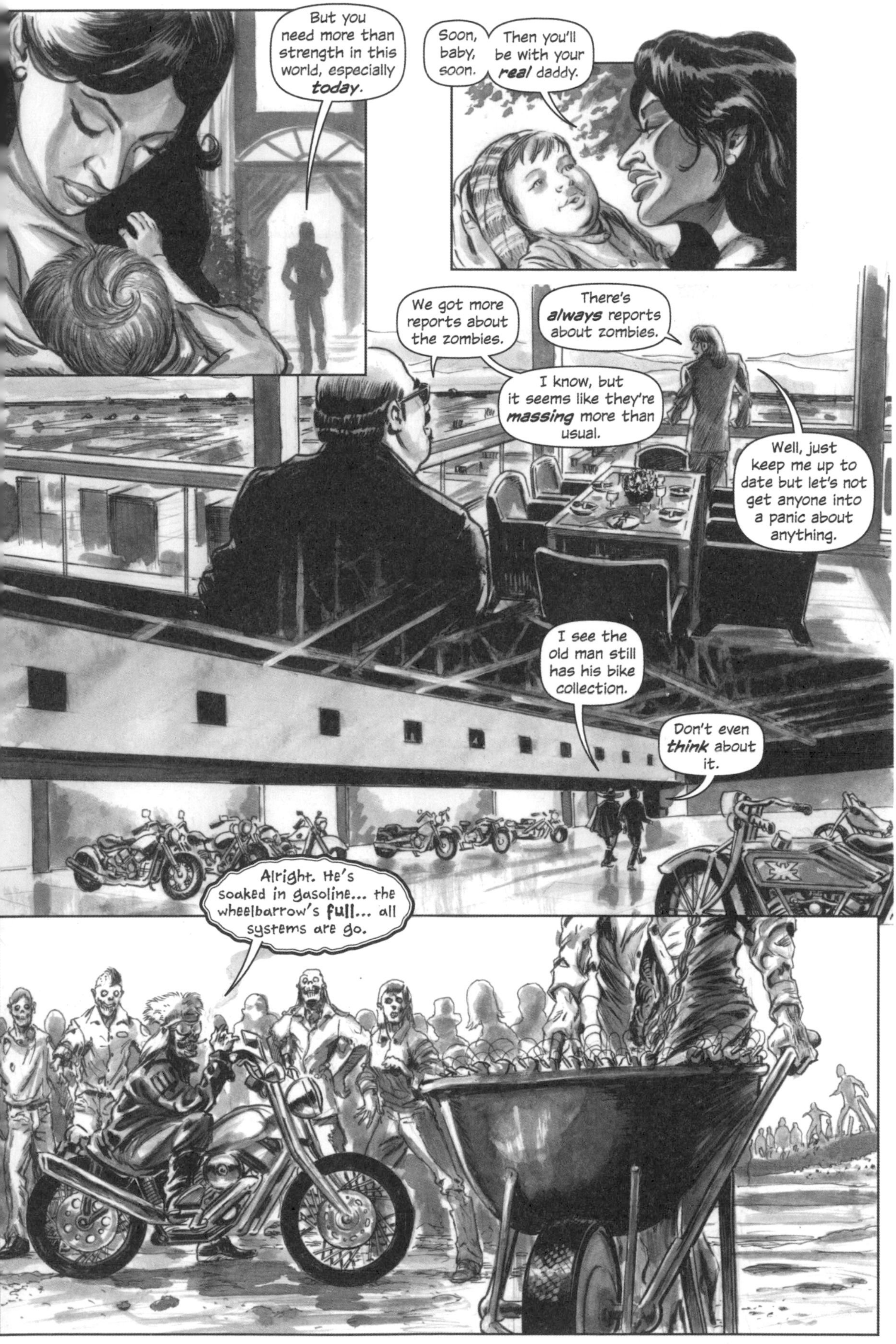
But you need more than strength in this world, especially today.
Soon, baby, soon.
Then you'll be with your real daddy.
We got more reports about the zombies.
There's always reports about zombies.
I know, but it seems like they're massing more than usual.
Well, just keep me up to date but let's not get anyone into a panic about anything.
I see the old man still has his bike collection.
Don't even think about it.
Alright. He's soaked in gasoline... the wheelbarrow's full... all systems are go.

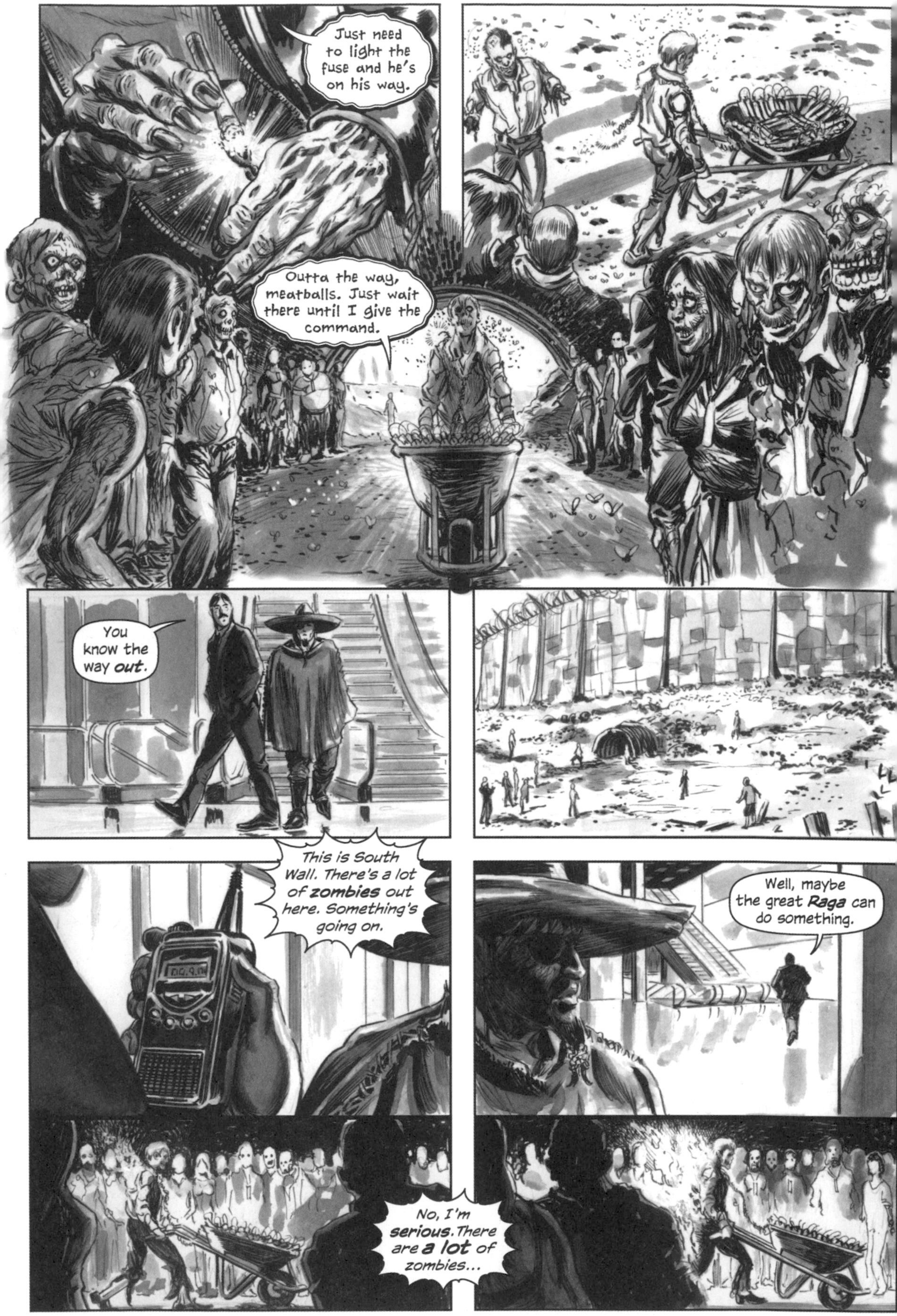

Just need to light the fuse and he's on his way.
Outta the way, meatballs. Just wait there until I give the command.
You know the way *out*.
This is South Wall. There's a lot of **zombies** out here. Something's going on.
Well, maybe the great ***Raga*** can do something.
No, I'm **serious**. There are **a lot** of zombies...

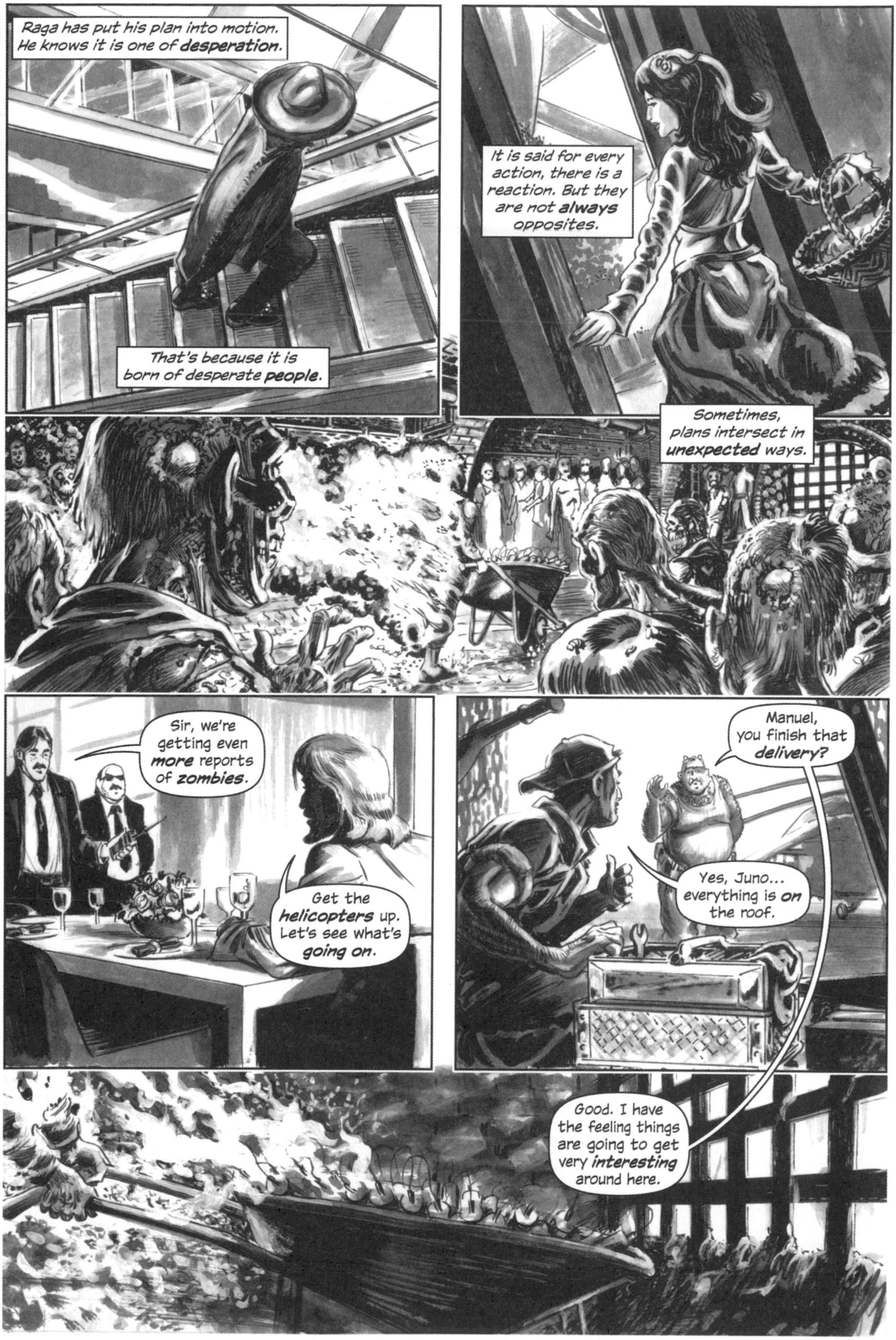
Raga has put his plan into motion. He knows it is one of desperation.
That's because it is born of desperate people.
It is said for every action, there is a reaction. But they are not always opposites.
Sometimes, plans intersect in unexpected ways.
Sir, we're getting even more reports of zombies.
Get the helicopters up. Let's see what's going on.
Manuel, you finish that delivery?
Yes, Juno... everything is on the roof.
Good. I have the feeling things are going to get very interesting around here.

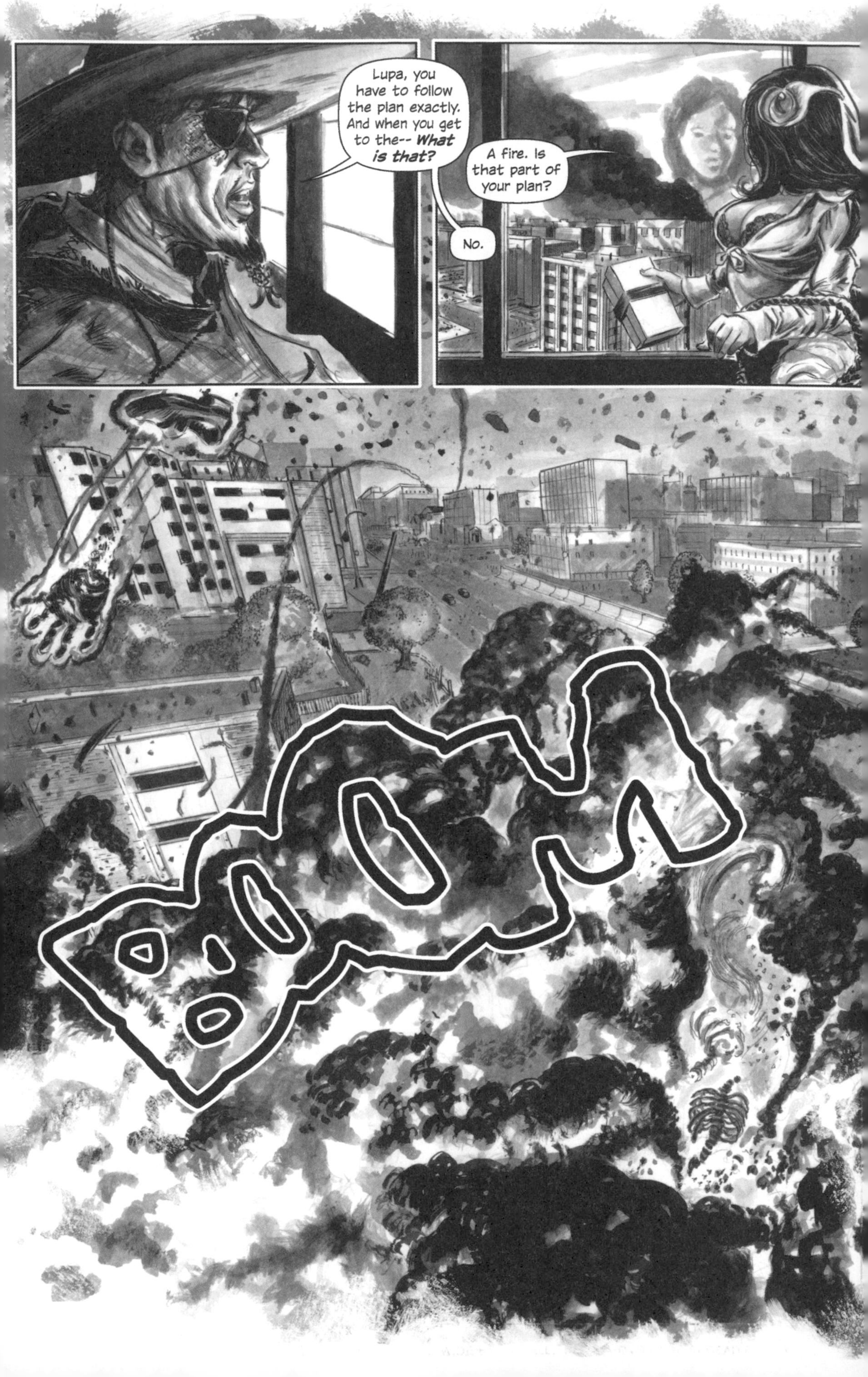
Lupa, you have to follow the plan exactly. And when you get to the-- ***What is that?***
A fire. Is that part of your plan?
No.
BOOM

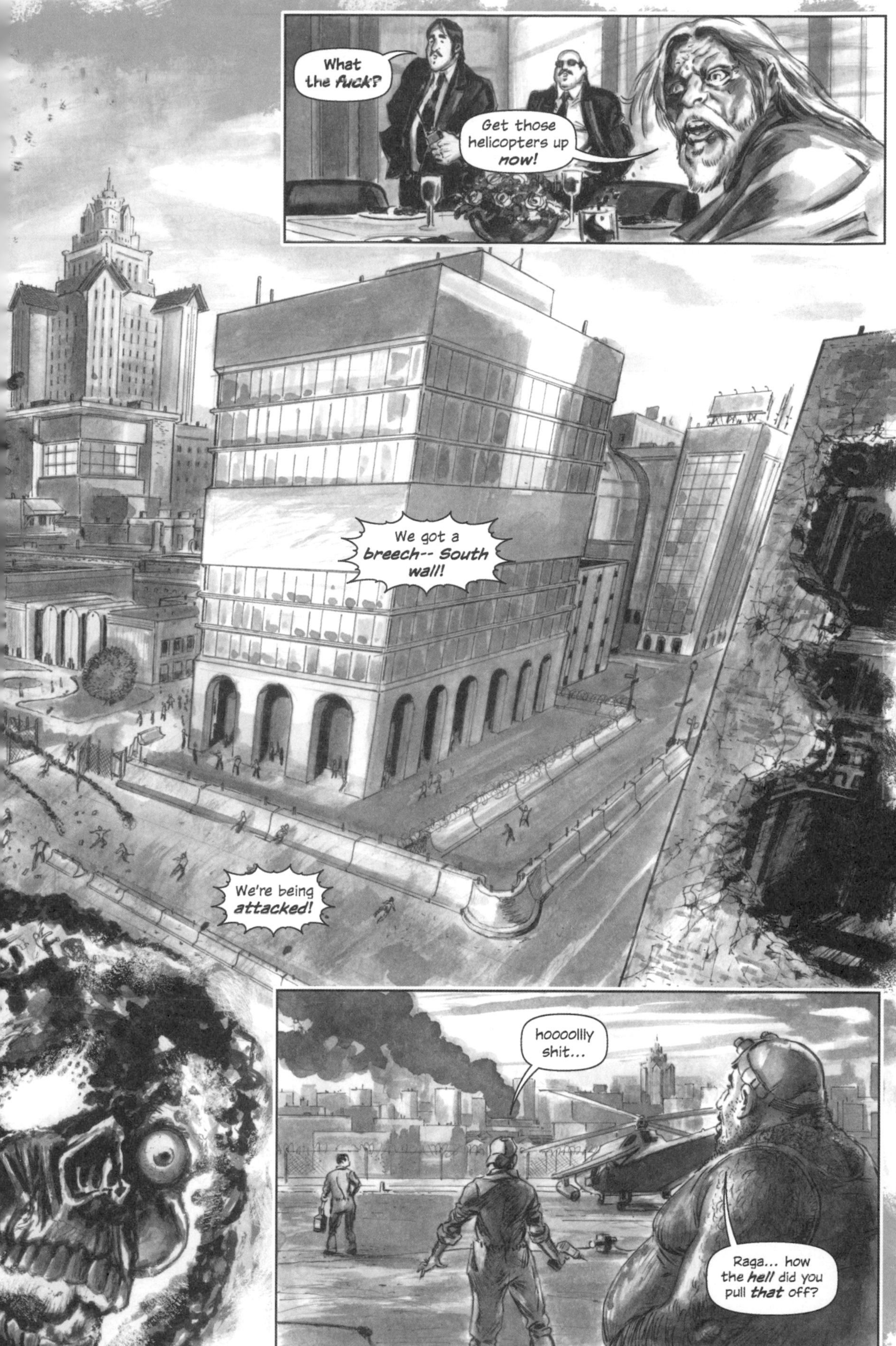

What the fuck?
Get those helicopters up now!
We got a breech-- South wall!
We're being attacked!
hoooollly shit...
Raga... how the hell did you pull that off?

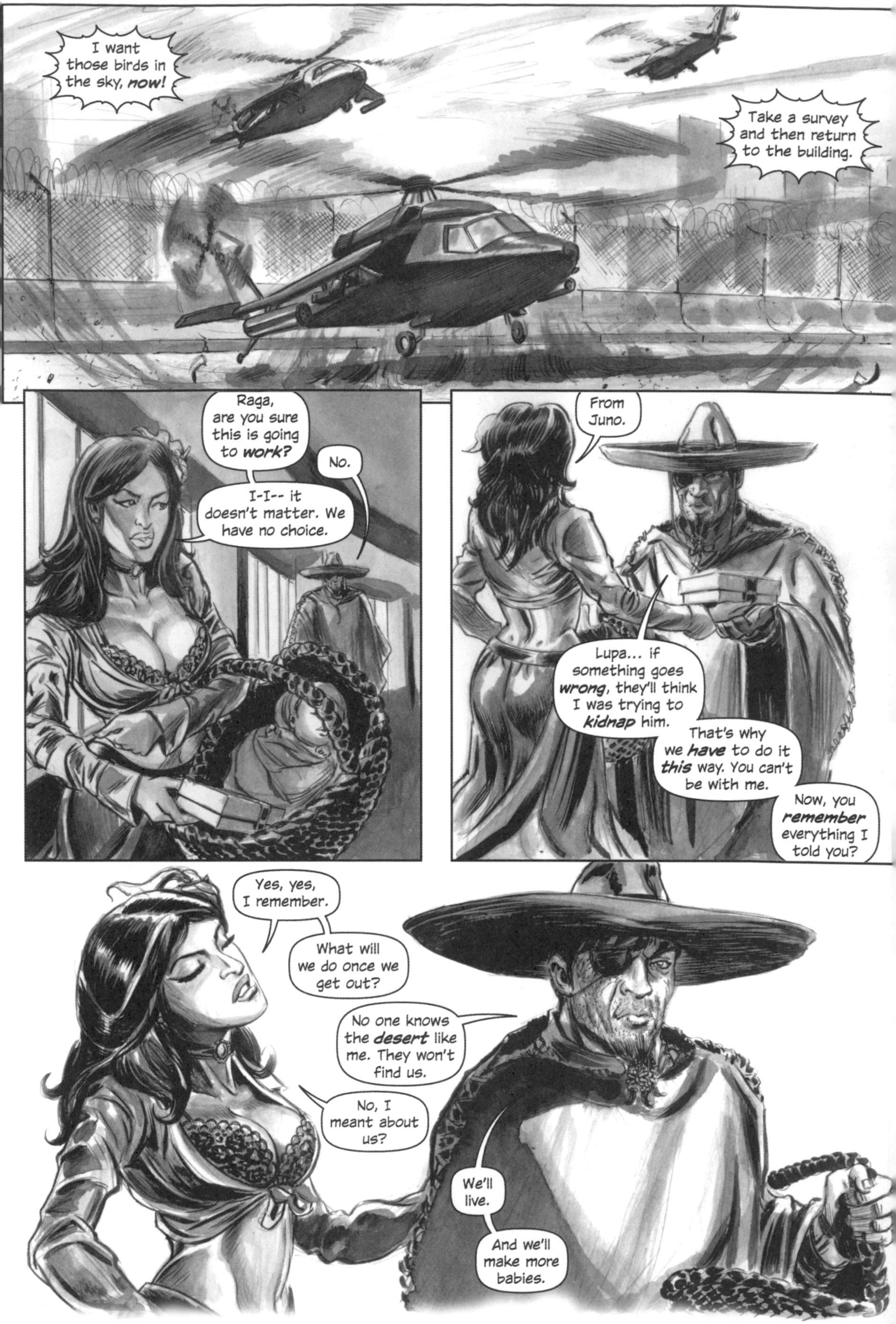
I want those birds in the sky, **now!**
Take a survey and then return to the building.
Raga, are you sure this is going to **work?**
No.
I-I-- it doesn't matter. We have no choice.
From Juno.
Lupa... if something goes **wrong**, they'll think I was trying to **kidnap** him.
That's why we **have** to do it **this** way. You can't be with me.
Now, you **remember** everything I told you?
Yes, yes, I remember.
What will we do once we get out?
No one knows the **desert** like me. They won't find us.
No, I meant about us?
We'll live.
And we'll make more babies.

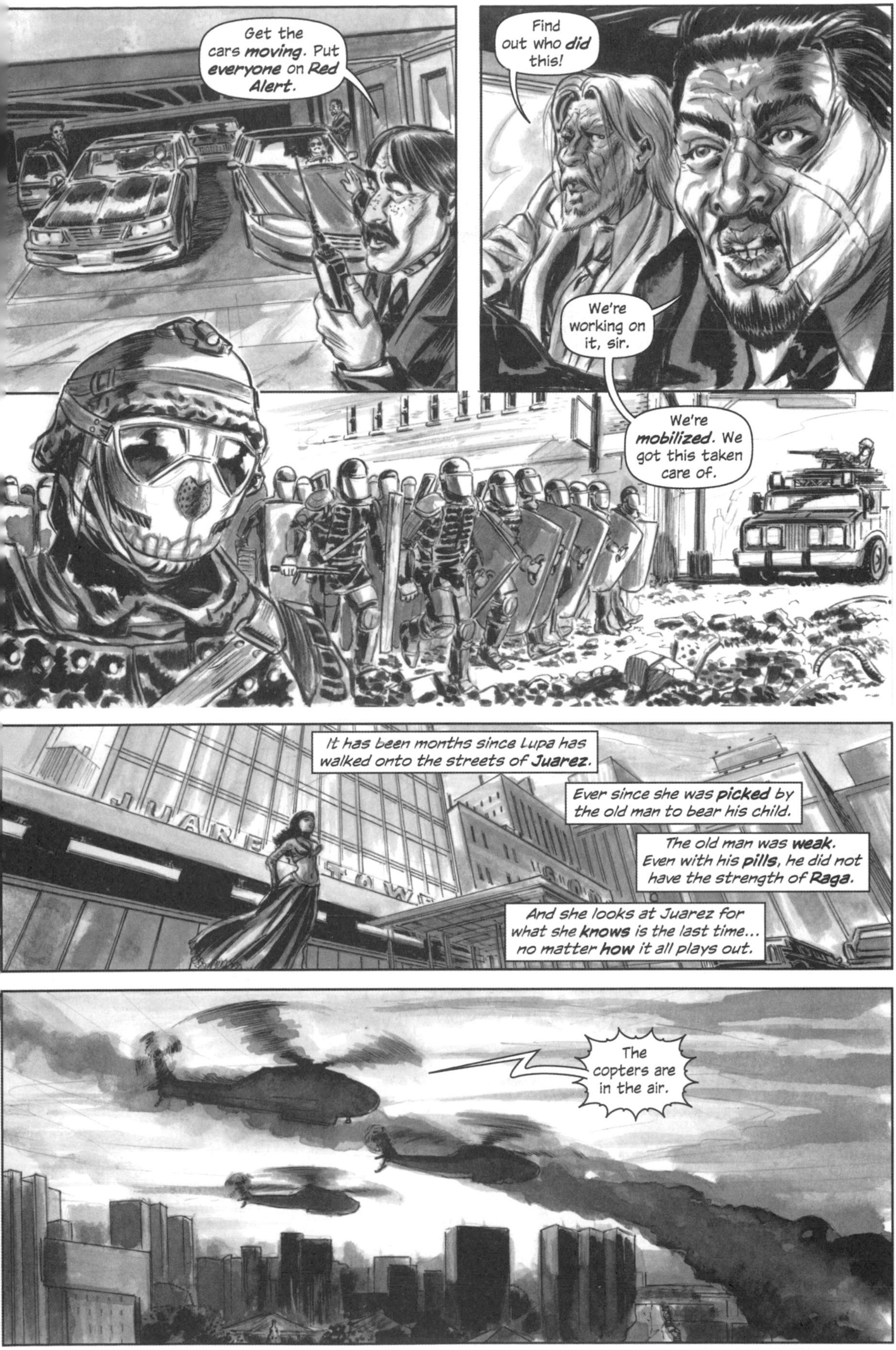
Get the cars **moving**. Put **everyone** on **Red Alert**.
Find out who **did** this!
We're working on it, sir.
We're **mobilized**. We got this taken care of.
*It has been months since Lupa has walked onto the streets of **Juarez**.*
*Ever since she was **picked** by the old man to bear his child.*
*The old man was **weak**. Even with his **pills**, he did not have the strength of **Raga**.*
*And she looks at Juarez for what she **knows** is the last time... no matter **how** it all plays out.*
The copters are in the air.

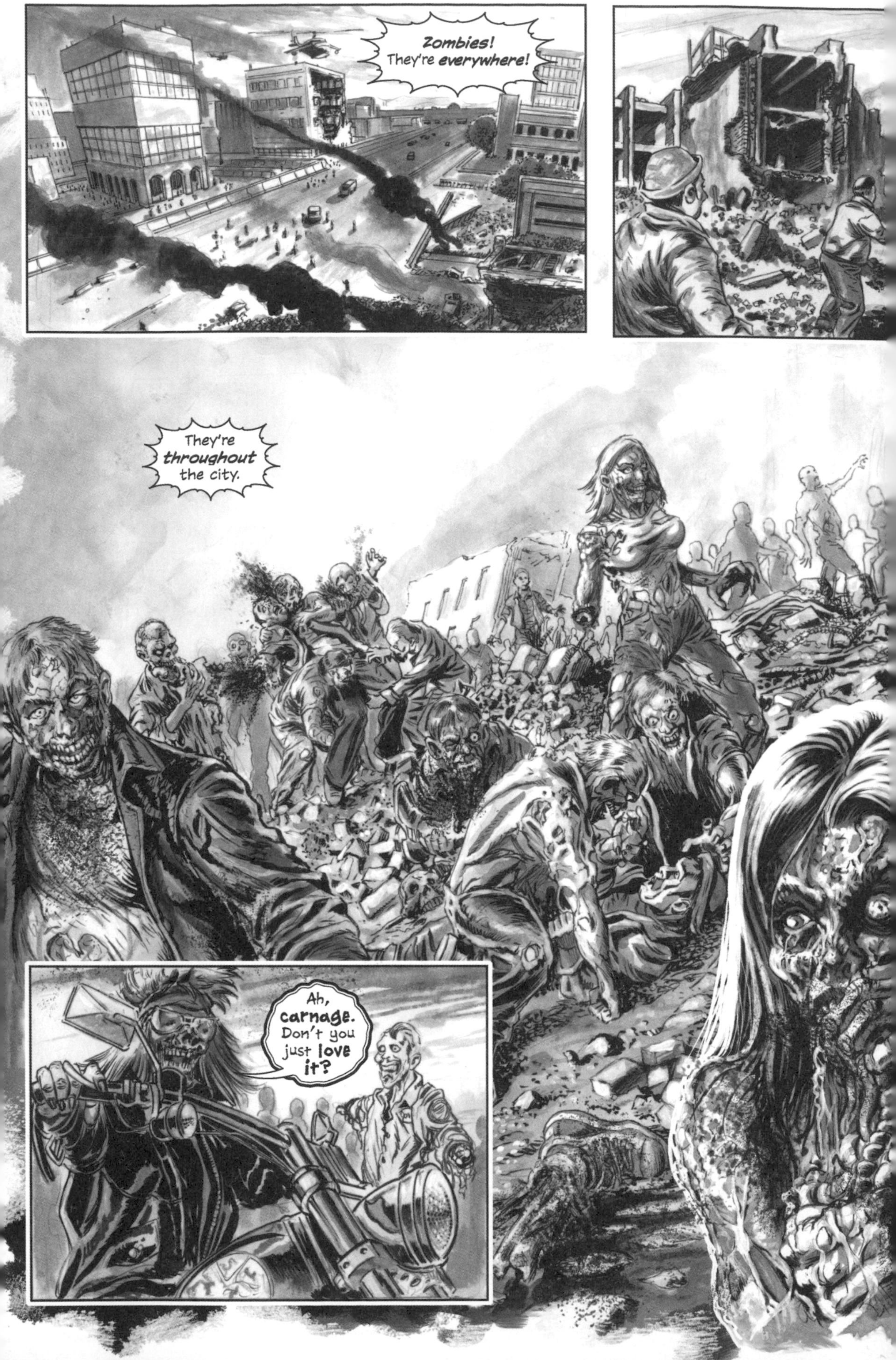
Zombies! They're everywhere!
They're throughout the city.
Ah, carnage. Don't you just love it?

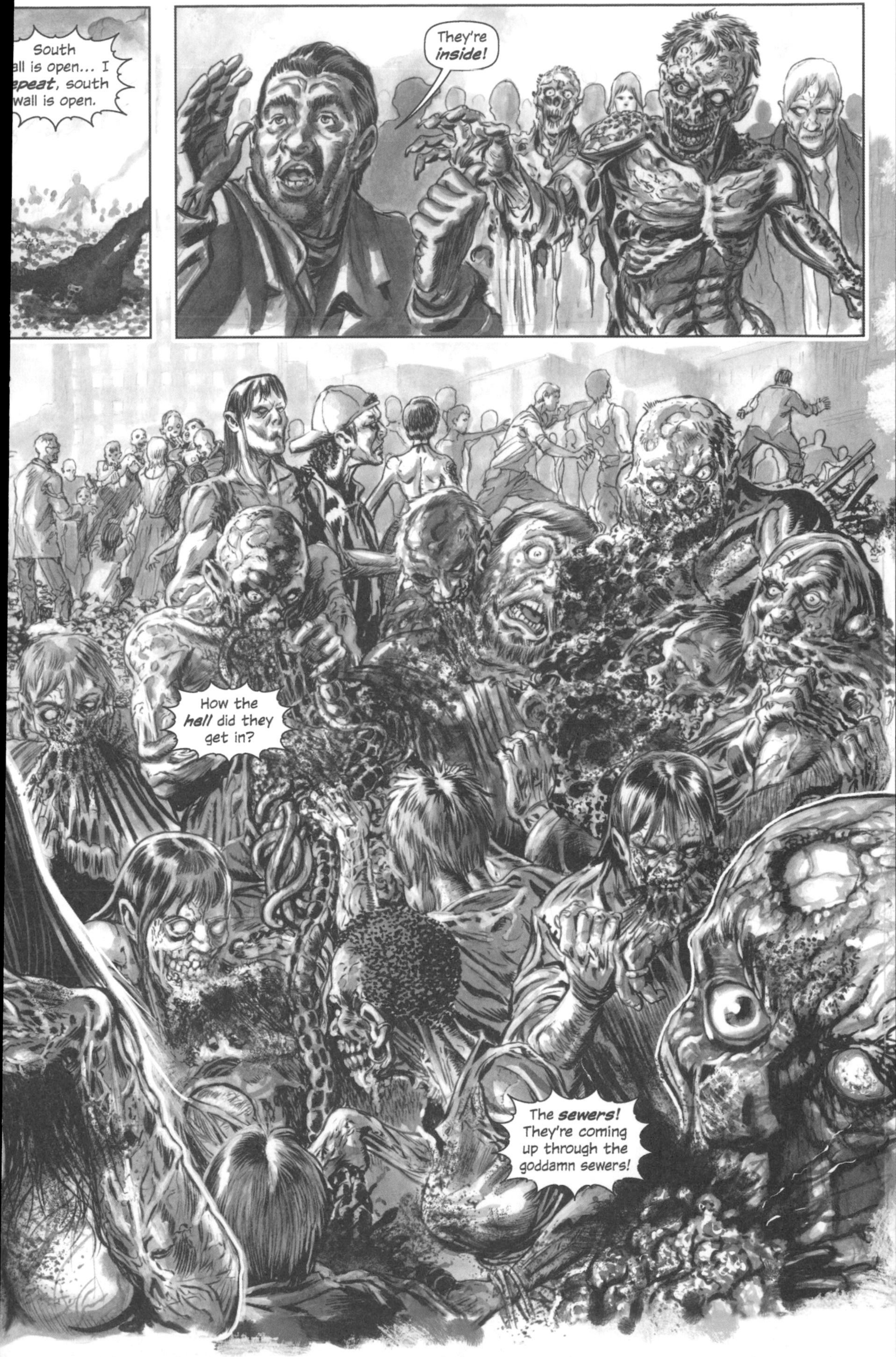
South
all is open... I
epeat, south
wall is open.
They're
inside!
How the
hell did they
get in?
The sewers!
They're coming
up through the
goddamn sewers!

Chapter five

the DESPERATE

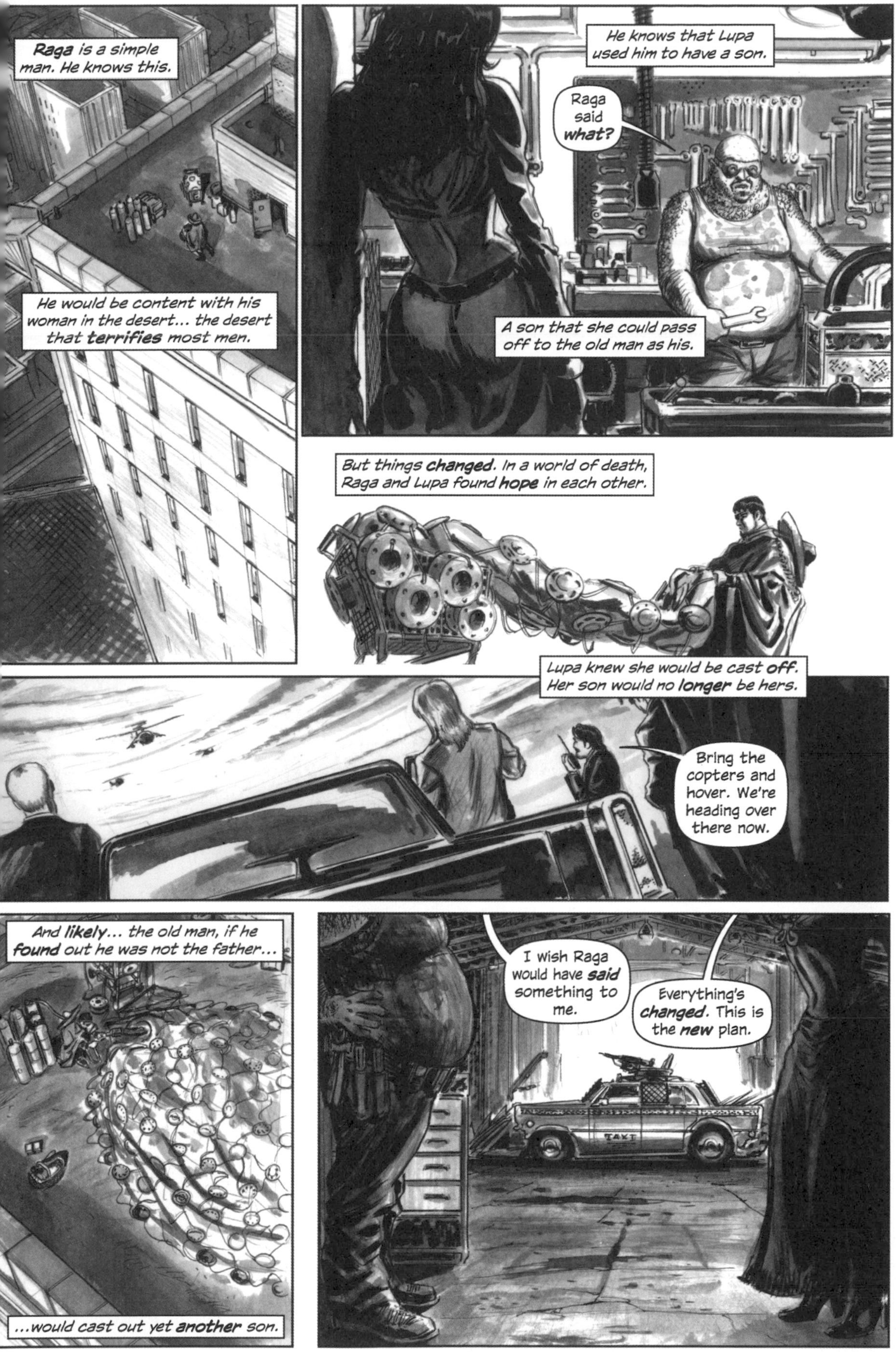

Raga is a simple man. He knows this.
He would be content with his woman in the desert... the desert that terrifies most men.
He knows that Lupa used him to have a son.
Raga said what?
A son that she could pass off to the old man as his.
But things changed. In a world of death, Raga and Lupa found hope in each other.
Lupa knew she would be cast off. Her son would no longer be hers.
Bring the copters and hover. We're heading over there now.
And likely... the old man, if he found out he was not the father...
...would cast out yet another son.
I wish Raga would have said something to me.
Everything's changed. This is the new plan.
TAXI

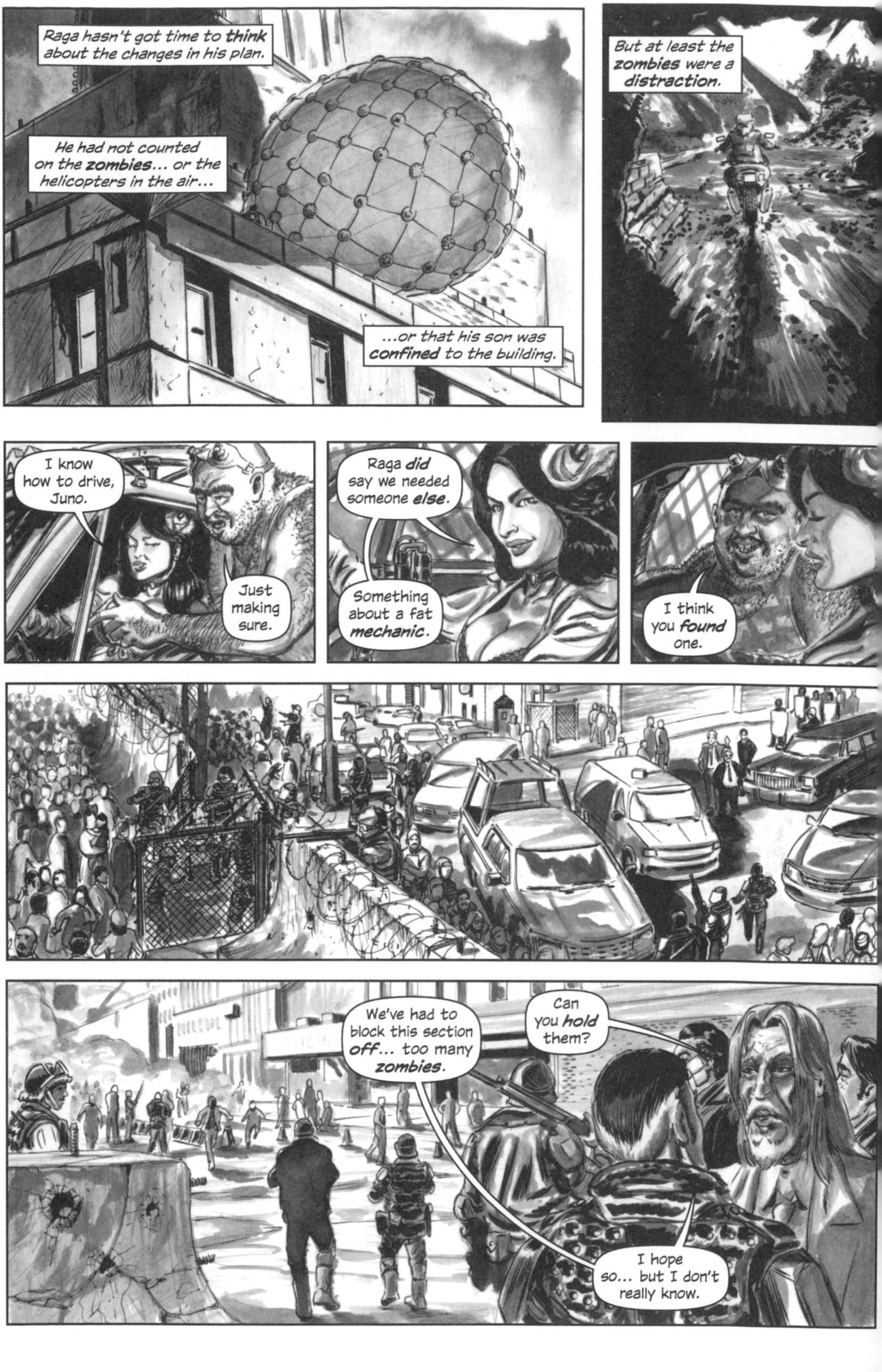
Raga hasn't got time to think about the changes in his plan.
He had not counted on the zombies... or the helicopters in the air...
...or that his son was confined to the building.
But at least the zombies were a distraction.
I know how to drive, Juno.
Just making sure.
Raga did say we needed someone else.
Something about a fat mechanic.
I think you found one.
We've had to block this section off... too many zombies.
Can you hold them?
I hope so... but I don't really know.

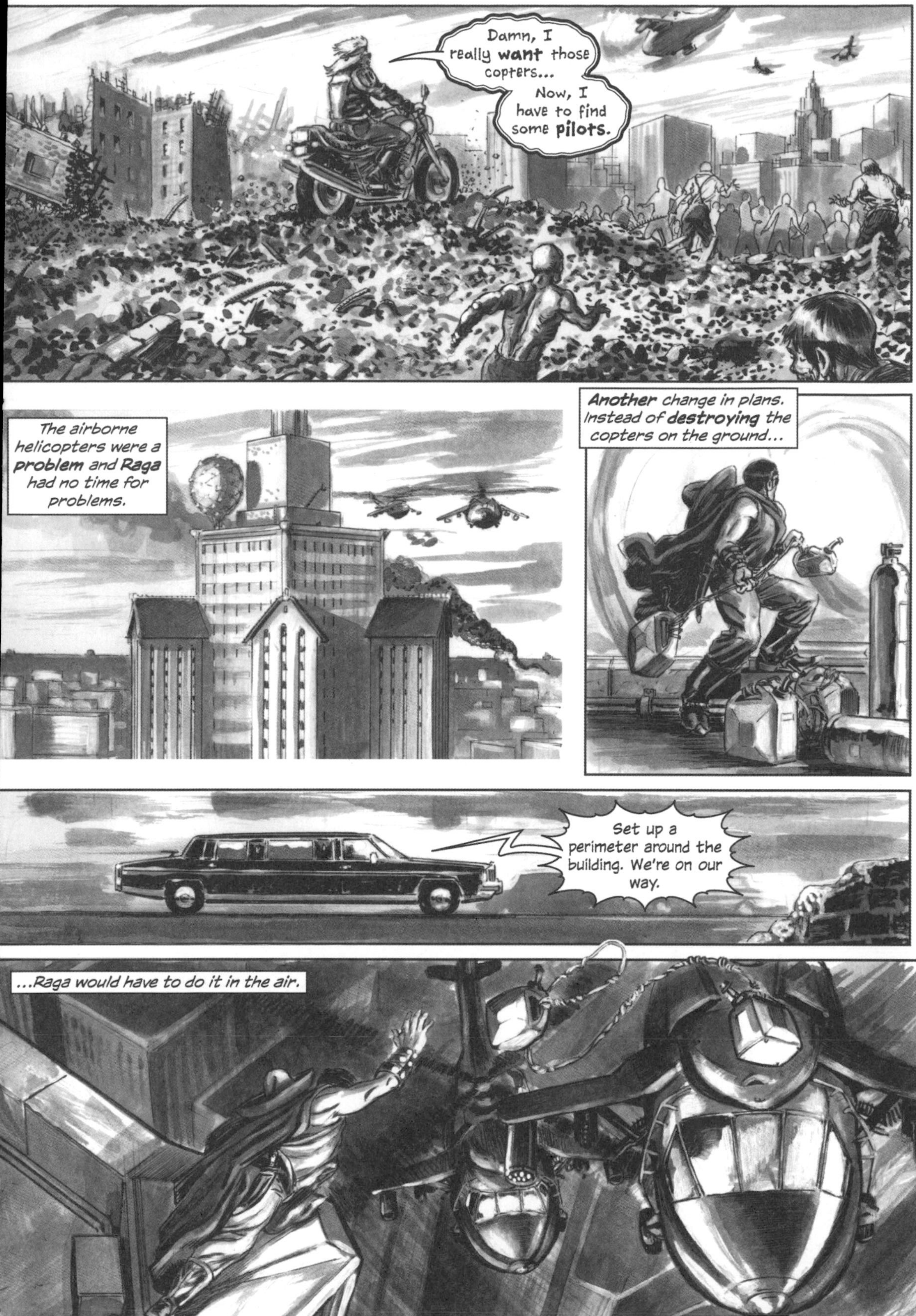
Damn, I really want those copters...
Now, I have to find some pilots.
The airborne helicopters were a problem and Raga had no time for problems.
Another change in plans. Instead of destroying the copters on the ground...
Set up a perimeter around the building. We're on our way.
...Raga would have to do it in the air.

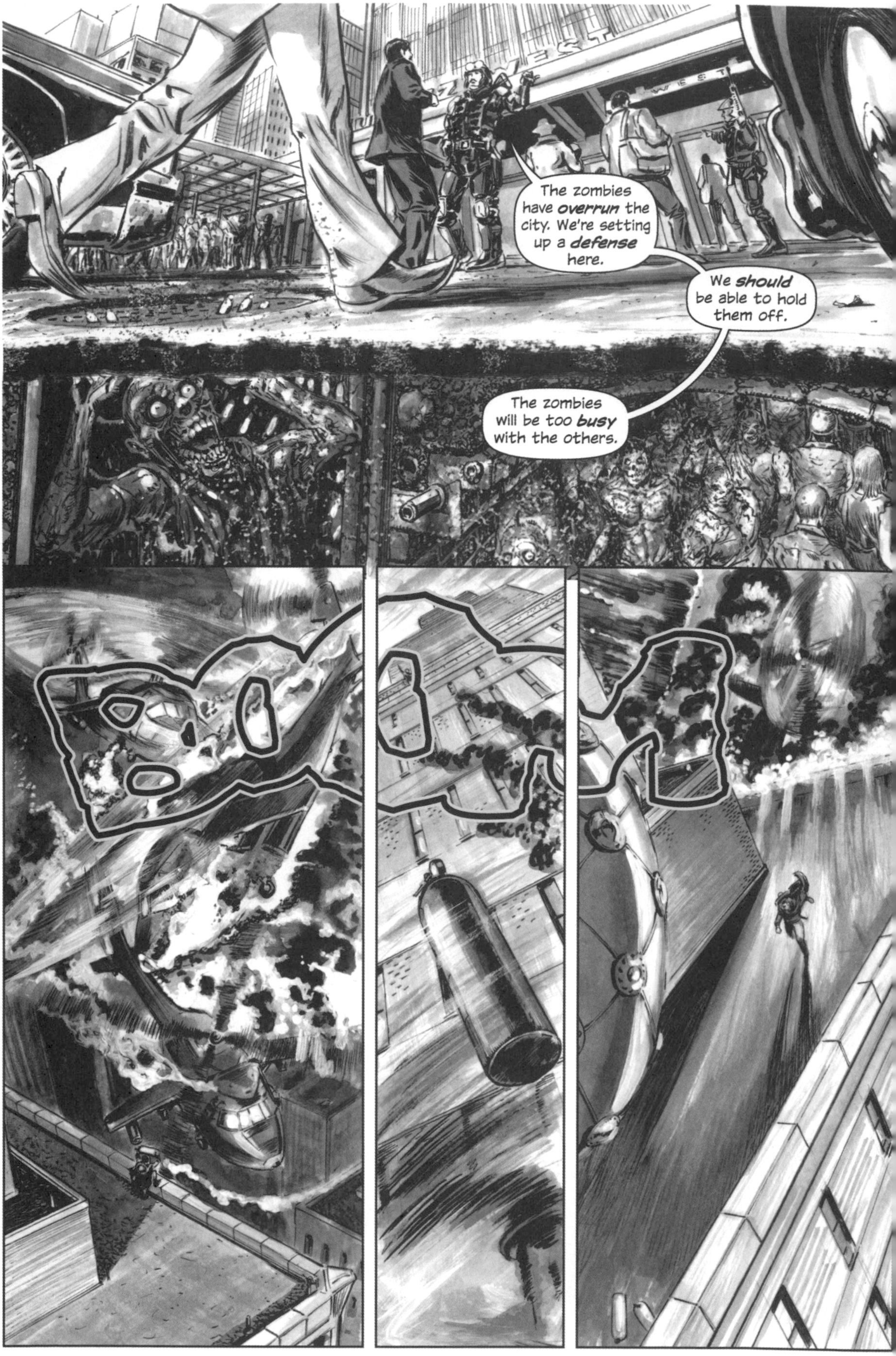
The zombies have ***overrun*** the city. We're setting up a ***defense*** here.
We ***should*** be able to hold them off.
The zombies will be too ***busy*** with the others.

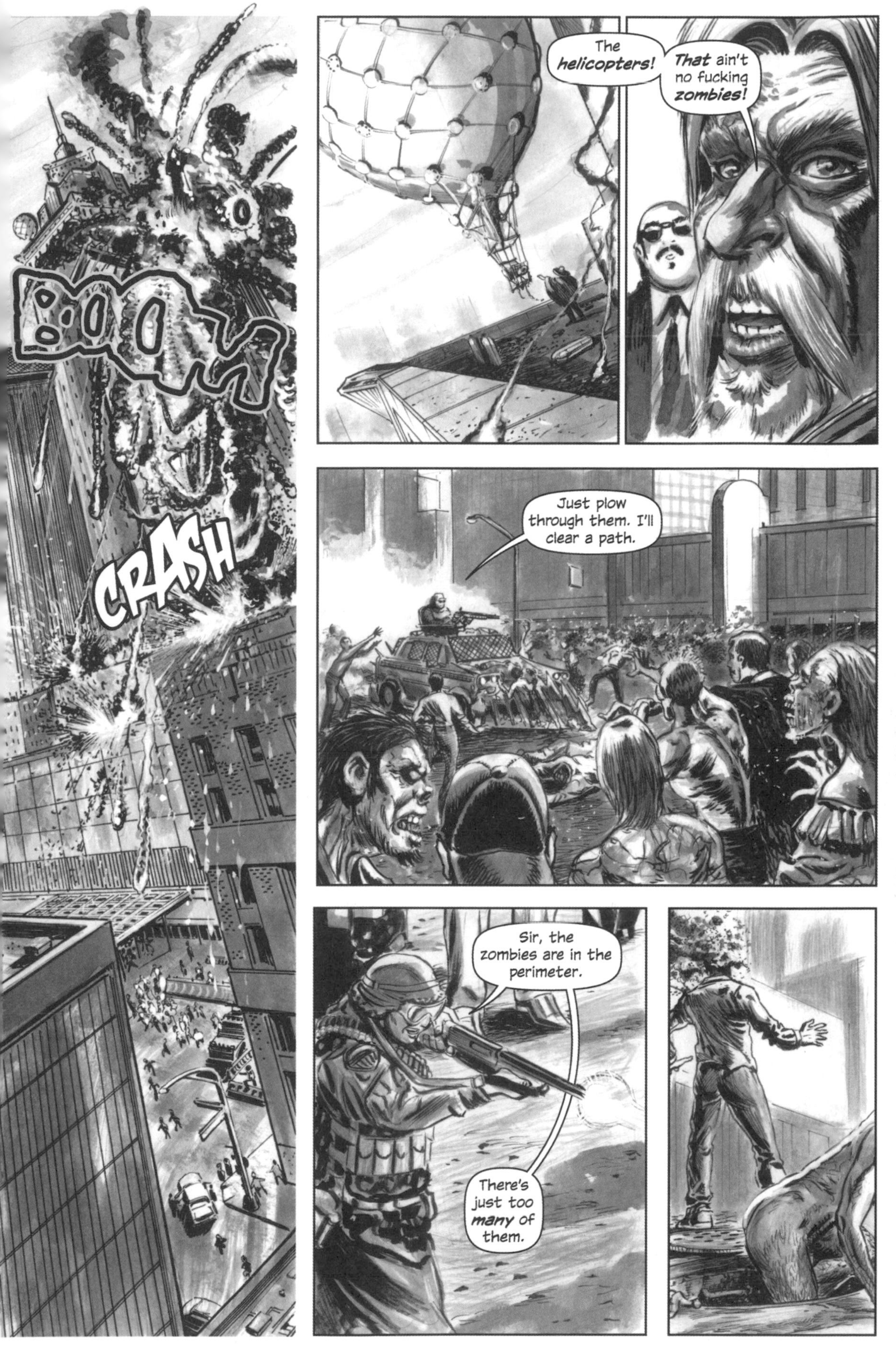
BOOM
CRASH
The helicopters!
That ain't no fucking zombies!
Just plow through them. I'll clear a path.
Sir, the zombies are in the perimeter.
There's just too many of them.

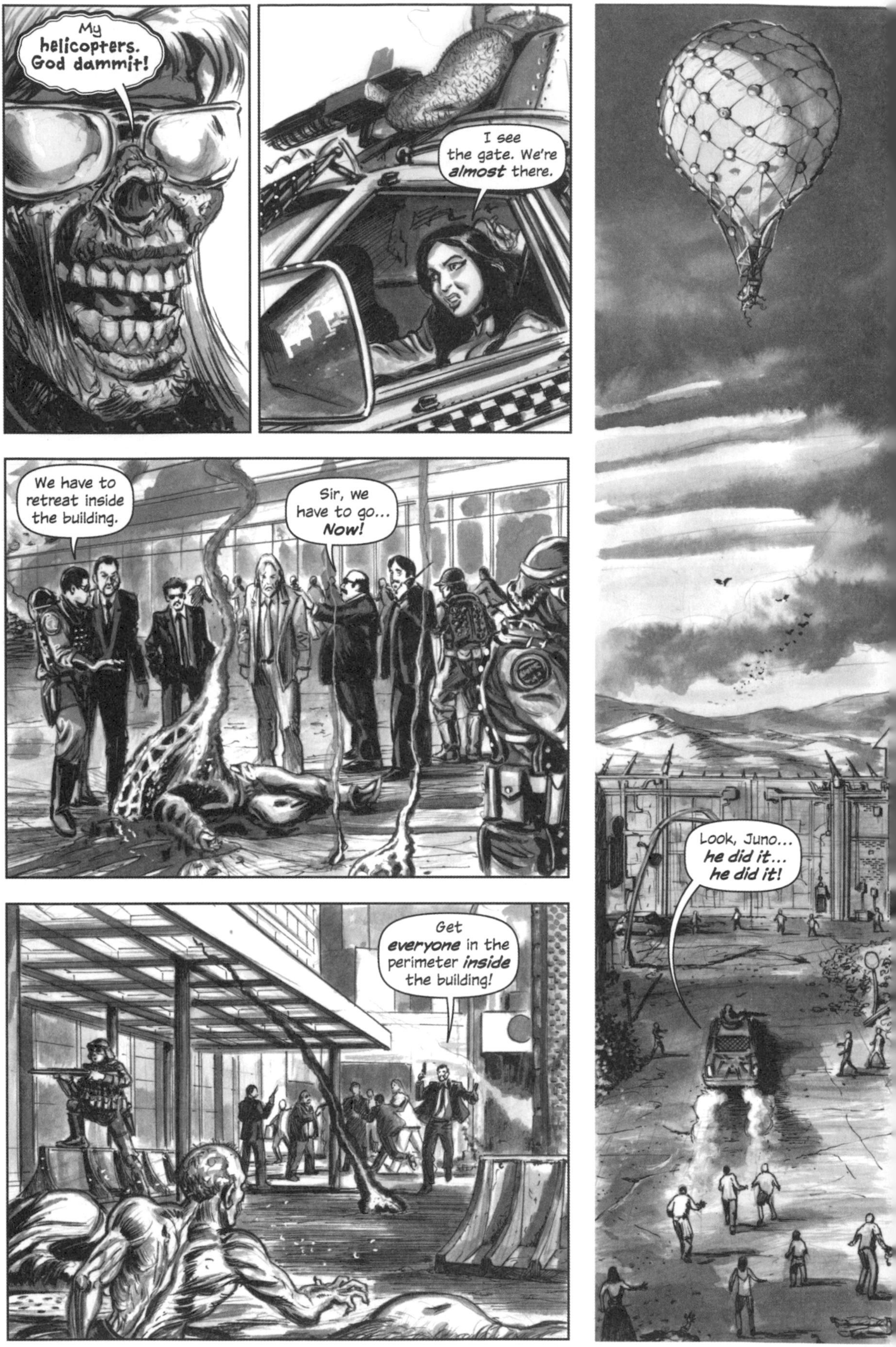
My helicopters. God dammit!
I see the gate. We're almost there.
We have to retreat inside the building.
Sir, we have to go... Now!
Get everyone in the perimeter inside the building!
Look, Juno... he did it... he did it!

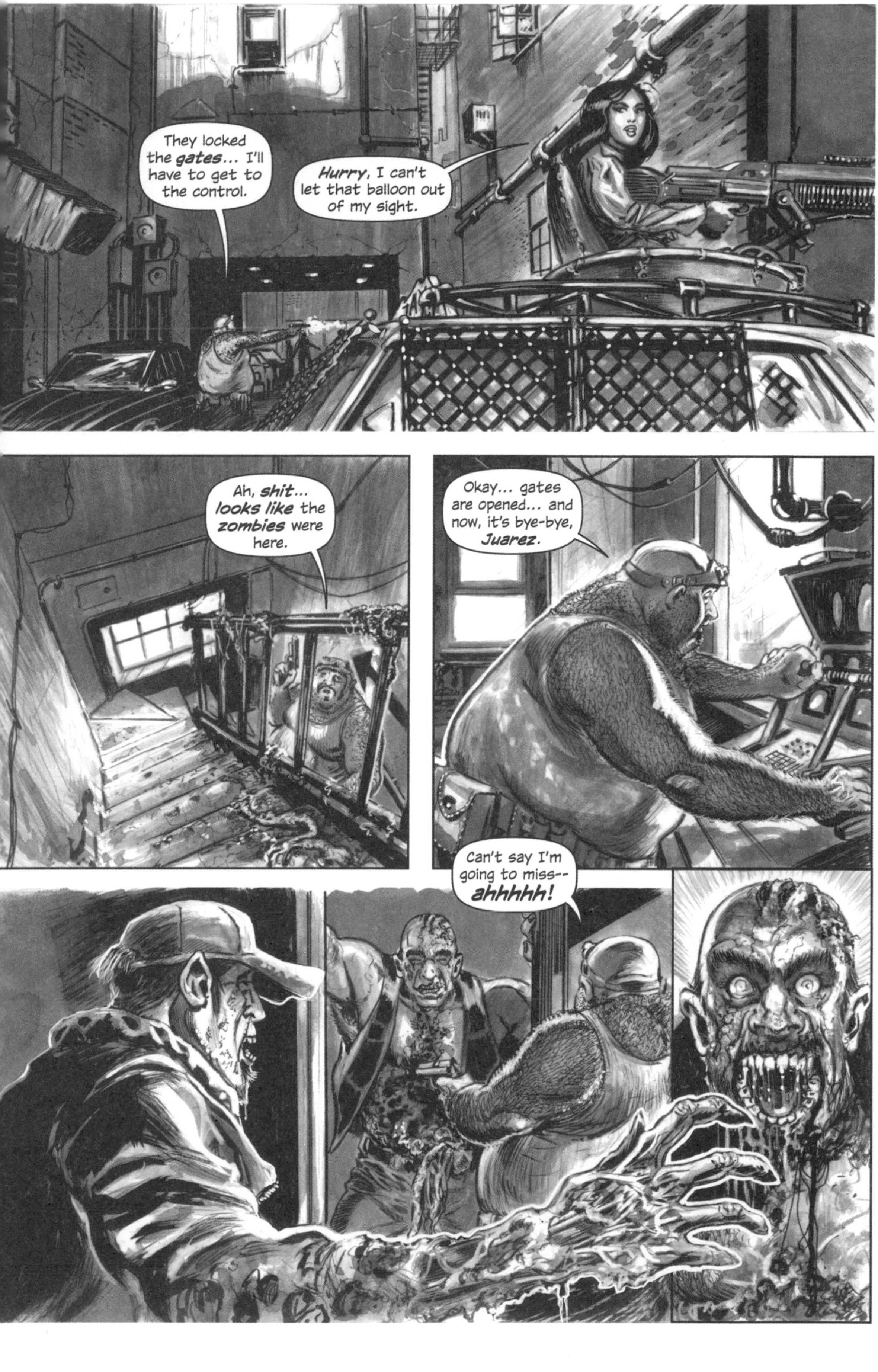
They locked the *gates*... I'll have to get to the control.
Hurry, I can't let that balloon out of my sight.
Ah, *shit*... *looks like* the *zombies* were here.
Okay... gates are opened... and now, it's bye-bye, *Juarez*.
Can't say I'm going to miss-- *ahhhhh!*

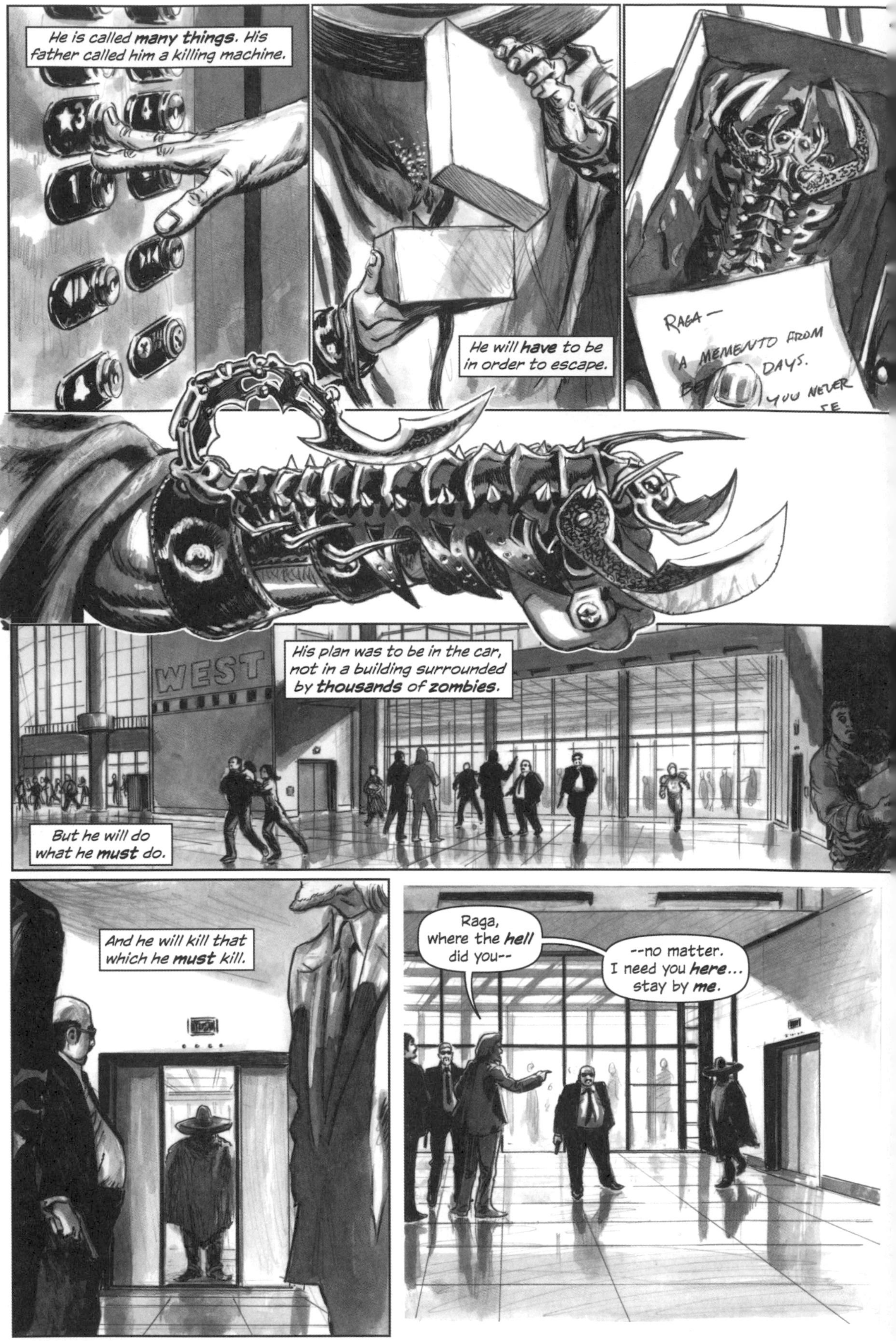
He is called **many things**. His father called him a killing machine.
He will **have** to be in order to escape.
RAGA —
A MEMENTO FROM
DAYS.
YOU NEVER
WEST
His plan was to be in the car, not in a building surrounded by **thousands** of **zombies**.
But he will do what he **must** do.
And he will kill that which he **must** kill.
Raga, where the ***hell*** did you--
--no matter. I need you ***here***... stay by ***me***.

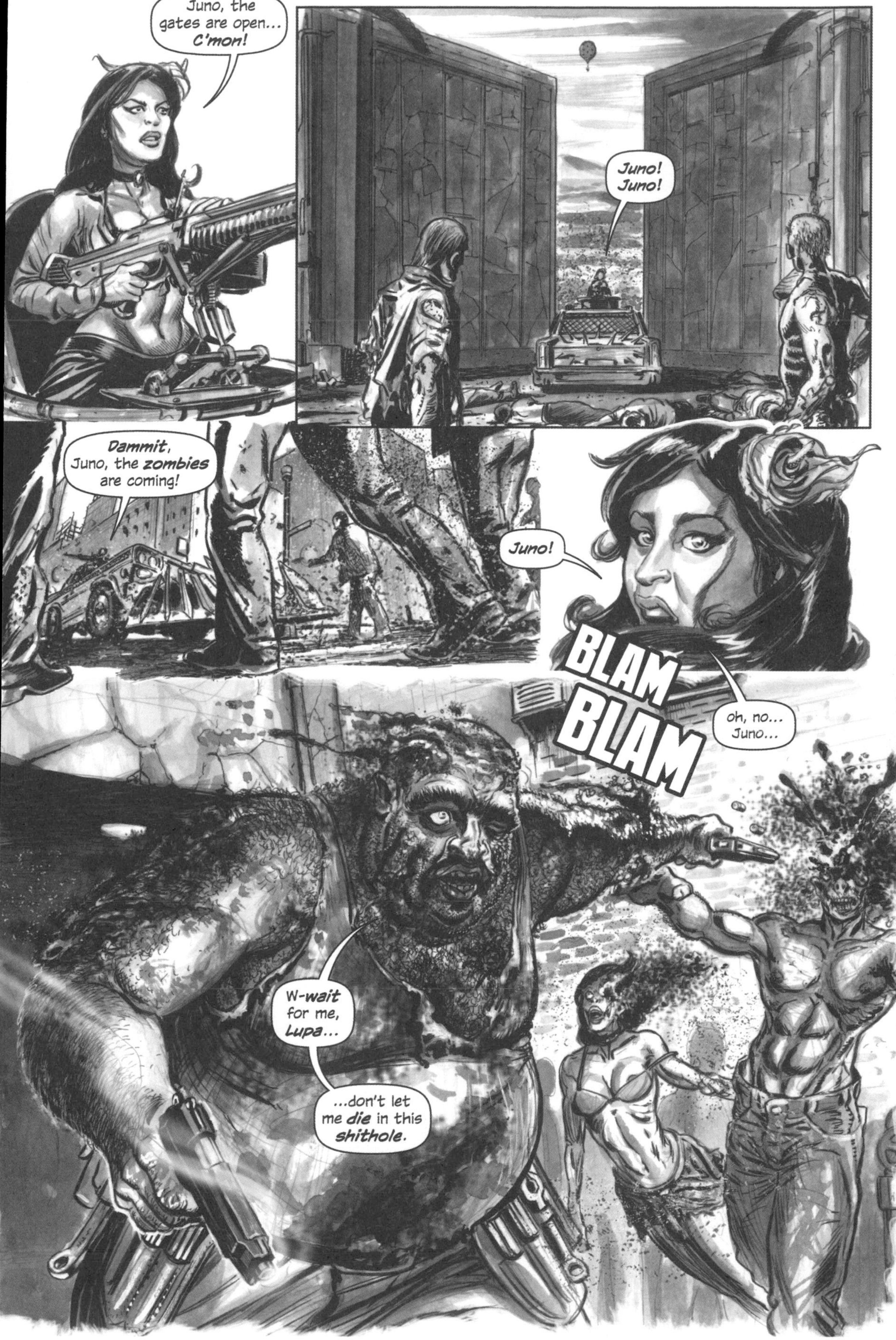
Juno, the gates are open... *C'mon!*
Juno! Juno!
Dammit, Juno, the *zombies* are coming!
Juno!
BLAM BLAM
oh, no... Juno...
W-*wait* for me, *Lupa*...
...don't let me *die* in this *shithole*.

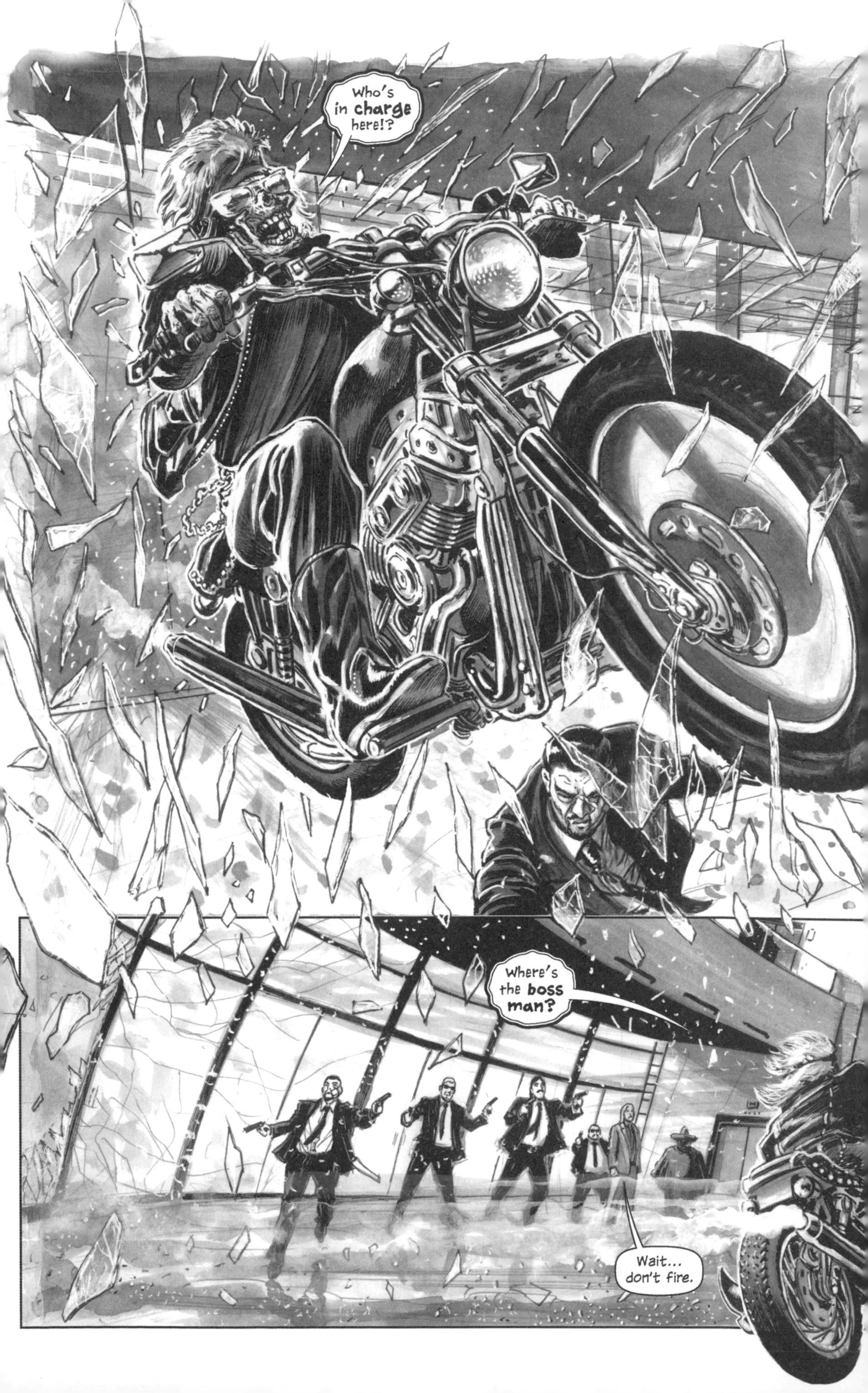
Who's in charge here!?
Where's the boss man?
Wait... don't fire.

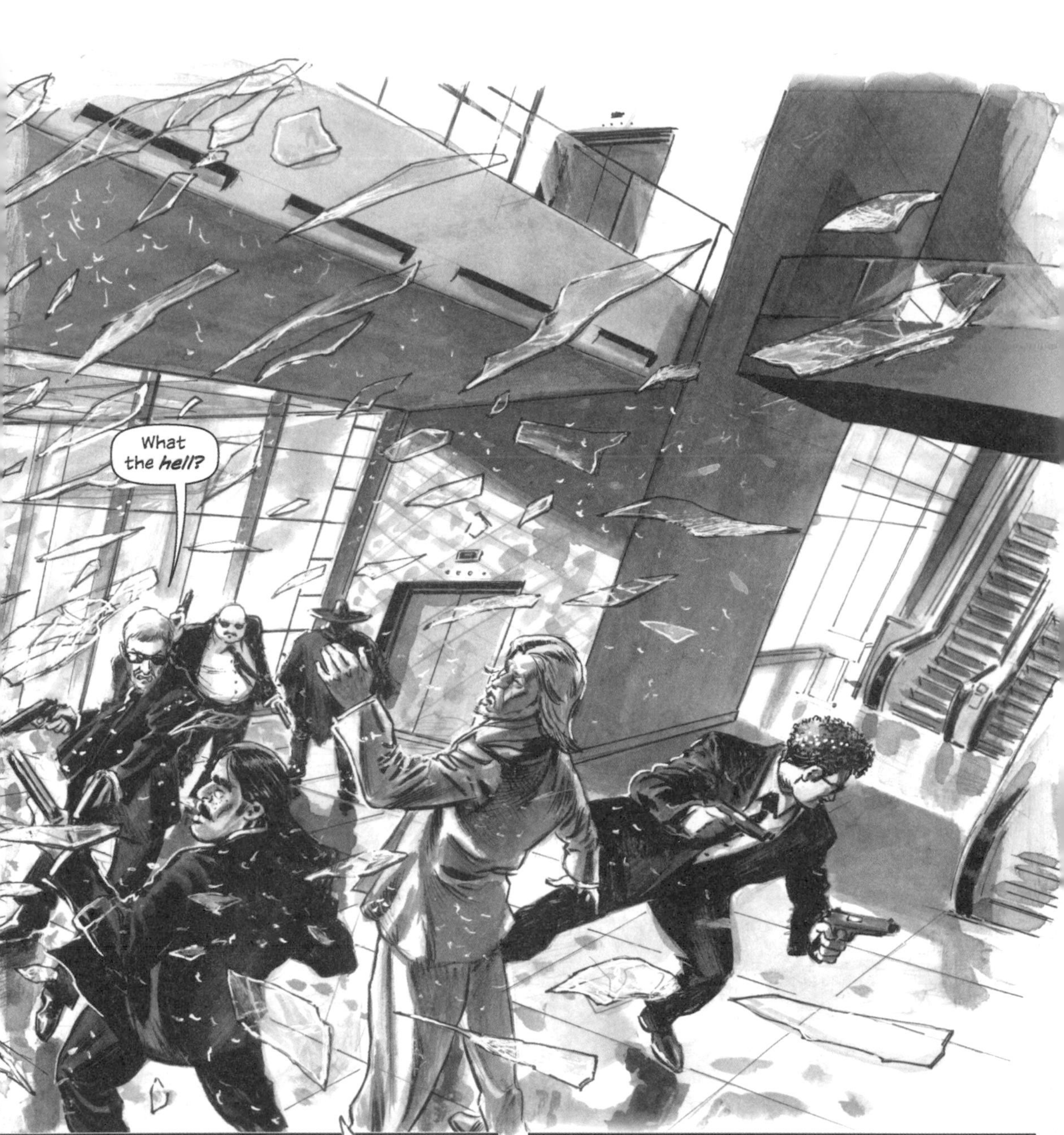
What the *hell?*

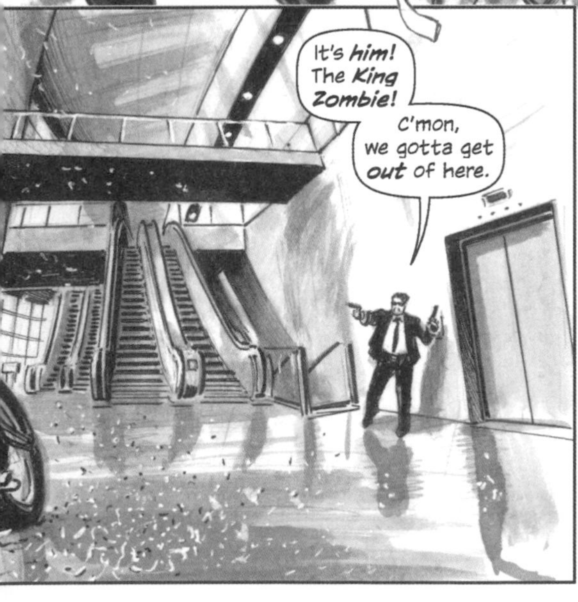
It's *him!* The *King Zombie!*
C'mon, we gotta get *out* of here.

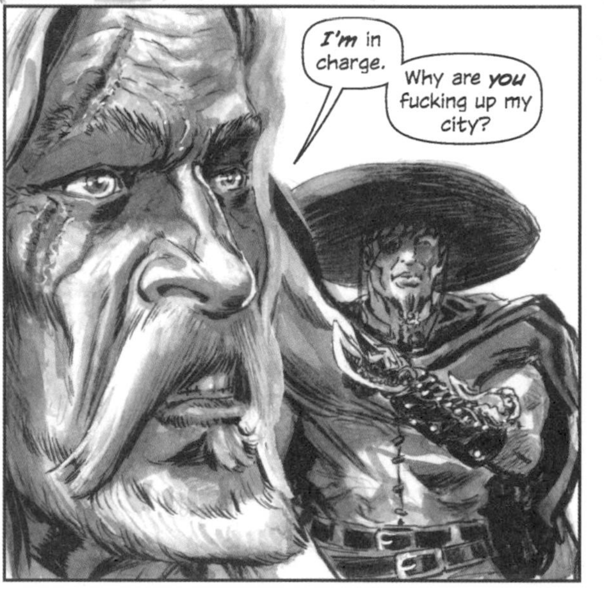
I'm in charge.
Why are *you* fucking up my city?

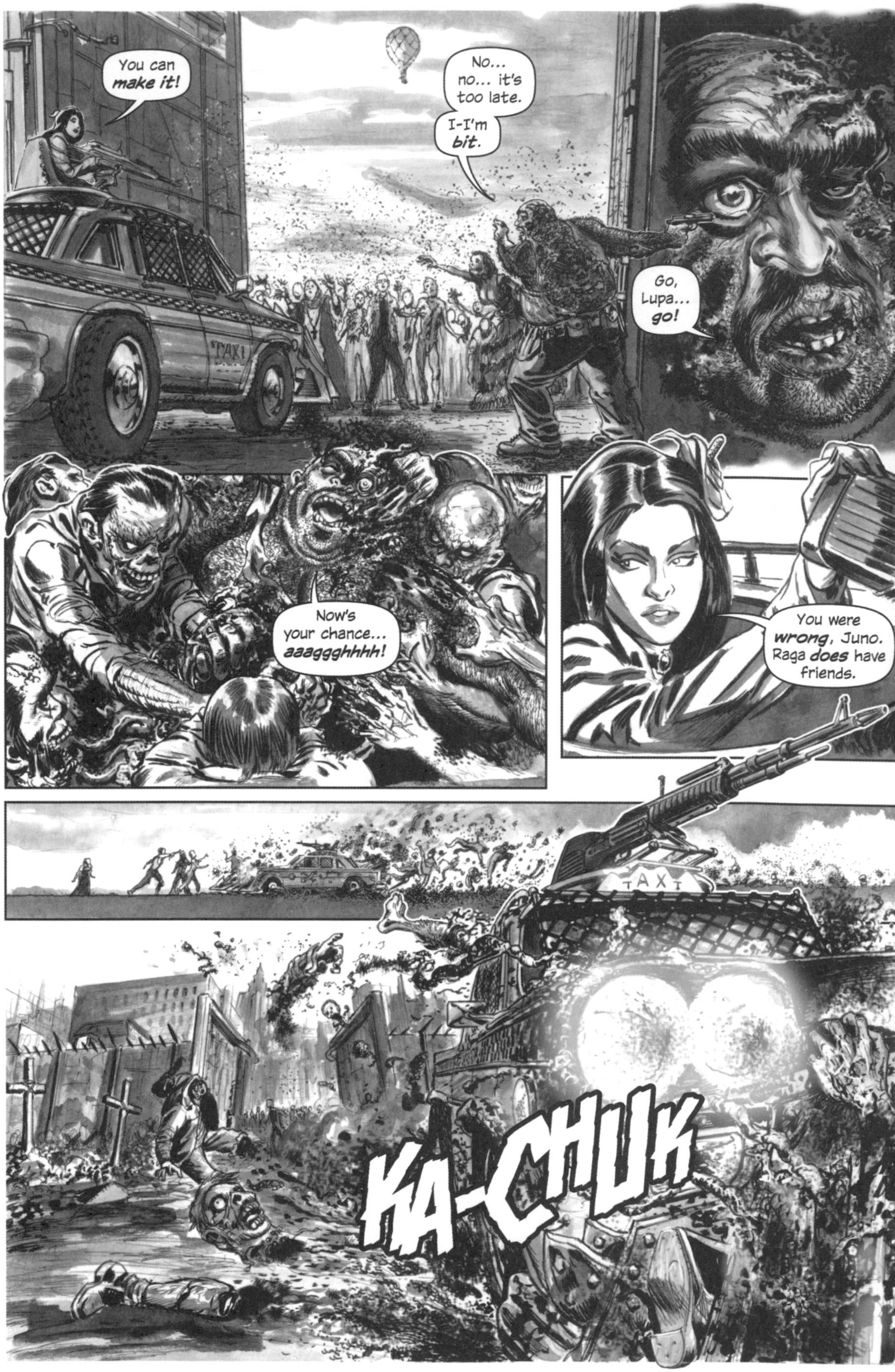
You can *make it!*
No... no... it's too late.
I-I'm *bit*.
Go, Lupa... *go!*
Now's your chance... *aaaggghhhh!*
You were *wrong*, Juno. Raga *does* have friends.
TAXI
KA-CHUK

Chapter six

the DEPARTED

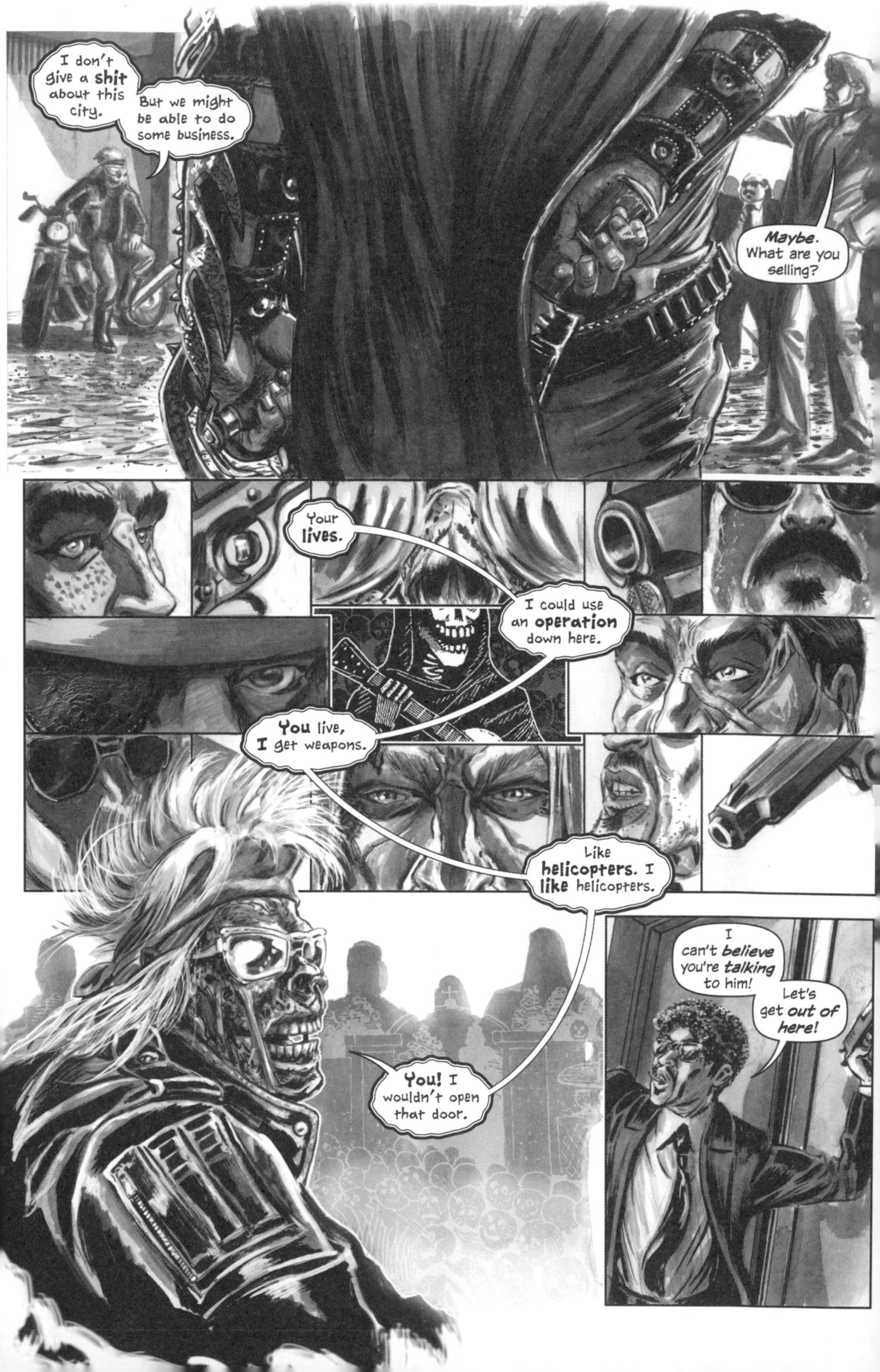
I don't give a shit about this city.
But we might be able to do some business.
Maybe. What are you selling?
Your lives.
I could use an operation down here.
You live, I get weapons.
Like helicopters. I like helicopters.
You! I wouldn't open that door.
I can't believe you're talking to him!
Let's get out of here!

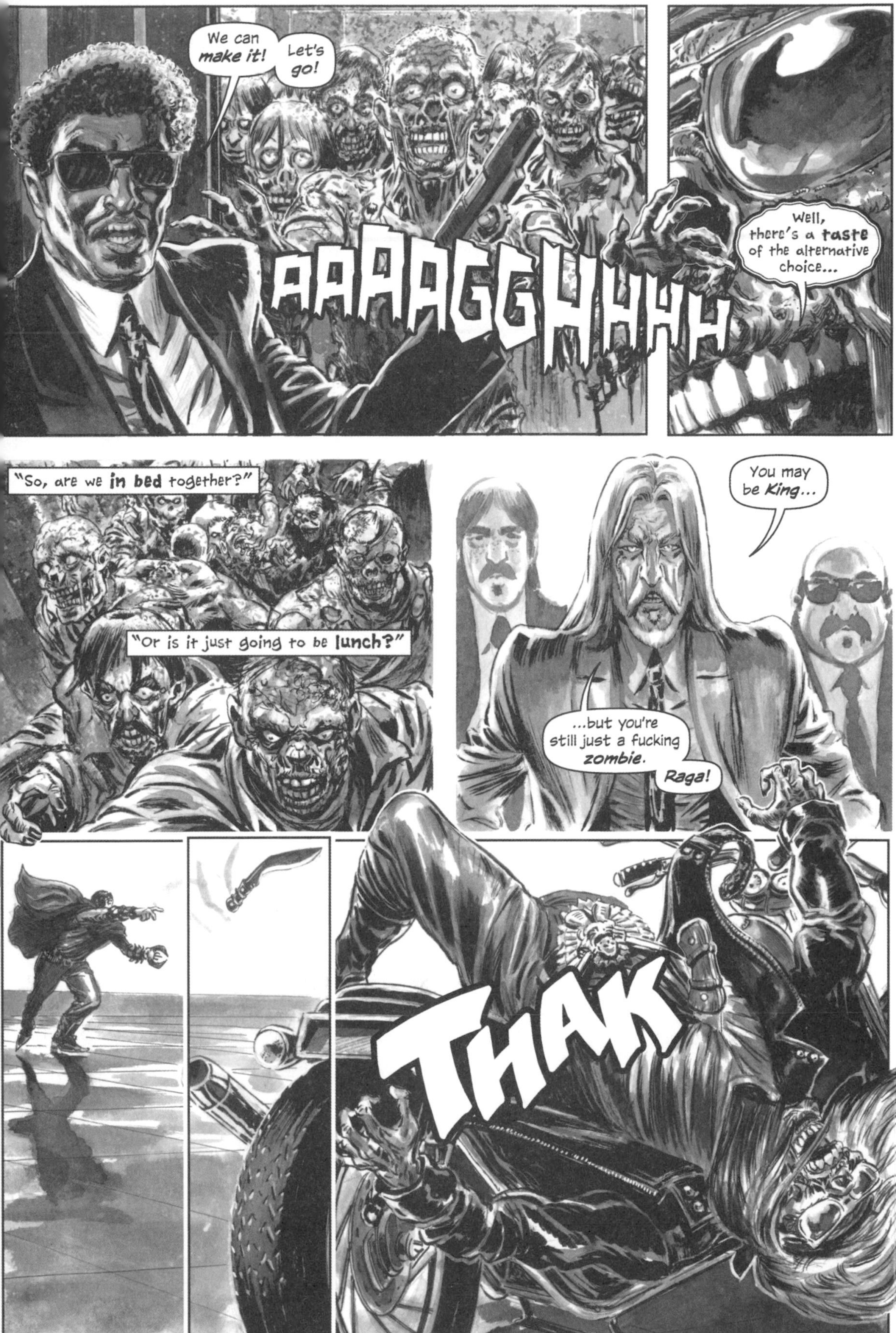
We can make it!
Let's go!
AAAAAGGHHHHH
Well, there's a taste of the alternative choice...
"So, are we in bed together?"
"Or is it just going to be lunch?"
You may be King...
...but you're still just a fucking zombie.
Raga!
THAK

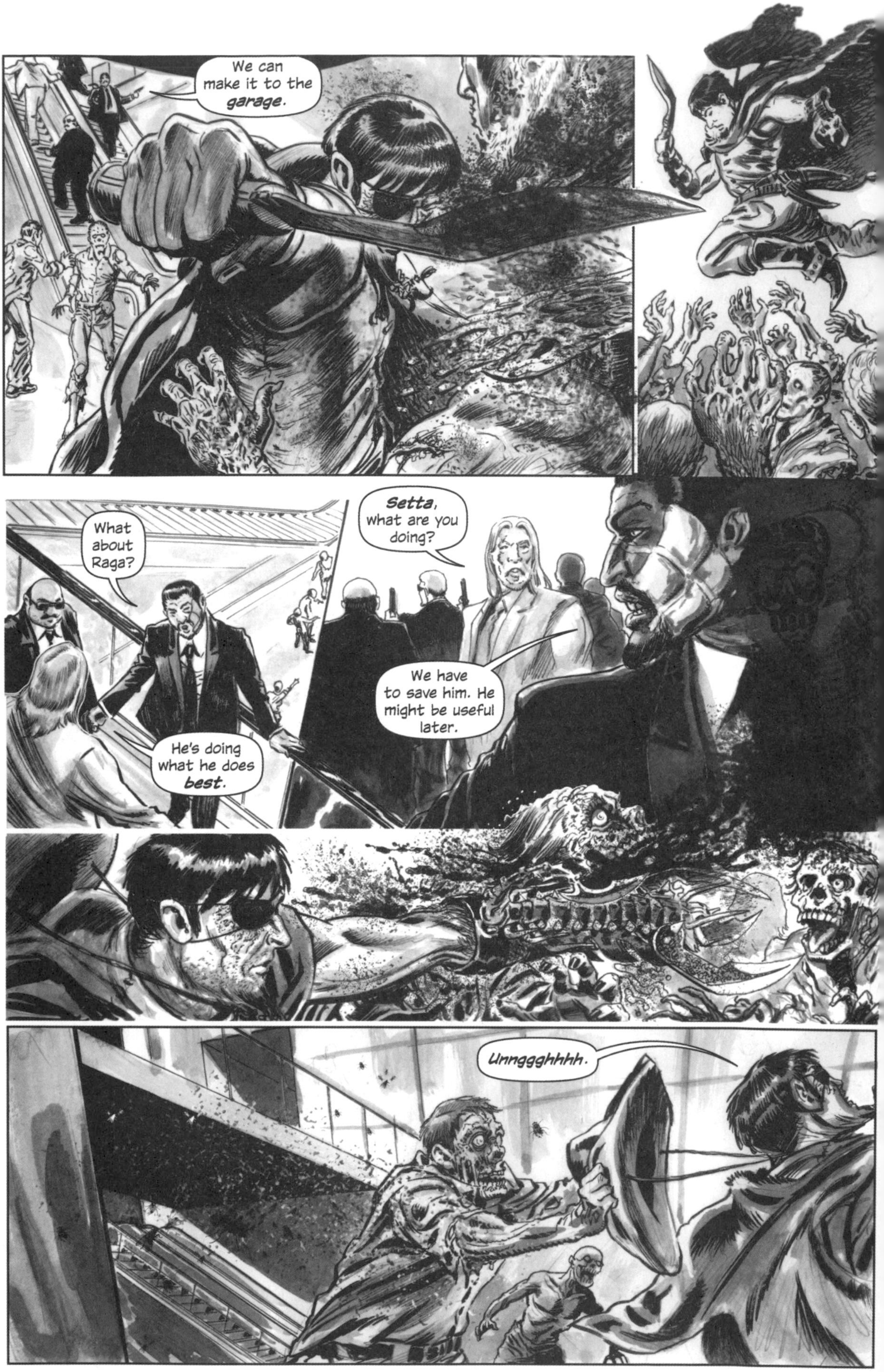
We can make it to the *garage*.
What about Raga?
He's doing what he does *best*.
Setta, what are you doing?
We have to save him. He might be useful later.
Unnggghhhh.

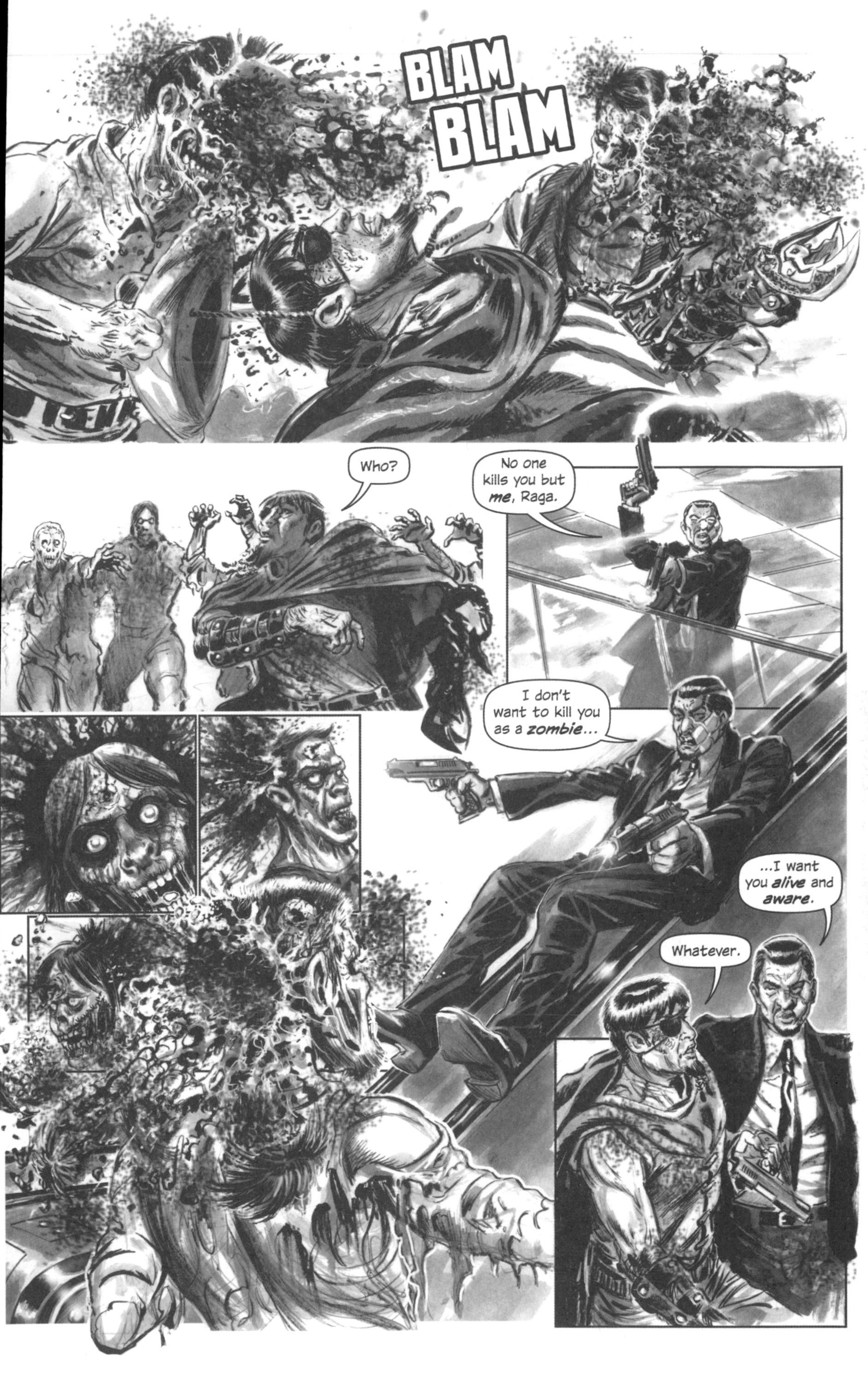
BLAM
BLAM
Who?
No one kills you but *me*, Raga.
I don't want to kill you as a *zombie*...
...I want you *alive* and *aware*.
Whatever.

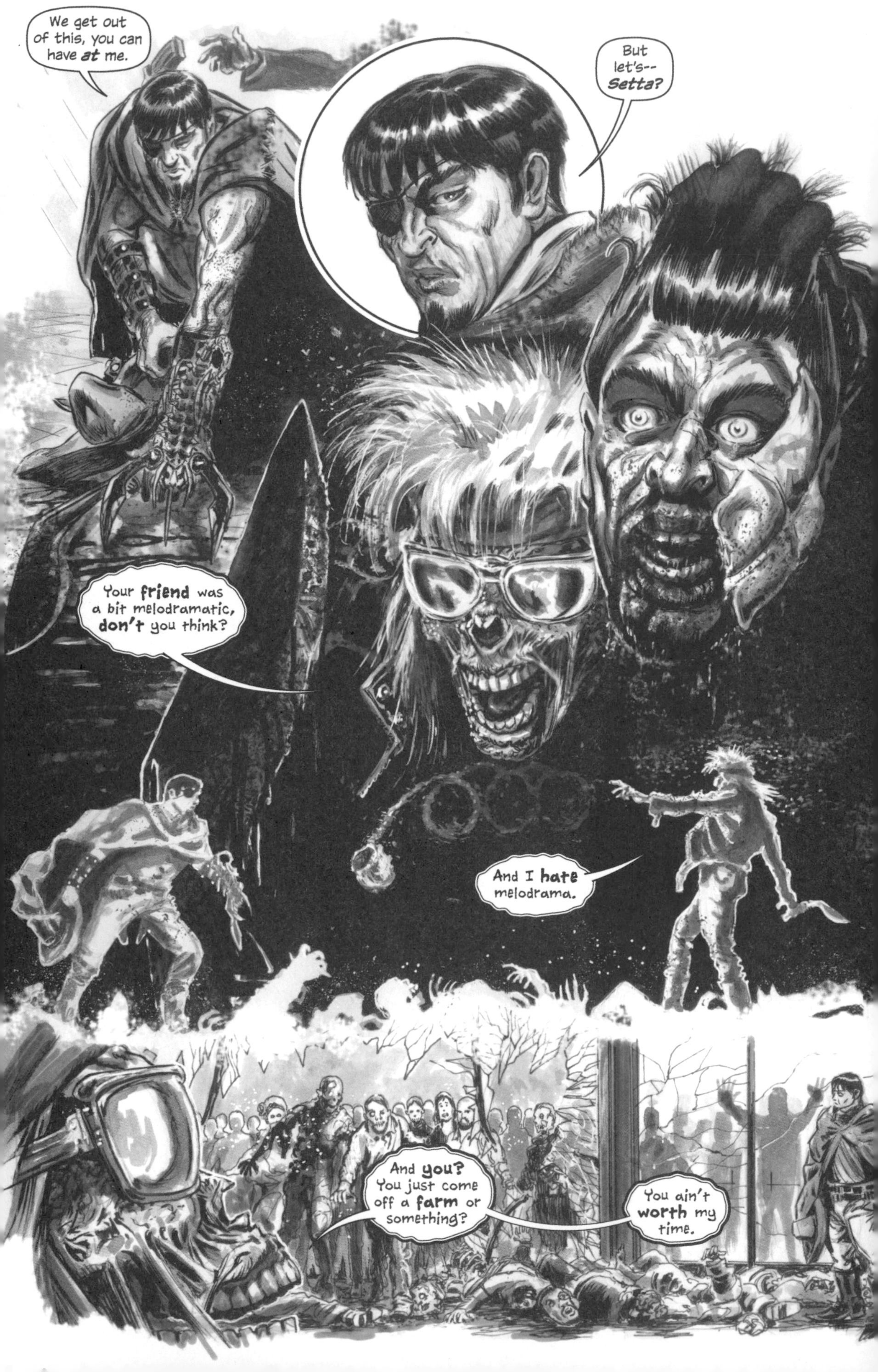
We get out of this, you can have at me.
But let's-- Setta?
Your friend was a bit melodramatic, don't you think?
And I hate melodrama.
And you? You just come off a farm or something?
You ain't worth my time.

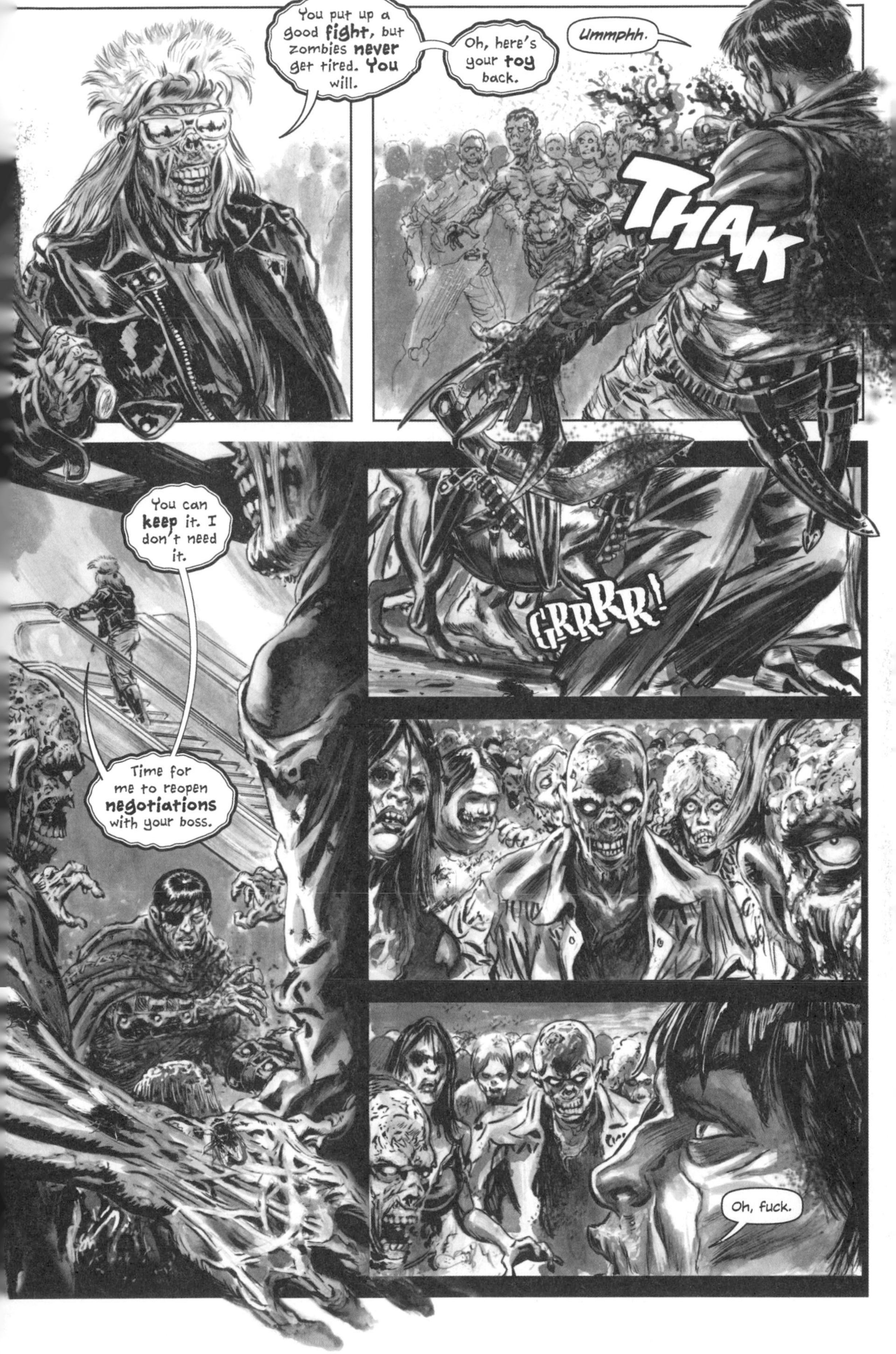
You put up a good fight, but zombies never get tired. You will.
Oh, here's your toy back.
Ummphh.
THAK
You can keep it. I don't need it.
Time for me to reopen negotiations with your boss.
GRRRR!
Oh, fuck.

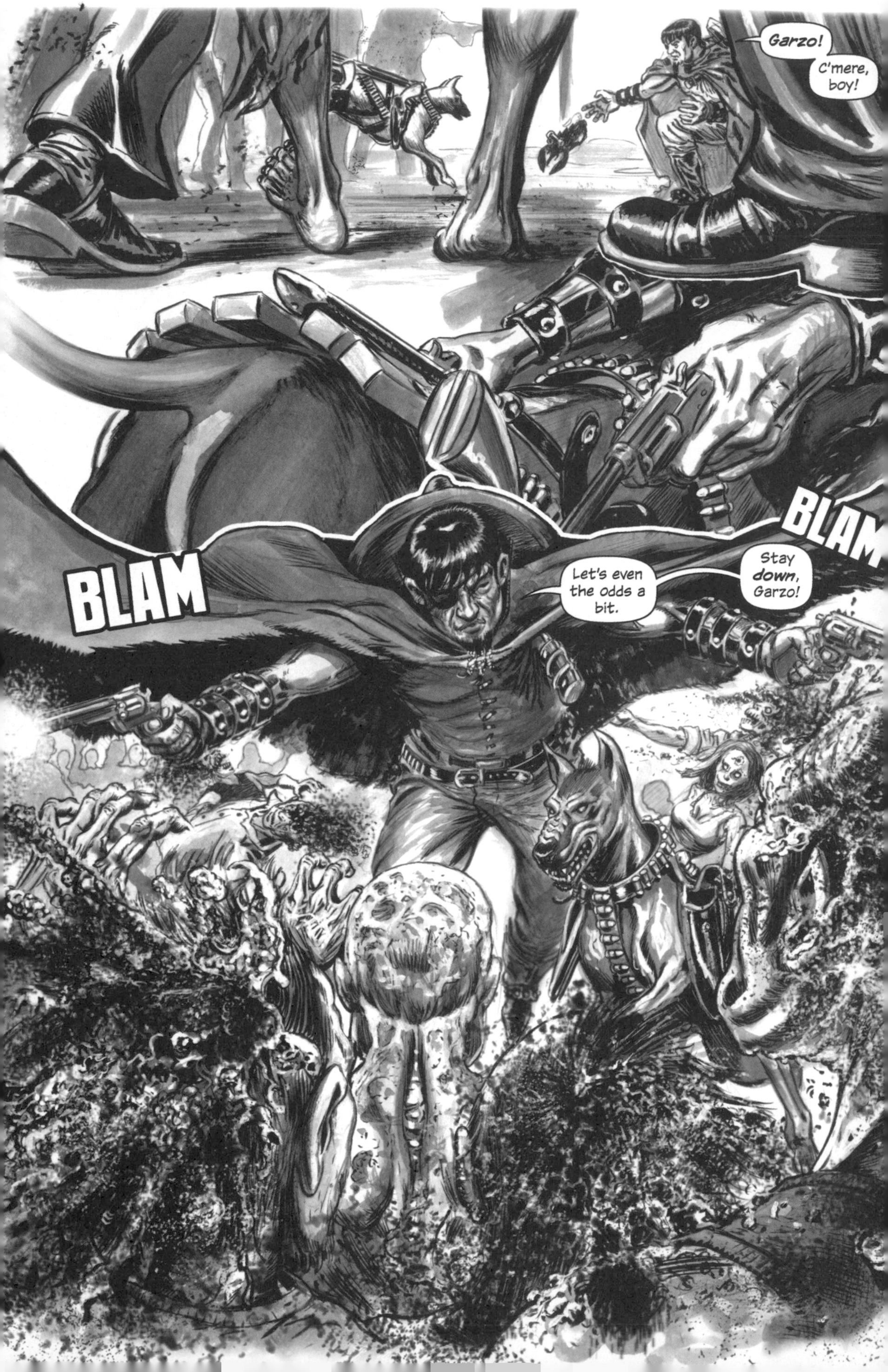
Garzo!
C'mere, boy!
BLAM
Let's even the odds a bit.
BLAM
Stay *down*, Garzo!

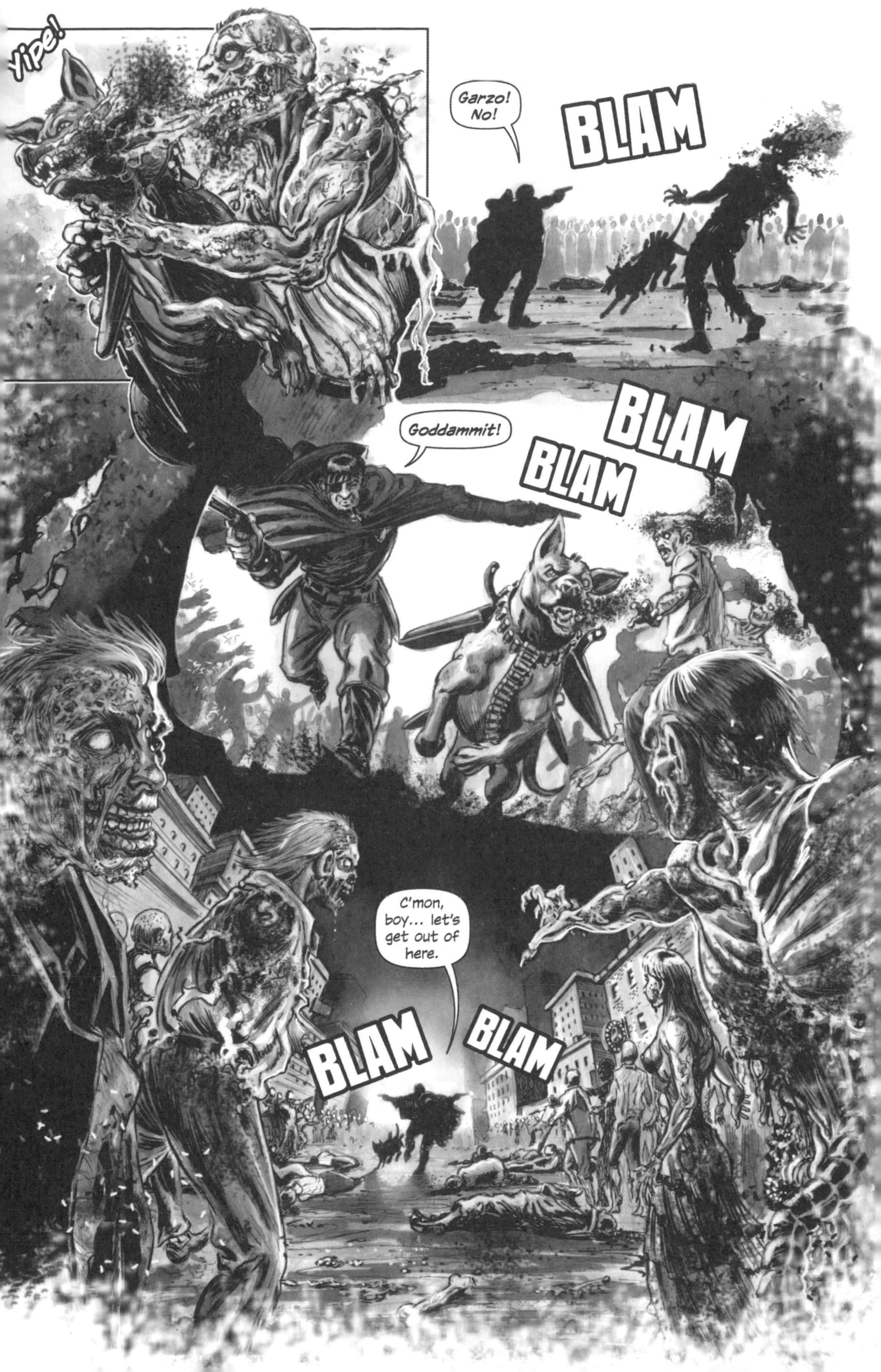
Yipe!
Garzo! No!
BLAM
BLAM
Goddammit!
BLAM
C'mon, boy... let's get out of here.
BLAM
BLAM

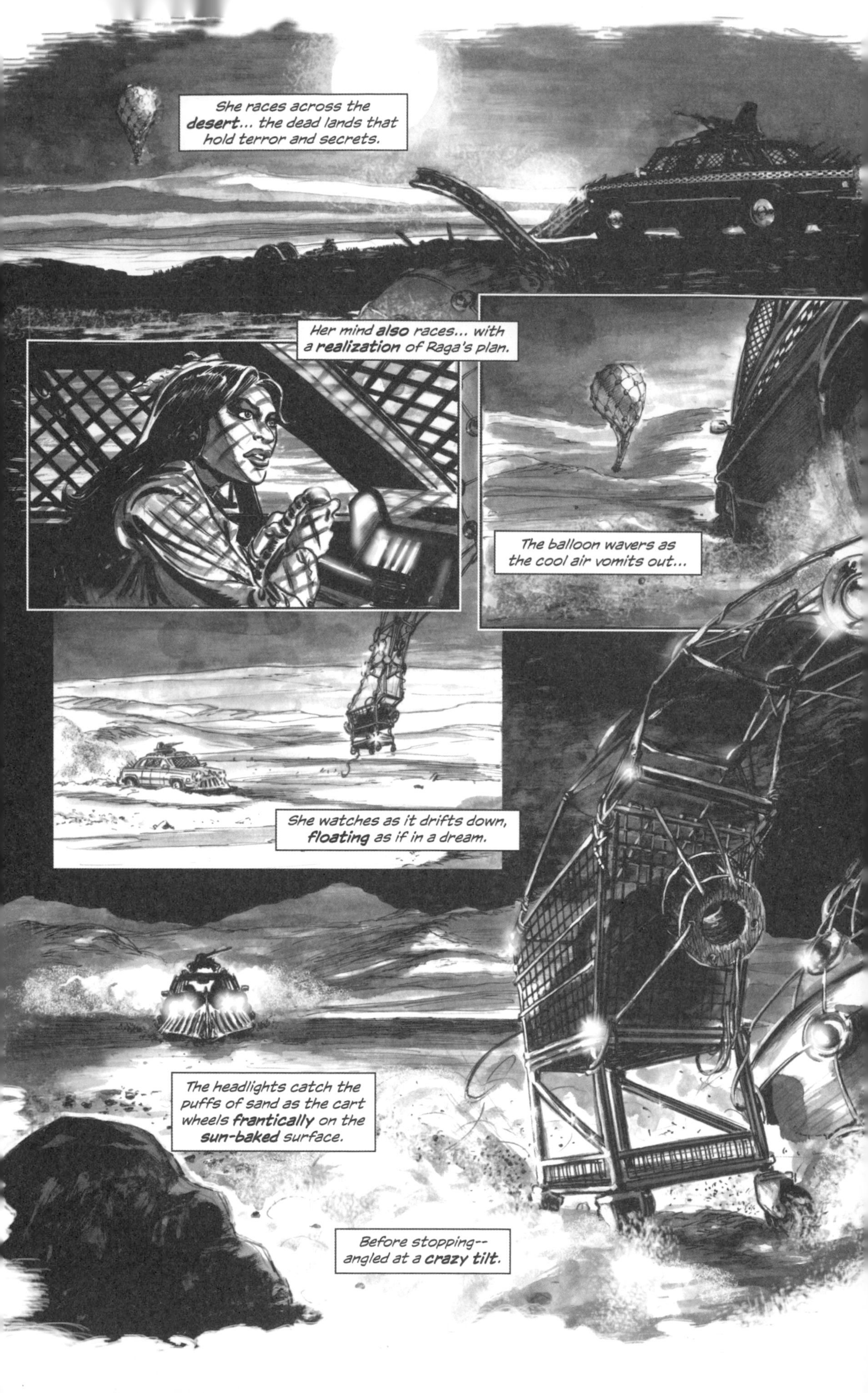
She races across the desert... the dead lands that hold terror and secrets.
Her mind also races... with a realization of Raga's plan.
The balloon wavers as the cool air vomits out...
She watches as it drifts down, floating as if in a dream.
The headlights catch the puffs of sand as the cart wheels frantically on the sun-baked surface.
Before stopping-- angled at a crazy tilt.

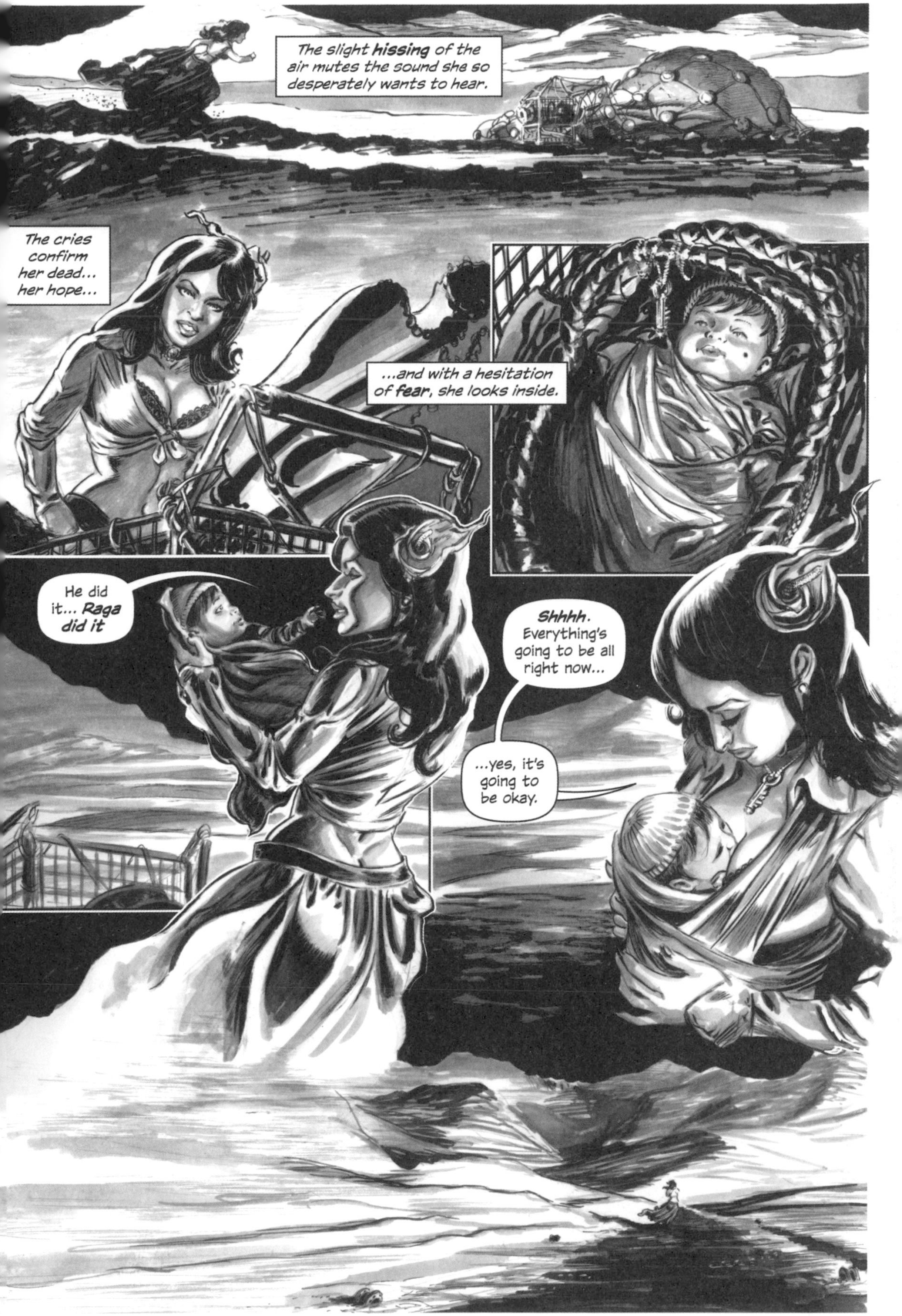
The slight hissing of the air mutes the sound she so desperately wants to hear.
The cries confirm her dead... her hope...
...and with a hesitation of fear, she looks inside.
He did it... Raga did it
Shhhh. Everything's going to be all right now...
...yes, it's going to be okay.

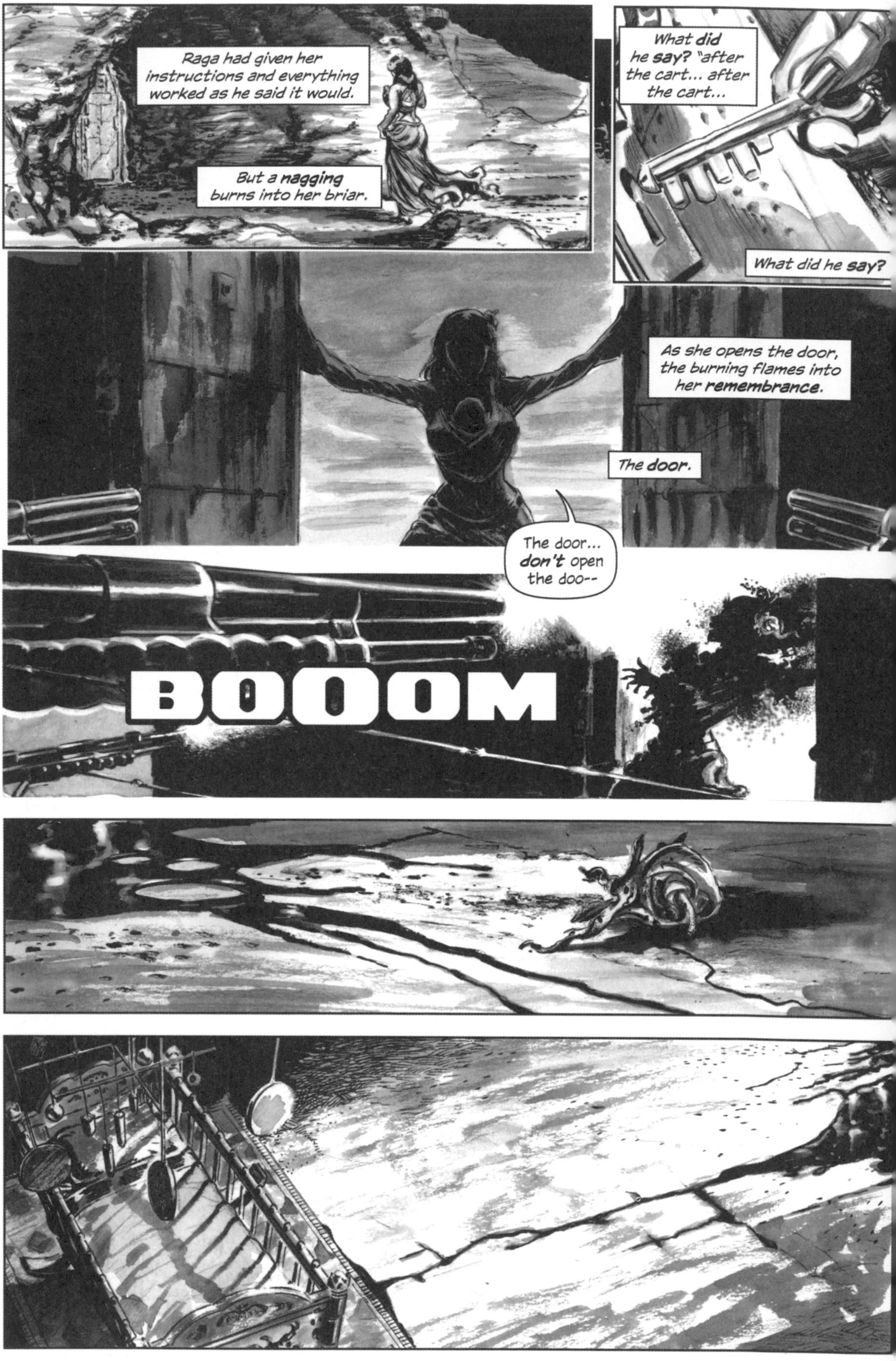
Raga had given her instructions and everything worked as he said it would.
But a nagging burns into her briar.
What did he say? "after the cart... after the cart...
What did he say?
As she opens the door, the burning flames into her remembrance.
The door.
The door... don't open the doo--
BOOOM

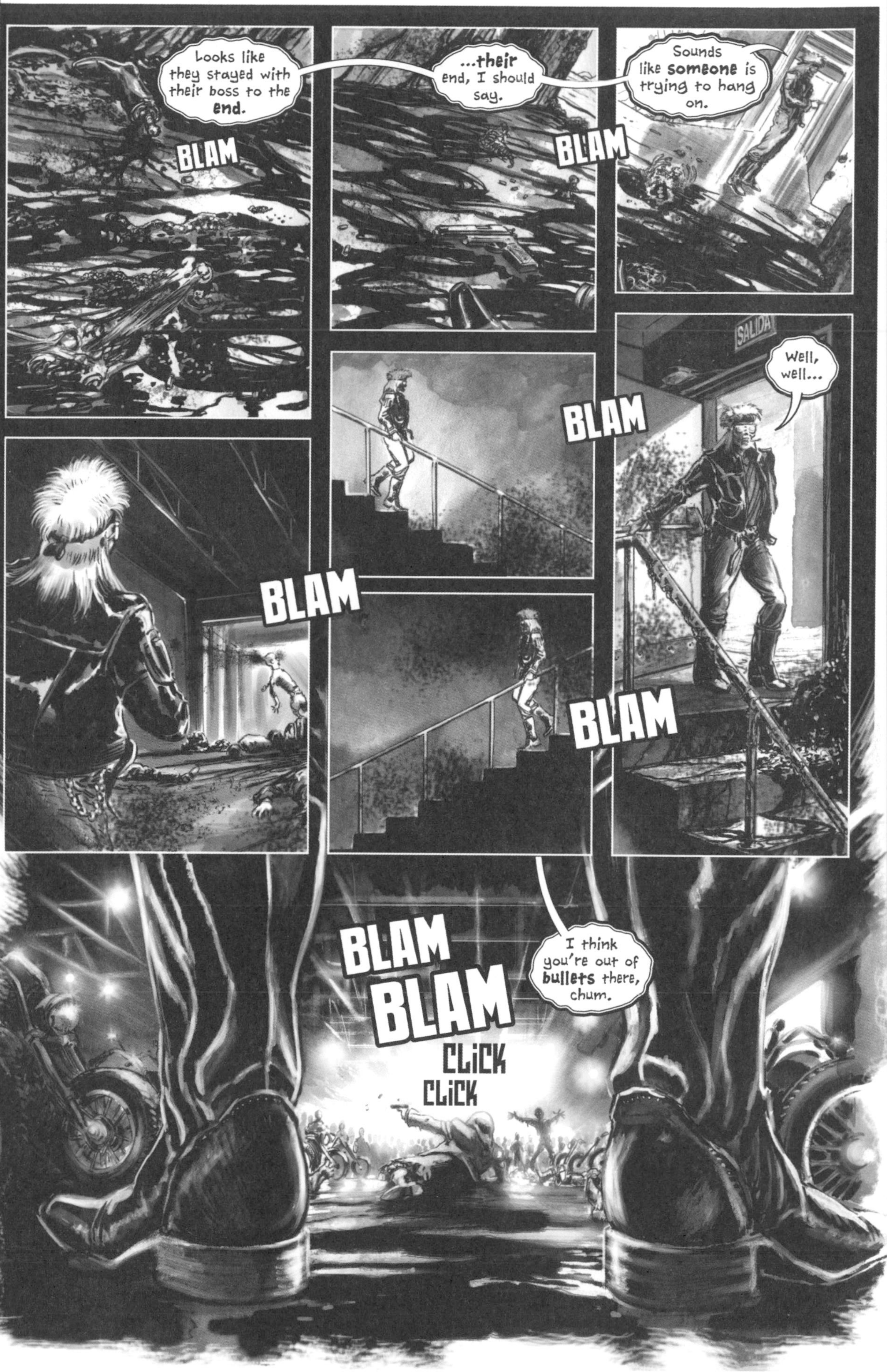
Looks like they stayed with their boss to the end.
BLAM
...their end, I should say.
BLAM
Sounds like someone is trying to hang on.
SALIDA
Well, well...
BLAM
BLAM
BLAM
BLAM
BLAM
CLICK
CLICK
I think you're out of bullets there, chum.

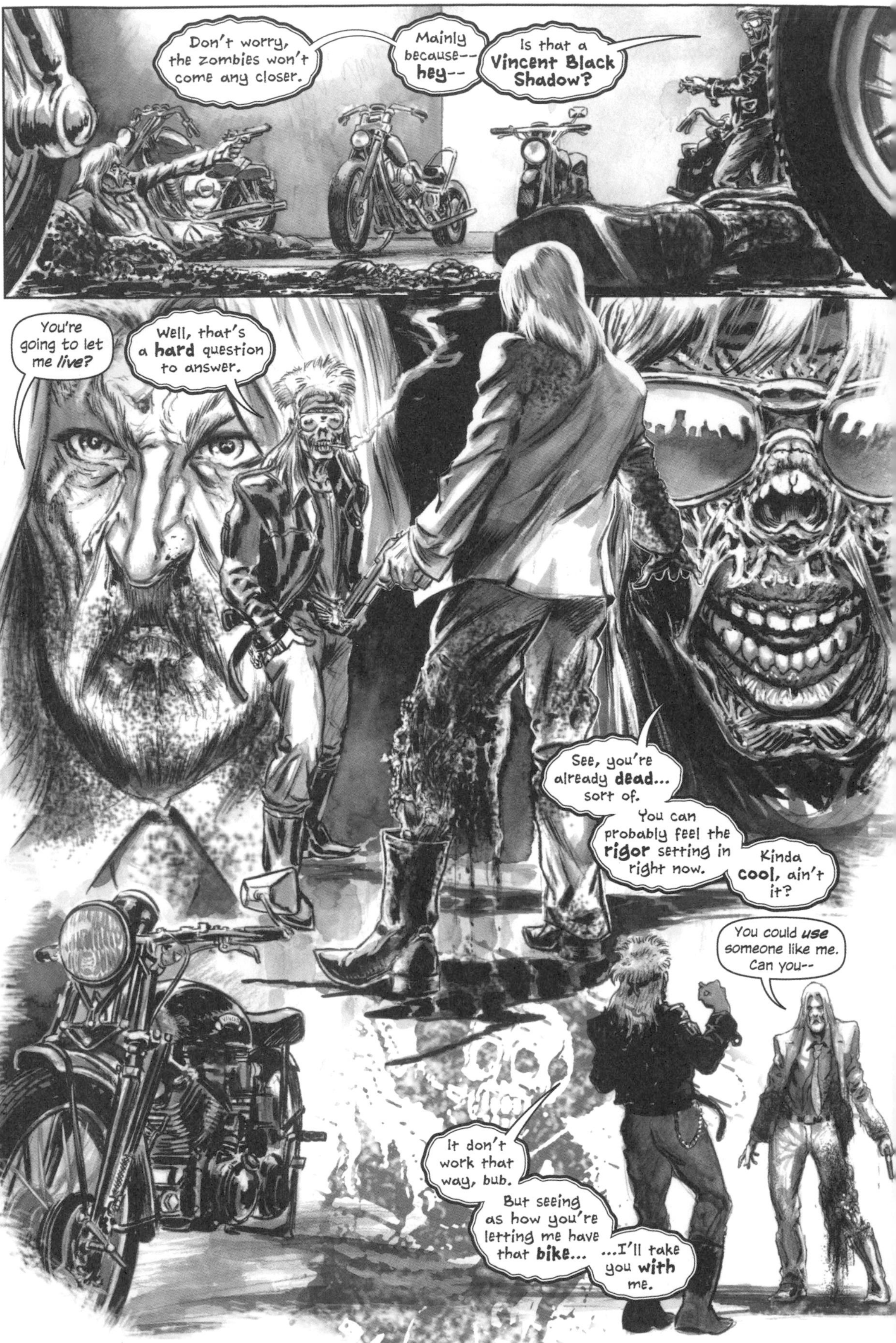
Don't worry, the zombies won't come any closer.
Mainly because-- hey--
Is that a Vincent Black Shadow?
You're going to let me live?
Well, that's a hard question to answer.
See, you're already dead... sort of.
You can probably feel the rigor setting in right now.
Kinda cool, ain't it?
You could use someone like me. Can you--
It don't work that way, bub.
But seeing as how you're letting me have that bike...
...I'll take you with me.

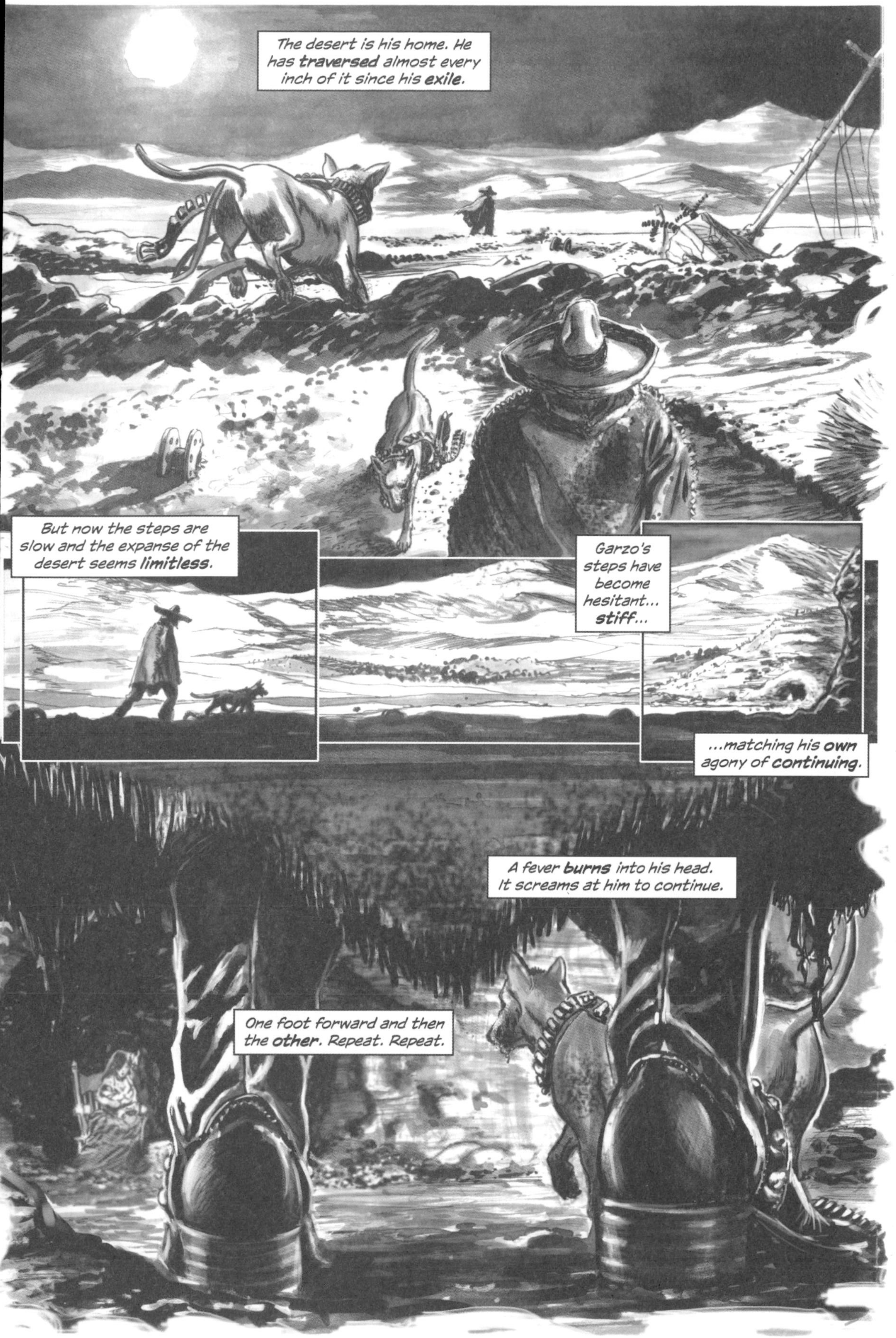
The desert is his home. He has traversed almost every inch of it since his exile.
But now the steps are slow and the expanse of the desert seems limitless.
Garzo's steps have become hesitant... stiff...
...matching his own agony of continuing.
A fever burns into his head. It screams at him to continue.
One foot forward and then the other. Repeat. Repeat.

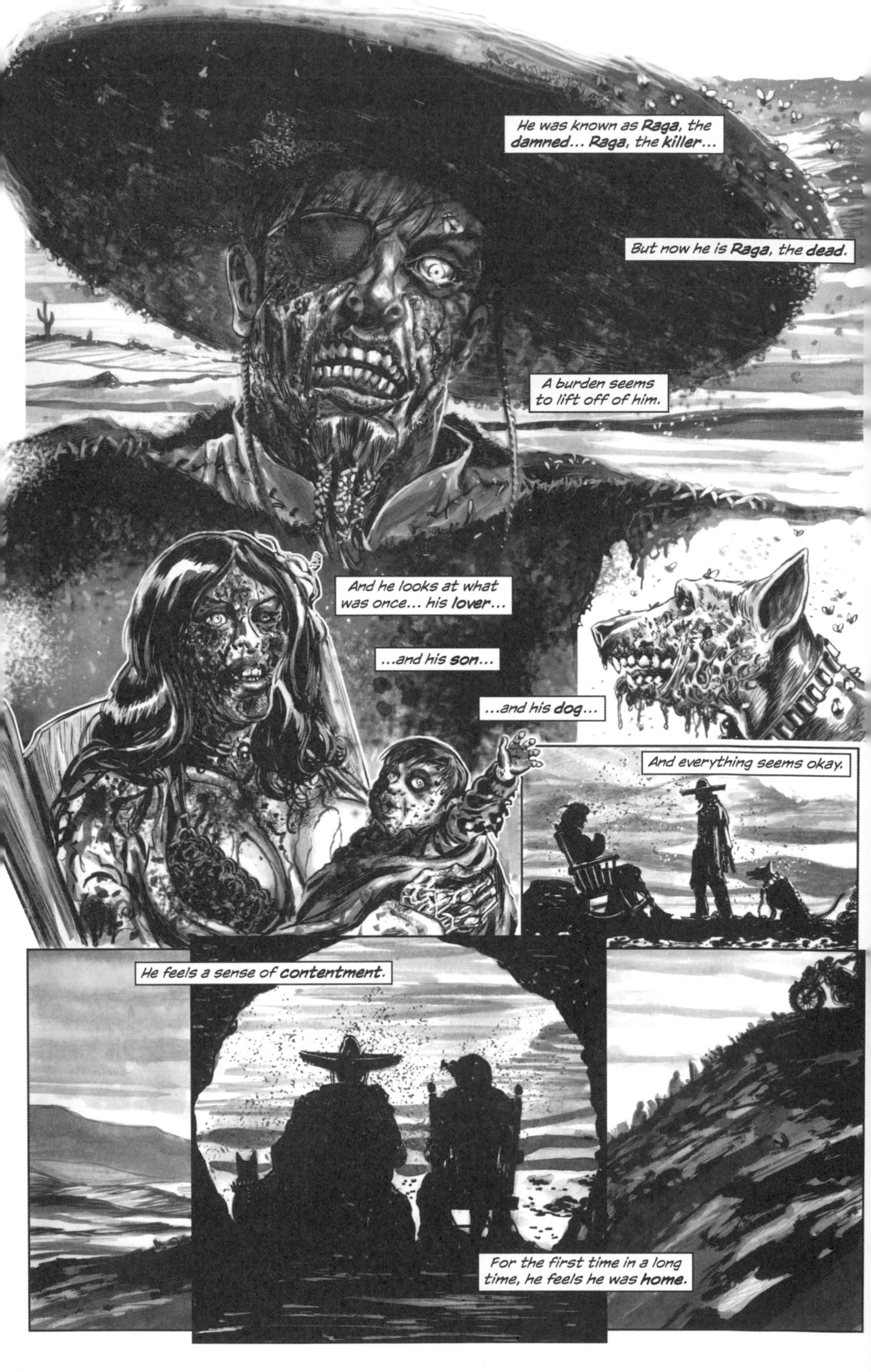
He was known as Raga, the damned... Raga, the killer...
But now he is Raga, the dead.
A burden seems to lift off of him.
And he looks at what was once... his lover...
...and his son...
...and his dog...
And everything seems okay.
He feels a sense of contentment.
For the first time in a long time, he feels he was home.

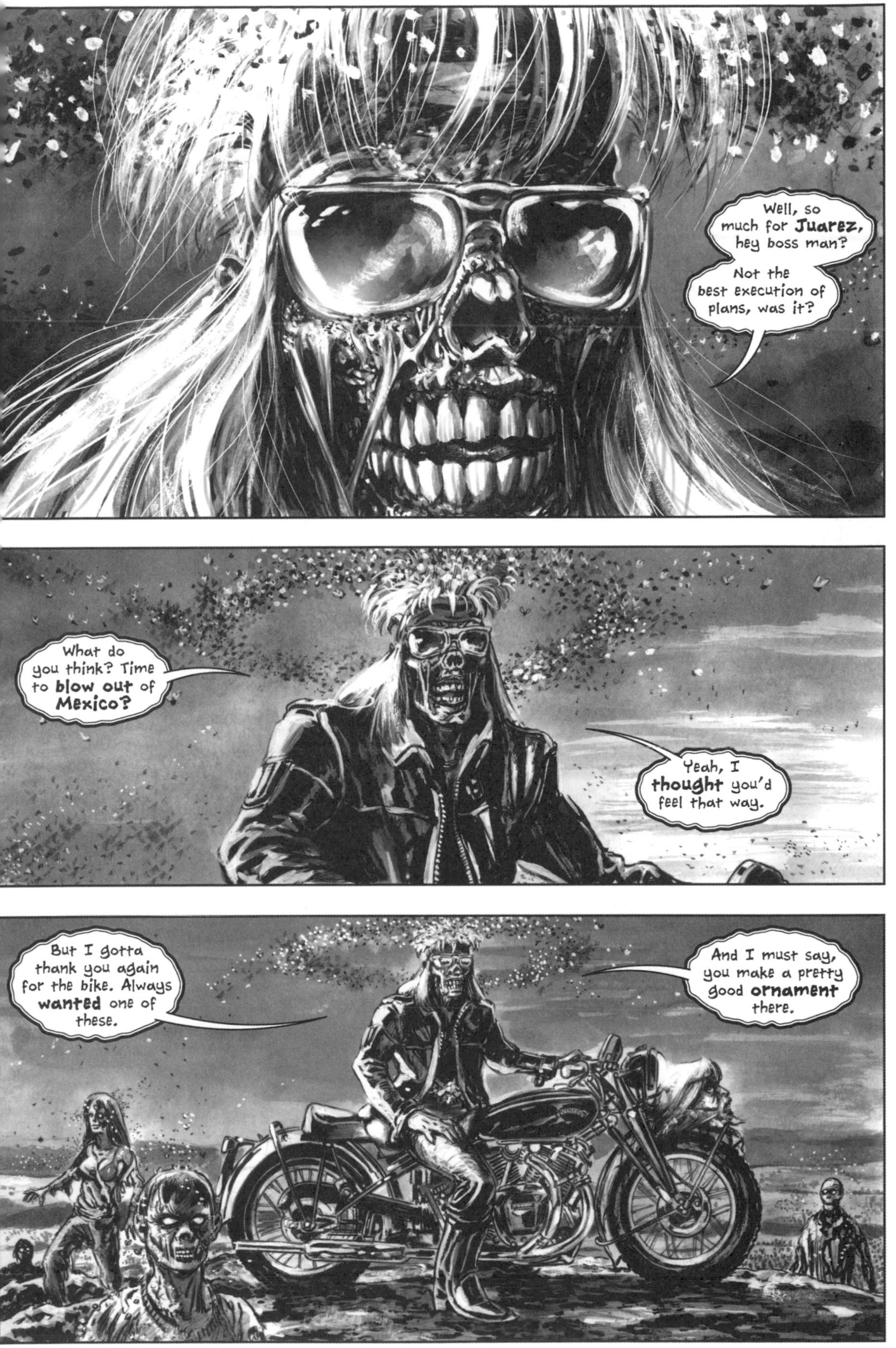
Well, so much for **Juarez,** hey boss man?
Not the best execution of plans, was it?
What do you think? Time to **blow out** of **Mexico?**
Yeah, I **thought** you'd feel that way.
But I gotta thank you again for the bike. Always **wanted** one of these.
And I must say, you make a pretty good **ornament** there.

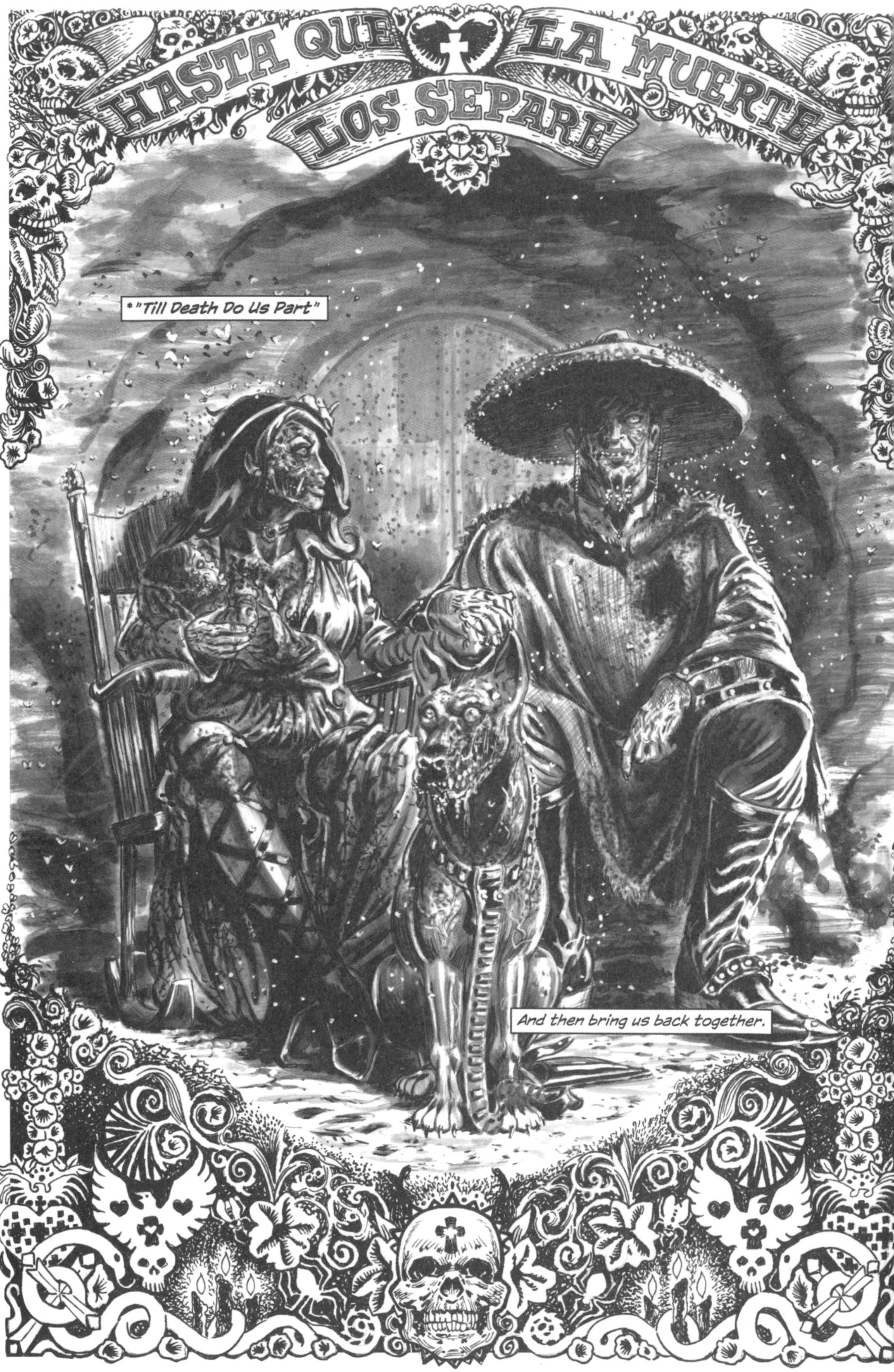
HASTA QUE LA MUERTE LOS SEPARE
*"Till Death Do Us Part"
And then bring us back together.

ABOUT DEADWORLD

Deadworld is the long-running horror series that originally came from Arrow Comics in the late '80s and was continued throughout the '90s by Caliber Comics. The original series, Volume One, ran 26 issues, and featured a group of teens in a yellow school bus plunged into a world of flesh-eating cadavers. But there was a twist. The world was not only populated with the mindless hordes of the walking dead, but also with intelligent zombies… ones that rode Harleys and had their own guns. Leading the way was the sarcastic, chain-smoking, King Zombie.

As the series branched off into many subplots and scenarios, it was decided to pare things down and Volume Two was structured, which ran 15 issues. In between the two volumes was a mini-series called *To Kill a King*, featuring a character introduced in the first volume, the Dead-Killer. This mini-series, along with the original short stories from the first volume, was collected into the *Deadworld: The Dead Killer* trade paperback.

In 2005, Deadworld was re-launched as a new series by Desperado Publishing, in association with Image Comics. The six-issue "Requiem for the World" storyline was a "re-boot" of the franchise which started at the beginning of the saga. It is not a re-telling of the original series, but rather a new start. Following that, the *Deadworld: Frozen Over* arc moved the action from the Louisiana heat to the wintry streets of New York. This limited series was followed by the *Deadworld: Slaughterhouse* hardcover, the first Deadworld original graphic novel. All three of the "re-booted" storylines have been collected into a single book, the *Deadworld Omnibus*, published by Desperado and IDW.

During the years, *Deadworld* has had some activity in Hollywood, including a stint with George Clooney's production company and Warner Bros., and is currently optioned with a screenplay by David Hayter. There have been some licensed material such as Halloween masks, t-shirts from Rotten Cotton Graphics, a CD-rom which holds PDFs of the first 46 issues, an upcoming action figure from Shocker Toys, and a role-playing game from Seraphim Guard is also in the works. All the latest news and information can be found on the Deadworld website: www. deadworld.info

Artwork by Sami Makkonen

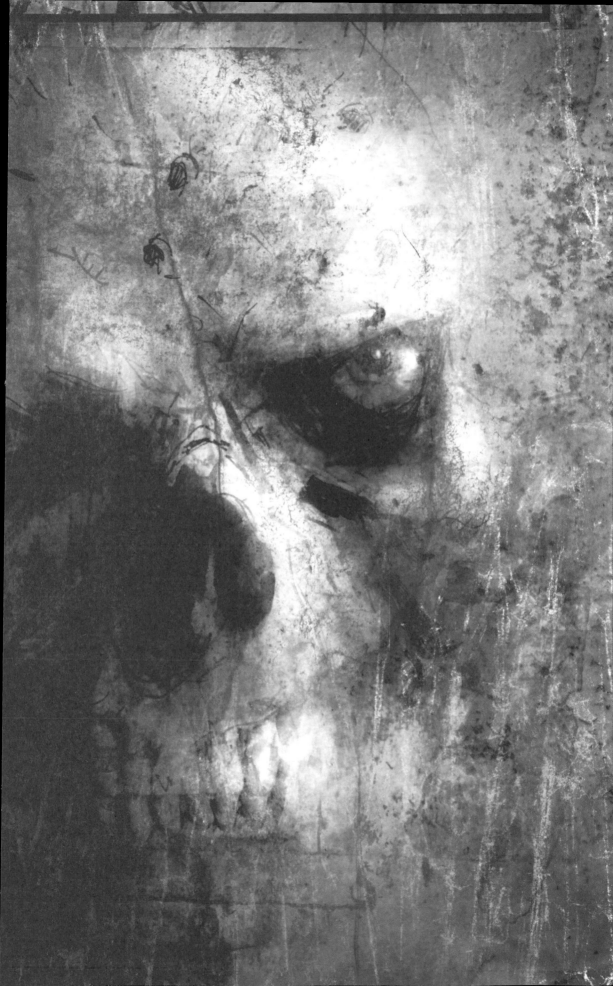

ALSO AVAILABLE

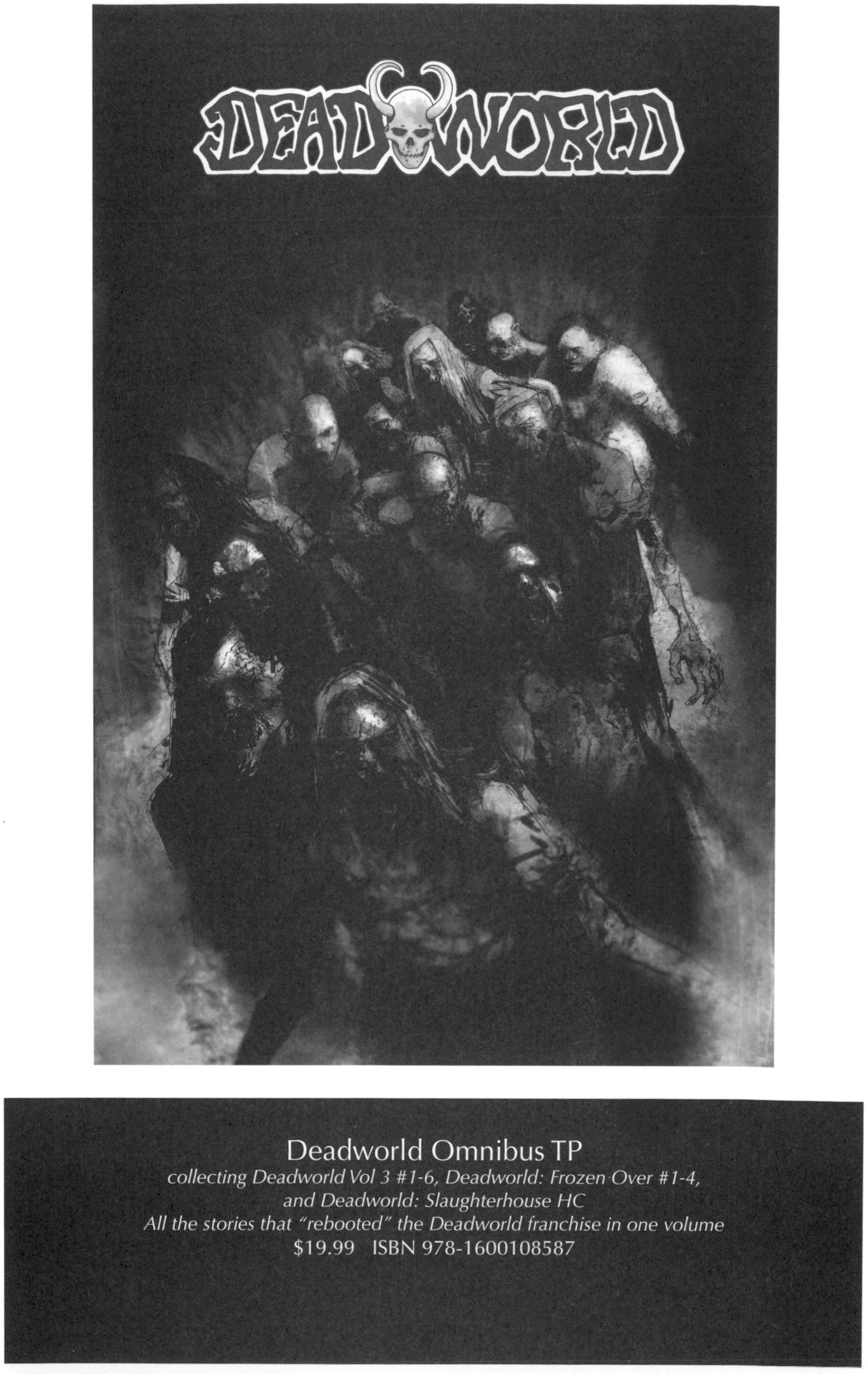
DEADWORLD

Deadworld Omnibus TP

collecting Deadworld Vol 3 #1-6, Deadworld: Frozen Over #1-4, and Deadworld: Slaughterhouse HC

All the stories that "rebooted" the Deadworld franchise in one volume

$19.99 ISBN 978-1600108587

Deadworld Classics TPs

Collecting the stories of the original Deadworld artist, Vince Locke. In addition to the comic tales that ran in the original series, short stories and miscellaneous artwork are also included, often with commentary by Vince.

Volume 1

collecting Deadworld, Volume 1 #1-7
$24.99   ISBN 978-1600108174

Volume 2

collecting Deadworld, Volume 1 #8-16
$24.99   ISBN 978-1600108587

GARY REED

Gary is the author of many titles, with the most notable being *Deadworld*, *Saint Germaine*, *Renfield*, and *Baker Street*. He has also written film scripts, short stories, role-playing games, and a video game storyline. He was the publisher of Caliber Comics, currently the publisher of Transfuzion Publishing, and one of the co-organizers of Detroit Fanfare.

GARY FRANCIS

Gary is the co-writer of *Deadworld, The Last Siesta*. He is a hard-working, meat and potatoes problem solver and feels lucky to be working in a creative capacity in such an amazing field. Gary likens approaching a project to being a mechanic who enjoys popping the hood and busting his knuckles until he hears the engine rev like a Hemi.

MARK BLOODWORTH

Mark created the critically favored, urban crime comic book *Nightstreets* before taking over art chores on the first volume of *Deadworld*. He was then hired by Marvel to work on *Clive Barker's Hellraiser*. His other works include *Jack The Ripper*, *Raven Chronicles*, *The Ripper Legacy*, *Abel*, and *Midnight Mortuary*. In recent years, he has worked illustrating a number of children's books, *Short Tales*.